Outlines of
Classical Literature

FOR STUDENTS OF ENGLISH

Outlines of
Classical Literature

FOR STUDENTS OF
ENGLISH

H. J. ROSE

M.A., LL.D., F.B.A.

*Professor Emeritus of Greek
in the University of St Andrews*

LONDON

METHUEN & CO LTD

36 ESSEX STREET · STRAND · WC2

First published 1959
© *1959 H. J. Rose*

Printed in Great Britain by
Butler & Tanner Ltd., Frome and London

CATALOGUE NO. 6184/U

Contents

Contents

Preface

FOR SOME YEARS IT HAS BEEN MY PLEASANT DUTY to lecture to Honours students in the Department of English at St Andrews on the classical background of our literature. A friendly suggestion was made to me that such students were likely to find the existing manuals of the literatures of Greece and Rome, my own included, too long and too detailed for their wants, since they are primarily meant for classical students, at universities or elsewhere. I have therefore tried to embody the substance of the lectures I have been giving in a work of moderate size which makes no attempt to cover the entire ground but confines itself almost wholly to a straightforward and non-technical account of such ancient authors as have demonstrably had an effect, direct or other, on later writers, especially those who have used the English tongue. Other literatures have been touched upon here and there, by way of illustration, but no more; to discuss successively what has been learned and used from classical sources by Frenchmen, Germans, Italians, Spaniards and so on would need not one volume but several, probably one for each nation, and each would have to be written by someone acquainted, not only with Greek and Latin literature, but with those of the nations in question, and that in far greater detail than I am master of. It is my hope that what I have written will prove of service to those for whom it is intended, those in fact who, while intelligently studying our own great literary heritage, have not had opportunity to delve deeply into the writings of a remoter past, the works of authors who lived from about fifteen hundred to perhaps as much as three thousand years ago.

Western Europe learned of Greek literature, history and

myths at first through Latin sources, and therefore took over the names in Latinized forms. These were attempts, generally quite close, at spelling the foreign words in Latin fashion. Greek K (*kappa*) was represented in Latin by C, which was always pronounced as in English *care*, never as in *civil* or *Cecil*. Greek P (*pei* or *pi*) and PH (*phei* or *phi*) were at first often confused. The reason was that P was pronounced by the Greeks as it is in French, with no perceptible expiration, while PH was not our F-sound but P with aspiration, a little like the sound in *up-hill*; whereas a Latin or Italian P was more like an English one, and thus P and PH were apt to be confused, or the latter identified with the voiced mute (B). Later, i.e. in the 'golden age' of Latin literature and afterwards, this was put right. The simple vowels were merely transliterated, since they had nearly the same sounds in both languages, except that for a while U (V) was used for the Greek U (written like our Y and sounded as in French or Dutch). Later, the letter Y was adopted for writing Greek words, which is why it (and Z, *zeta*, a double consonant which has no precise equivalent in Latin) comes at the end of the Latin, and our, alphabet, instead of much higher up, as they do in Greek. Of the diphthongs, Greek *ai* was spelled *ae*, both at that time being pronounced much alike, about like French *ê* in *être*; *oi* was spelled *oe*, and *ou*, which had the same sound as it has in French, simplified to *u*. In like manner, *ei* was simply written *i*, as indeed it often was by the Greeks themselves, since it then had exactly the same sound (our *ee* as in *seem*), when the *i* was long. The endings of names were modified to suit the Latin declensions; thus -ŏs became -us, -ŏn changed to -um, -ē to -a, -ōn to -ō. With a very few exceptions, in which the Latin form is so well established in modern languages that it can hardly be changed now (as Thucydides for Thoukydides, Apollo for Apollon), I have simply transliterated the Greek names; but in the Index, the Latin form of every name is given after the Greek.

My especial thanks are due to the head of the Department of English here, Professor Falconer, who has been so obliging as to read through my work chapter by chapter and make many encouraging and useful suggestions and criticisms.

H. J. ROSE

St Andrews
   September 1958

traces on the existing literatures.) In any given age, the strength
of the classical influence may be small or great. In the Dark
Ages, all learning being in the hands ... once the writers of the
time (they were not many) knew little of how their great
predecessors had expressed themselves. The late Middle Ages

Introduction

T O UNDERSTAND A RIVER THOROUGHLY, IT IS
necessary to know its springs and its tributaries, as
well as its main course. To study such a literature as
ours properly, attention must be paid to at least the principal
sources on which the writers drew for their inspiration and
for their training in arrangement and other important formal
matters. Among these sources, and certainly among the
agencies which have taught English authors to give form to
their ideas and clothe them in becoming words, the literatures
of Greece and Rome occupy an important place. It would
indeed be absurd to say that they are the only source. A great
deal of what is most characteristic in our literature is due to
the Germanic element in our ancestry, something no doubt
to the Keltic strain. Much has been learned from the literature
of other nations, not least the French. Very much is due to the
experiences through which the peoples of Great Britain, the
Commonwealth, and the United States have passed (for by
'English' literature I of course mean that written in one dialect
or another of the tongue which originated among the Saxon
ancestors of the English, wherever that tongue is in general
use). The literatures of France and Spain began with compositions in Latin, while that was still the spoken tongue of all
civilized Western Europeans; or, the literature of Rome was
written partly by natives of these countries, whichever way
we choose to look at it. Yet there is definitely a new note
struck in the vernacular compositions, especially perhaps in
the lyric poems, of both these regions, once provinces of the
Roman Empire though they were, and demonstrably non-
Roman influences at work, from the Franks in the north to
the Moors in the south, many of which have left very distinct

traces on the existing literatures.[1] In any given age, the strength
of the classical influence may be small or great. In the Dark
Ages, all learning was at a low ebb, hence the writers of the
time (they were not many) knew little of how their great
predecessors had expressed themselves. The later Middle Ages
saw a slow revival of classical learning, and with it felt an
increasing influence of the ancient writers, confined at first,
in the West, to those who had written in Latin, for knowledge
of Greek was all but extinct and such acquaintance as there
was with writers in that tongue came through translations,
direct or indirect, into Latin, often very bad both in their
style and as a guide to the meaning of the originals. As the
New Learning made its way from the East, one Greek author
after another was re-introduced to Western readers, who
edited them, published them in various forms, commented
on them, imitated them, and often misunderstood them, but
never failed to be influenced by them, directly or indirectly.
One school of writers after another in more recent times had
felt the influence especially of the Greeks, now as a rule better
understood as modern scholarship interpreted them and
knowledge of ancient history became more exact and wider
spread. At the present time, some writers seem to be cut off
entirely from this source of ideas and from the models their
predecessors followed, while others again adapt the old plots
to modern forms or experiment with ancient forms, dramatic
and other, modified to suit the taste and technique of today.
But there are few, if any, who express themselves in any kind
of literature without owing something, whether they know
it or not, to those who composed in Greek or Latin from
Homer down to the late Roman Empire. Indeed it is amusing
to notice how often a highly original and modern method of
expression proves to be but a modification, conscious or
unconscious, of some old one. The very latest medium, tele-

[1] For Spain in classical and medieval times, see G. Brenan, *The Literature of
the Spanish People* (1951), pp. 1-100.

vision, but the other day produced an opera by having it sung in one studio and mimed in another. The ghost of Livius Andronicus perhaps listened with approval; for he it was who relieved the strain on his voice by setting an assistant to sing his arias while he, on the stage, provided the appropriate gestures.[1]

It need hardly be said that I have not set out to write a complete history of either classical or English literature. For one thing, to do so would need a far larger book than this, and a complete study of the effects produced by the older on the more recent writers might well extend to many volumes. Elsewhere I have sketched the literatures of both Greece and Rome;[2] there are many excellent works on our own literature in English and other languages. To those, any who need fuller information are referred. What I have attempted is to give a brief account of such ancient writers as have demonstrably influenced the moderns by providing them with technique, subject-matter, or both, omitting the many, often important in themselves, who have exercised no such influence. Following on this account I have something to say of the form the influence has taken, the more outstanding writers who have imitated the ancients in question, and the trends or schools of writing which have resulted. The order is chronological, but this is not to say that the older Greek or Roman authors are paired with the older English ones, for it may often happen that the first modern imitations were of writers comparatively late. Ovid was known, studied and imitated by Englishmen for centuries before Sophokles was anything but a name to them, if even that, and the like is true in many other cases. Hence the chronology is that of the ancients only. Moreover, nothing is said of those moderns in whom there is no visible trace of ancient influence. This involves no judgement of their value. Mark Twain would, I think, have been approved by some of the best writers of antiquity, for he went for inspiration

---

[1] Livy vii, 2, 9; see below, p. 149. [2] See Bibliography.

where they went, to his knowledge of mankind and his mother-wit; but he was no classicist, nor had he much knowledge of history, literary or other. On the other hand, there have been books written in sundry modern tongues which showed considerable acquaintance with the ancients, but were not worth a page of *Huckleberry Finn*, because they lacked life and originality. He who merely classicizes is not likely himself ever to become a classic, for he is apt to be slavish in his following of the forms and ideas which another originated, whether a few weeks or two thousand years earlier does not matter. The true imitator learns from his model how to set his thoughts, be they serious or trifling, to fitting words in verse or in prose, with due observance of the proper length, whether that is small or great. This is done, not by catching at superficial mannerisms, which when transferred will perhaps suit neither the language nor the age into which they are introduced, but by a more profound study of what is essential in the original's combination of form and matter, which will show him, among other things, what to alter in his own adaptation. We shall have occasion to note examples of both the right and the wrong ways of imitating in the course of this work; for the present, let it suffice to remark that Shakespere is never more thoroughly Shakespere than when he is almost transcribing whole pages out of Plutarch or Boece, Molière never more completely himself than when he is copying Plautus.

Every ancient author, then, will be treated in such detail as space permits and followed by an account of those who have used him well or ill in producing their own works. Here and there examples will be given of a fascinating matter, deserving of a treatise to itself, the echoes of some well-turned phrase or acute sentiment down the ages, from one language to another. It is my hope that some who read will be moved to pursue the whole subject for themselves, by mastering the necessary languages and forming their own first-hand opinions.

I

Homer, Epic and the Troy-Saga

WHEN THE ANCESTORS OF THE HISTORICAL
Greeks (it is convenient to call them Achaians) began
to enter Greece, probably about 2000 B.C., they were
an illiterate people with no more than the beginnings of a
political organization. But they brought with them a copious
and flexible language, especially well equipped in its elaborate
verb-system, by which it was possible to convey a very wide
range of meanings, both temporal and other. Moreover, as
even we, who are but imperfectly acquainted with its pronunciation, can make out, its sound was melodious, rich in
vowels and diphthongs and lacking the harsher elements, such
as gutturals.[1] They had also, at the earliest times of which we
can form any conception, definite ideas of what constituted
verse, both sung and recited. Of the former kind we shall hear
something in a later chapter;[2] the latter was based wholly on
quantity, that is to say on the differing length of syllables,
according as they had or had not either long vowels, diphthongs,
or a consonant-group between one vowel and the next which
made the pronunciation slower than if there had been but
one intervening consonant, or none. The accent, which seems
to have been purely one of pitch, not of intensity, had nothing
to do with metre. At some date, so early that we cannot conjecture when it was, a convention grew up that one long
syllable was equal in time to two short ones, and therefore that
a dactyl (one long followed by two shorts) and a spondee

---

[1] A guttural is a sound produced actually in the throat; consonants like the
'hard' g and German ch, sometimes miscalled gutturals, are palatals or velars,
i.e. made on the hard or the soft palate.

[2] See below, pp. 26-48.

(two longs) were of equal length, each being, to use modern musical terminology, the equivalent of a bar of 'common time' (four beats to the bar). On this foundation arose, again at an unknown but certainly early date, the verse known as the hexameter ('six-measure'), whereof every foot but the last might be a dactyl but could also be a spondee, while the last was invariably a spondee, with, however, the small licence that a trochee (one long syllable followed by one short) might serve instead, at the end of the verse, the slight natural pause filling the gap, as a rest of one beat might in a bar of modern music. The line therefore might vary considerably in length, from twelve to seventeen syllables, but not at all in time (twenty-four beats). So far as we know, this noble and flexible verse was the earliest which Greeks used for narrative, indeed their earliest medium for literature of any kind, for prose, as is usual, was a later discovery. It, or something like it, was therefore what was used by the bards, *aoidoi* in Greek, who recited or chanted to the accompaniment of a small stringed instrument, *phorminx* or *kitharis*, tales of the doings of gods or men. There was no lack of material in either case, for this people had a rich imagination and a lively curiosity regarding the nature and occupations of the beings whom they worshipped, and therefore one of the most extensive mythologies of the world,[1] enriched, there is little doubt, by adaptations of the tales told among neighbouring peoples, such as the Hittites and members of the other great cultures of the Near East. As to human adventures, it was a disturbed time, a 'heroic age' in fact, full of wars, piratical enterprises, and on occasion trading-voyages as well, from all which stories would come back, to be improved, not only by the imagination of the first tellers but by that of the bards, whether professional or amateur, with all manner of wonderful episodes, including of course the intervention of gods to help or harm men according to their deserts or the divine preferences.

[1] For works on mythology, see Bibliography.

Towards these gods the Achaians felt no doubt considerable reverence, but not of a slavish kind; they were superior to men in knowledge, power, and immortal or at least very long life, and no human being, however distinguished, could hope to attain divine rank, or indeed to look forward after death to anything better than a pale shadowy existence, in which his breath-soul (*psyche*) became an empty phantom of the living man or woman, quite lacking inward parts (*phrenes*) and no more substantial than a cloud of smoke, which went drearily through some imitation of the actions of real life. The only exceptions were some few especial favourites of the gods, who were snatched away, body and soul together, to a blissful place (the Islands of the Blessed, or the Plain of Elysion), where they never died and led a life of happy, unforced activities, and a few sinners who had directly insulted or otherwise deeply offended the deities and so were tormented for ever; for these chosen offenders had one and all somehow gained immortality, to their everlasting sorrow. Yet, despite this wide gap between men and gods, the respect paid to divinity was merely that due to an acknowledged superior, and did not in the least prevent the worshippers telling all manner of stories, not always edifying, about the objects of their perfectly sincere worship. The idea that there are absolute standards of right and wrong to which every being deserving of respect must conform was due to later Greek thought. The gods of early times might quarrel among themselves, have intrigues with goddesses or with mortal women, intervene for all manner of reasons in the fortunes of mankind, and so forth, without derogation of their godhead or, apparently, the least resentment on the part of their worshippers. However theologically unsound, this attitude provided the bards with an excellent divine machinery for their poems. A spear for instance does not always miss merely by chance or because the man aimed at sees and avoids it in time, for it may be turned aside by a god. A man in danger need not avoid an

B

enemy simply by slipping away in the confusion of battle, for a god may snatch him away. A clever idea is often suggested by a deity; a disaster is often due to divine wrath, manifesting itself in a violent storm or the like; and continual interventions take all manner of forms from the giving of good advice to open force or even fraud. As to how the bard was to know all this, the answer was plain. He was himself a favourite of deity, inspired by one of the Muses (perhaps 'reminders', a group of goddesses who presided over all arts), or by Apollo himself, god among other things of music and all that went with it. They of course knew what their fellow-deities were doing and had done, and therefore could dictate the whole true story to the teller, who of his own knowledge could but hear the report (*kleos*) of it, as Homer distinctly says, and so would be as likely to get it wrong as right.

Having created the civilization known to us as Mycenaean, from the fact that Mycenae (*Mykenai*) in the Peloponnesos was one of its chief sites, the Achaians declined, for reasons both economic (they were rather plunderers than producers) and political (they were continually at war), till their culture gave place to the much poorer sub-Mycenaean, and the decline was hastened by the invasion of a more backward stock of the same people, the Dorians, about 1200–1000 B.C. Their great age receded into the past, and the men of that time seemed to the imagination of their greatest poet far superior to his contemporaries, 'mortals such as now are'. To this poet we give the traditional name of Homer (*Homeros*), a word of unknown meaning, though it happens to sound like the Greek word for a hostage. Of his life we know nothing at all, save that he must have been a poet by profession, for the biographies of him which survive are the merest products of folklore eked out by pedantic attempts to fit in the various works ascribed to him at one time or another, and are very much later than any possible date for him. By the nearly universal consent of antiquity he is the author of two long epics, the

Iliad (*Ilias*, understand *poiesis*, 'poetry about Ilion' or Troy) and the *Odyssey* (*Odysseia*, sc. *poiesis*, 'poetry concerning Odysseus', the legendary king of the island of Ithaca whose name appears in Latin under the dialectical form Ulixes[1]). Some ancient scholars, however, were of opinion that Homer composed the *Iliad* only, some other poet having produced the *Odyssey*, and a modification of this view is held by a number of moderns. What is generally agreed now, however, is that Homer is one poet, not a number of ballad-makers whose works were patched together by some unknown editor. For some time a very different view was current, and is not yet entirely given up.

Cicero, writing in 55 B.C.,[2] that is to say when the great age of Alexandrian scholarship (see below, Chapter V) was over and its results were available to every educated man, says that Peisistratos, the sixth-century tyrant of Athens, is reported to have 'arranged the books of Homer, which previously were disordered, as we now have them', and several later authors support the statement. After several less important modern acceptances of this, an excellent scholar, F. A. Wolf, brought out, in 1795, his *Prolegomena to Homer*, in which he asserted that the *Iliad* could not have been preserved in writing in an illiterate age, nor remembered unwritten, because of its length. He therefore concluded that it had been put together in the time and under the direction of Peisistratos from a number of shorter pieces, and that the like process had been undergone by the *Odyssey*. The thesis was taken up by many other scholars, and a great array of arguments, linguistic, archaeological and literary, advanced in support of it. To give

---

[1] The familiar English form Ulysses results from medieval mis-spellings. At that time, *x* and *s*, or *ss*, were pronounced alike, a confusion which survives in such French spellings as *Bruxelles*, *beaux*, etc., while in Italian *x* has gone out of use, Xenophon, for instance, becoming Senofonte. Also, *y* (properly pronounced like French *u*) was pronounced exactly like *i*. Hence this and several other strange orthographies.

[2] Cicero, *de oratore* iii, 137. For a longer sketch of the 'Homeric question', see *H.G.L.* pp. 34-46, with the authors cited there.

anything like a complete account of the variations of theory and the facts, or alleged facts, brought up in support of them is quite impossible here, but in general it may be said that none of the separatist arguments is cogent and the case for the unity of authorship has regularly had the support of the best literary critics especially. It is the personal conviction of the present writer that the same poet composed both poems, and he is much inclined to believe that he literally wrote them, for some kind of writing seems to have been known to the Mycenaeans some centuries before any reasonable date for Homer, and it is likely that a professional poet, that is to say a man in the forefront of such learning as there was in those times, would have acquired the new art enough at least to set down a kind of *aide-mémoire*, enough to prompt him if his memory failed and to serve as a guide to others who would learn to recite his masterpieces.[1]

This is of course not to say that once the poems were composed (whether written down or not) they remained absolutely unalterable for all time. There was then nothing corresponding to the many safeguards which a modern author enjoys. There was no reading, but only a listening, public; the nearest approach to the publication of any work was its recitation – such recitation as Homer describes as occurring in the houses of nobles for their entertainment, and as we know took place, at all events in later times, at sundry festivals. The reciters, *rhapsodoi*, literally stitchers together of songs, might not remember perfectly the text of the poems they presented, although the memory of a trained reciter can be marvellously good, and to have the entire *Iliad* and *Odyssey* by heart was not an unknown thing even among persons who were not of the poetic gild, the *Homeridai* (clan of Homer; names of this form are occasionally found applied to associations of pro-

[1] The reference is to the adaptation of the Linear B script of Minoan Crete to Greek use. As this, the discovery of Messrs Ventris and Chadwick, is at present under criticism from many angles, the above must be taken as provisional.

fessional men, who seem to have been organized into fictitious groups of kindred). Local demand might easily cause the insertion of a new passage containing a mention of some hearer's ancestor, for to claim descent from one of the men who took Troy was no uncommon boast of a noble house. The curiosity of the audience might lead them to ask, for instance, what song Demodokos sang for the Phaiakians to dance to, or what became of the wall the Achaians put around their camp, and thus give rise to two passages somewhat doubtful on internal grounds, *Iliad* xii, 6–35 and *Odyssey* viii, 267–366. Here and there our text, after all the efforts of ancient critics (see below, p. 124), may be thought to bear a trace of some reciter forgetting for a moment what came next and 'gagging' in consequence (*Iliad* xvi, 611–15 tells us twice over what happened to the spear which Aineias threw at Meriones). But all such insertions amount to but a few hundred lines at most out of the total of nearly 28,000 which the two poems contain. Substantially, we have what Homer composed.

The *Iliad* is a poem of war, and its material is part of the long and complicated saga of Troy.[1] This rests, like all genuine saga, on historical facts. On the Asian shore of the Hellespont (Dardanelles) a strong Achaian kingdom had arisen. It grew rich, partly at least through its control of the straits and the consequent tolls it could level on traffic, in return presumably for protection against pirates or brigands. It maintained friendly relations with neighbouring powers and was to some extent orientalized, though its language probably remained a dialect of Greek. Through commercial jealousy or for some other reason a quarrel broke out between it and the Achaian power in mainland Greece, and after a long and exhausting war of blockade Troy fell and was destroyed. This much at all

---

[1] Strictly speaking, Troy (*Troia*) is the name of the district, the city being Ilios or Ilion, but after Homer the names are often used loosely, *Troia* being very often the city itself.

events we may accept as historically true; the traditional date of the city's fall, as computed by ancient chronologers, was 1184 B.C. The cause of the war, in the tale as we have it, was the carrying off by Paris, or Alexandros, son of Priam (*Priamos*) king of Troy, of Helen (*Helene*) wife of Menelaos king of Sparta (not the historical city but an older, Mycenaean settlement across the river Eurotas from it); which cannot be fact, for Helen's name is not Greek and there are reasons for supposing that she was a local goddess, not a human princess. It might however be supposed that some elopement or kidnapping was among the grievances which finally provoked the war. Menelaos' brother Agamemnon, king of Mycenae, was commander-in-chief of the Achaian forces, which blockaded Troy for nearly ten years, finally taking and destroying it. The action of the *Iliad* consists of an episode of the tenth year, and its plot is as follows.

Agamemnon having wronged Chryses, priest of Apollo, the latter prays to his god for revenge, and Apollo, who in any case favoured the Trojans, sends a plague. Learning that this will not cease until he has returned the priest's daughter Chryseïs ('the girl from Chryse', a town in the neighbourhood), who is his prisoner, Agamemnon reluctantly consents, but insists on recompensing himself by appropriating the female prisoner of one of the chieftains. His anger being roused against Achilles (properly Achilleus), the handsomest, swiftest and bravest of the Achaians, he seizes his prisoner Briseïs ('girl from Brysa', another local town), and Achilles refuses to fight or obey Agamemnon's orders, and prays to his mother, the sea-goddess Thetis. She in turn entreats Zeus to avenge her son; he consents, for he owes Thetis a debt of gratitude, and sends a deceitful dream to Agamemnon, assuring him that if he leads out his army against the Trojans he will take the city. So far from this proving true, the two hosts, after an attempt at making peace, brought to nothing by the treachery of Pandaros, one of Priam's allies, who is inspired by the goddess Athene to shoot an arrow at Menelaos, fight inconclusively with heavy losses on both sides. Now Priam, who can get reinforcements from nearby states, can afford this much better than Agamemnon, whose only possible reserves are across the sea in Greece. He and his followers are much discouraged; they retire on their camp, fortify it, and send an embassy to Achilles offering him the return of Briseïs, together with large compensation. He puts himself in the wrong by contemptuously refusing to be reconciled, and Agamemnon is almost in despair and talks of giving up the expedition, a suggestion indignantly opposed by the valiant young chieftain Diomedes. In the night, Diomedes and Odysseus sally out and obtain a success against a party of Thracians who have come to reinforce Priam; they kill the Thracian leader Rhesos and capture his splendid chariot-horses. This rouses Agamemnon's spirits, and in the morning he leads out his army again and fights bravely (for he is physically courageous, though morally a weakling), until he is wounded. Several other leading fighters have also to retire, and finally the Achaians are forced back to their camp, which the Trojans, led by their great champion Hektor,[1] proceed to attack with varying success. Despite the help given by Here, who beguiles Zeus with her love-making and so distracts his attention from the battle which he is guiding, the wall is finally broken through and Hektor begins to set one of the beached ships (which form the inner line of defence) on fire. Now at length Achilles is persuaded to let his followers, the Myrmidones, and his dearest friend Patroklos go out to battle. Patroklos puts on Achilles' armour, to make the Trojans think the great hero himself is coming. He drives off the Trojan attack, kills Sarpedon, leader of the Lykian contingent and one of the most formidable opponents of the Achaians, pursues the enemy to the walls of their city, which he tries to storm, but then is first checked and later stunned

[1] A most sympathetically drawn character, perhaps Homer's own invention.

by Apollo in person. In his weakened condition he is wounded by Euphorbos, a minor Trojan leader, and dispatched by Hektor, who takes the armour of Achilles and puts it on.

The action now approaches its climax. Achilles, when told of the death of his friend, is nearly mad with grief. He cannot go out to battle, for he has now no armour (the tale of his invulnerability is much later than Homer, who even describes a slight wound inflicted on him by an insignificant opponent), but encouraged by Athene, he frightens the now triumphant Trojans away from the camp with his war-cry. But for the cool good sense of Odysseus, he would neglect the formal reconciliation with the accompanying honour-price which Agamemnon offers, thus staining his own reputation, and he can hardly be persuaded, on the next day, to let the army have time for breakfast before joining battle; for he is now armed anew, Thetis having persuaded Hephaistos, the smith-god, to make him magnificent equipment, which is described at length, especially the elaborately decorated shield. Once in action, he completely routs the enemy and engages, pursues and kills Hektor, although he knows that his own death must soon follow the Trojan leader's. He subjects the corpse to brutal indignities, for Achilles is in several ways not a normal Achaian, but something of a splendid savage from an out-lying district (Phthia in Thessaly) of the Mycenaean world. Patroklos is given an elaborate funeral, accompanied by races and other sports, after the Greek manner. Twelve days after Hektor's death, Achilles is in somewhat softened mood. Warned by Thetis, he consents to let Priam ransom the body of his son, and the old king, divinely counselled and guided, comes by night to visit him. Hektor's body, miraculously preserved from decay and mutilation in reward of his piety in life, is taken to Troy and the lamentations and funeral rites conclude the poem.

The *Odyssey* has an entirely different plot, still belonging to the Troy-cycle, but really folktale and not saga. The theme is the widespread motif of the man who is so long away from home that everyone supposes him dead and he returns just in time to prevent his wife marrying another. The poem begins with a council of the gods in the absence of Poseidon the sea-god, Odysseus' implacable enemy. Athene asks why Odysseus, long detained on a lonely island, is not helped to return home. Zeus agrees that something should be done, despite Poseidon's hostility, and sends Hermes to bid Kalypso, the nymph of the island, to let Odysseus go, while Athene visits Telemachos, Odysseus' son, at his home in Ithaca (*Ithake*). There, Penelope, Odysseus' faithful wife, is besieged by a number of noble suitors who urge her to marry one of them and meanwhile spend their days in her house, putting her to great expense for their feasts. Acting on the advice of the goddess, Telemachos calls a folkmoot and formally asks the suitors to go. They laugh at him, and he then, helped by Athene in the disguise of Mentor, an old friend of Odysseus, borrows a ship, collects a volunteer crew, and departs to the mainland, where he seeks news of his father, first from Nestor king of Pylos (Navarino) and then from Menelaos at Sparta. Menelaos, who has a tale of his own wanderings to tell, informs Telemachos that Odysseus is not dead but has been stayed for years on Kalypso's island, where she has been trying to induce him to marry her, promising to make him immortal if he does so. Hermes meantime goes and bids Kalypso let Odysseus go. She reluctantly agrees, being unable to resist a command of Zeus, and gives him tools and materials for a makeshift ship, on which he sails away till he is wrecked by a storm sent by Poseidon and gets ashore, exhausted and naked, in the country of the Phaiakians (*Phaiekes*), a fairyland people who possess wonderful ships that steer themselves and sail faster than a bird can fly. Nausikaa, daughter of their king Alkinoos, meets him next morning and gives him food and clothes; her father receives him hospitably, and he and his nobles give him presents and listen to the tale of his wanderings.

After leaving Troy, he tells them, he was beaten off from the country of the Kikones, upon whom he attempted a piratical raid. Thence a gale from the north drove him to the land of the Lotos-Eaters, who gave some of his men the fruits on which they lived, thus making them forget home and kindred and desire only to live in Lotos-Land. Putting these on board by force, Odysseus sailed away and got to the country of the Kyklopes, monstrous one-eyed savages, one of whom, by name Polyphemos, was a son of Poseidon. Captured by this monster, who ate two of his crew at every meal, Odysseus and the survivors managed to put out his eye as he lay in a drunken sleep and to escape from his cave the next morning by hiding among his sheep when he let them out by taking down the huge rock that served him as a door. Departing, Odysseus taunted the monster, incidentally telling him his true name, whereat Polyphemos prayed to Poseidon that Odysseus, if he reached home at all, might do so with loss of all his men, in a ship belonging to another, and find trouble awaiting him. Departing from this country, they came to the island of Aiolos, a man (he is not a god in Homer) who controlled the winds. He entertained them, and as a parting gift handed Odysseus a sack containing all the winds except the one which would blow him to Ithaca. But when they were in sight of home, Odysseus fell asleep and his followers opened the sack, supposing it contained treasure. The resulting tempest blew them to the land of the Laistry-gonians, cannibal giants who sank all the ships but the one on which Odysseus sailed, and ate the crews. Escaping, Odysseus next arrived at the island of Aiaie, where the goddess Kirke, daughter of the Sun and a dangerous witch, had her abode. She turned half his men into swine by her magic, but Odysseus, meeting with Hermes, was given the herb moly against which no charms had power. With this he subdued Kirke, who became his mistress, and made her turn his companions into men again. After a year, he asked her the way home. She bade him first cross the stream of Ocean (*Okeanos*, not a sea, but the river encircling the earth, thought of as a great disk, not a sphere) to the land of the dead, and there enquire of the ghost of the great prophet Teiresias of Thebes. This he did, was informed by him of the state of affairs in Ithaca and of his own future fates, and saw something of the wonders and terrors of the other world. Returning, he got directions for his voyage from Kirke and set out. First he came near the dwelling of the Sirens (*Seirenes*), whose sweet singing beguiled sailors into drawing near, only to be wrecked and drowned. By Kirke's advice, he stopped his men's ears with wax and had himself bound firmly to the mast, and so escaped this danger. Next he came to the straits between the terrible sea-monster Skylla and the deadly whirlpool Charybdis. Steering nearer Skylla, as the less dangerous, he lost six of his men to her, but got away with the rest. Now came the island Thrinakie, where the cattle of Helios (the Sun) pastured. These being sacred, he forbade his men to touch them, but when they were wind-stayed there and their provisions gave out, they disobeyed him. Helios called on Zeus for vengeance, and Zeus, after sending a favourable wind, destroyed their ship with a storm and a thunderbolt. Only Odysseus escaped and after many dangers landed on the island of Kalypso, where he remained for seven years.

The Phaiakians now send Odysseus home on one of their ships, and next morning he is met by Athene, disguised as a young man, who gives him information as to the state of things, tells him that he must overcome the suitors by guile, and changes his appearance into that of an old beggar.[1] Thus disguised, he makes his way to the house of Eumaios the chief swineherd, who is faithful to the memory of his master, receives the stranger hospitably and gives him shelter for the night. Meanwhile Athene brings word to Telemachos to

---

Greek gods deal little in magic, but they can change their own shapes and those of anyone else they choose.

hasten home, avoiding an ambush which the suitors have
set for him on the usual route to Ithaca. He takes leave of
Menelaos and Helen, returns, meets his father and is enabled
to recognize him, for his proper shape is restored for a little
while. They then plot the destruction of the suitors. Odysseus
makes his way to his palace and begs of the suitors, several of
whom abuse him, but he wins a certain amount of respect
and favour by easily defeating another beggar, one Iros, who
is set to box against him. He further learns that Philoitios the
cattleman is faithful to him, and that Melanthios the goatherd
is on the side of the suitors. At night, he has a long interview
with Penelope, who tells him of her troubles. For a while she
had kept the suitors at bay by pretending that she must weave
a garment in which to bury Laertes, Odysseus' aged father,
when he died, but every night she unravelled what she had
woven during the day and so the task bade fair never to be
completed. At last she was discovered and obliged to finish it,
and now she is at her wits' end. She has determined to set the
suitors a task; whichever of them can string Odysseus' great
bow and shoot an arrow from it through a kind of tube
formed by holes in the blades of twelve axes set up in a row
shall be her husband. The day comes when she had resolved
to do this, and she is reminded of it by Athene. All the suitors
fail,[1] and Odysseus asks to be allowed to try. Against the
protests of the suitors, the bow is handed to him, Penelope
(whom Telemachos now sends out of the men's hall) saying
she will give him a good suit of clothes if he succeeds. He
strings the bow and shoots through the axes without even
troubling to stand up, and then, saying he will try a new mark,
sends an arrow through the throat of Antinoos, the leading
suitor.[2] Revealing himself and refusing offers of compensation,

---

[1] It is a composite bow, of great strength, needing skill and not mere brute
force to string it. The trajectory being comparatively flat, the feat of skill
required would probably not be impossible.

[2] This (*Od.* xxii, 8 ff.) is the passage which Jules, in Browning's *Pippa Passes*,
had marked with a flower. It is indeed one of most satisfactory pieces of 'poetic

he continues to shoot down one man after another. The suitors have no weapons but the swords that every Homeric gentleman carried as a matter of course, for Odysseus and Telemachos have removed all the armour that used to hang in the hall, save four suits, with which they and the two faithful thralls equip themselves. But Melanthios gets several sets of equipment for them from the store-room until he is detected and caught by Eumaios and Philoitios. This makes the fight more equal, but in the end Odysseus and his three supporters kill all the suitors, sparing no one but the bard and the herald who had unwillingly waited on them. They then hang those of the maid-servants who had been the suitors' mistresses, mutilate Melanthios,[1] and purify the hall with burning sulphur. Eurykleia, Odysseus' old nurse (who had recognized him the night before from a scar on his thigh, and nearly betrayed him in her joy), brings word to Penelope, who declares it must be a god in disguise and comes down to see the wonder. Odysseus, by mentioning a secret which only he, she and one maid know, convinces her that he is indeed her husband, and the two retire to their room. In the morning, Odysseus goes to the farm where Laertes lives, makes himself known, and discusses ways and means of meeting the inevitable blood-feud, for meantime the killing of the suitors has become known, and their kindred, headed by Eupeithes, the father of Antinoos, are arming. Odysseus, Laertes, and their few supporters go out to meet them. Laertes, restored for the time being to something of his youthful vigour, is in the forefront of the battle, and with a prayer to Athene, hurls his spear at Eupeithes and kills him. As Odysseus and the rest advance to the charge, Zeus throws a thunderbolt to stop

---

justice' in all literature, though doubtless there are squeamish persons found to object to it.

[1] This is the one place in Homer where anyone is mutilated or otherwise tortured, but it is also the one instance of a thrall deliberately betraying his lord and siding with his deadly enemies.

them, and Athene, in the guise of Mentor, makes peace between the two parties.

It will be seen that the two poems have this much in common, that they do not attempt to tell the whole story of their central characters. Homer assumes that his hearers know who Achilles, Agamemnon, Odysseus and the rest were, how the Trojan war ended, and much else to which he sometimes alludes in passing, or even refers to in some detail. Odysseus' subsequent career, for instance, is briefly sketched by the ghost of Teiresias; the famous Wooden Horse by which Troy was taken is mentioned in the *Odyssey*; we are given glimpses of the visit of Paris to the home of Menelaos and his carrying off of Helen; and there are various episodes showing a knowledge of stories not germane to Homer's plots. In other words, he has selected two parts of a long and famous tale out of which he can construct unified poems, the one held together by the character of Achilles and his relations with sundry other leading Achaians, the other by the striking personality of Odysseus and his endless resourcefulness, paralleled in typical fashion by Athene's constant friendship towards him. That a wide difference exists between the two works is obvious, and to the present writer it seems equally obvious that it is due to their widely different themes, the action of one taking place in an armed camp with a busy crowd of warriors always present, while the other tells the story of one man, often isolated or surrounded by but a small group of other characters, in time of peace and partly in his own home. Hence the necessity for a different tone and a different vocabulary. A like difference is observable in Shakesperian plays of different periods and themes, for instance *Othello* and *A Winter's Tale*, despite the fact that jealousy plays a large part in both. From the point of view of sound literary criticism there is no sufficient reason for supposing the poems not to be the work of the same man.

Be that as it may, it is clear that the Homeric poems are

very far from being primitive. Although they are the beginning of surviving European literature, they come towards
the end of an age of active production. Homer, whoever he
was and whenever he lived (the more probable estimates of
his date vary between the tenth and the eighth centuries B.C.,
the present writer preferring the earlier date for several
reasons), had behind him a long heritage of poetic technique.
Not only did he take over from his predecessors the Epic
dialect, which is an artificial one, more like the Ionic than
any other but by no means identical with it, but he had at his
command a store of ready-made phrases, epithets, short
descriptions, transitional and other formulae. It is not too
much to say that a trained poet of his time could have produced extempore a fairly long passage, suitable for filling
a gap between one episode and the next, simply by piecing
together a sufficiency of these kennings, if they may be so
called. Thus to begin a new day in the narrative there is a
stock pair of lines, 'Dawn arose from her bed beside proud
Tithonos, to carry light to immortals and mortals.' To end it,
there are several formulae, for instance, 'And the sun set and
all the roads were shadowed.' A character is in doubt what
to do next: 'While he pondered on these things in heart and
mind' leads up to the next point in the story. Battle is joined
and two champions meet, defy one another, and prepare to
fight: 'So he spake, and brandishing his long-shadowed spear
he hurled it.' One character gives an order or a piece of advice
to another, 'Thus he (she) said, nor did . . . disobey.' And so
the narrative goes on from episode to episode. In addition,
numerous persons have stock epithets. Agamemnon is
regularly either 'king of men' or simply 'lord' (*kreion*).
Odysseus is 'much-enduring', 'of many wiles' or 'city-sacker'.
Diomedes is 'mighty at the war-cry', a phrase used also of
some other heroes. Gods and men alike have polite formulae
for addressing one another, usually composed of name,
patronymic and some epithet, as 'Child of aigis-bearing

Zeus, Atrytone' (Athene), 'O Nestor Neleus-son, great glory
of the Achaians'. Any king or baron is a 'shepherd of the
people'. Some of these epithets are obviously old and their
meanings very obscure. One instance has already been given
in Athene's title Atrytone; another is the stock adjective
applied to death, *taneleges,* perhaps 'out-stretcher', 'he who
makes men lie down'. It may very well be that Homer himself
did not understand them and used them simply as traditional
ornaments to his style. No one who is acquainted with our
ballads or the similar popular compositions of other nations
can fail to recognize the likeness. The difference, which makes
the greatness of Homer, is that he had the genius to use this
traditional material to make, not more ballads or other short
narrative poems, but epics of wide sweep and elaborate
structure.

As already said, there was then no reading public, and to
make a poem widely known it had to be recited, not copied
out and distributed. One occasion of recitations, from Homer
or other writers of Epic, was religious festivals, and from quite
early times it was felt to be seemly to prefix the actual recitation with something in praise of the appropriate god. Hence
there were composed a number of hymns, or proems (both
words are used in antiquity), of which we have thirty-three,
one incomplete, ranging in length from half a dozen lines to
several hundred and in date from perhaps the seventh century
B.C. to much later. Long or short, they show their purpose
by regularly ending with some such formula as 'But I will
make mention of thee (the deity of the festival) and of another
song', meaning the Epic recitation. Four are of such length
and elaboration as to be practically independent poems,
namely those to Apollo (if this is not two hymns loosely
joined together, one for the god's Delphic and the other for
his Delian shrine), Demeter, Aphrodite and Hermes. All are
of interest and considerable poetical merit. The Apolline
hymn, or one of them, seems to be the origin of the notion

that Homer was blind, for its composer says that if the chorus are asked who is the most delightful poet, they are to answer 'A blind man, and he dwells in craggy Chios.'[1] The hymn to Demeter tells at length the legend of the rape of Persephone and the foundation of the Eleusinian Mysteries; that to Aphrodite, of the begetting of Aineias by Anchises, while Hermes is given a most humorous account of his babyhood and his first theft, of the cattle of his half-brother Apollo; Shelley's translation has made this hymn well known to English readers.

Homer's poems seem to have won favour immediately and never ceased to be admired, even to idolatry, by later generations. Other poets set themselves, not to rival him, but to supplement him, telling the rest of the long tale of Troy or trying their hands at other traditional legends, as the story of Thebes. The works of these men, the so-called Epic Cycle, are lost to us save for some fragments and a jejune epitome of late date, but their matter is well known from the constant rehandling which it underwent in works of all manner of dates. More will be said later (pp. 215 ff.) of the further elaborations which the epic themes gave rise to, and their endless modifications in Latin, medieval and modern hands. For the present, it is enough to say that Homer took his place as the fundamental author for all Greeks and for those who learned from them in later times. Greek children learned to read from copies of the *Iliad* and *Odyssey*. Poets who used other dialects than the Epic were at liberty to use Homeric words and forms, even if they were quite alien to the speech in which the rest of their work was written. Prose writers more than once seem to have learned how to construct a long narrative from the epics; it is a commonplace that Herodotos, for instance (see pp. 115 ff.), composed a sort of prose epic on a grand scale.

This led in time to quaint misunderstandings of the poems.

---

[1] Hence Byron's 'The blind old man of Scio's rocky isle'. The original is line 172 of the Hymn to Apollo.

C

Naturally, the religious, political, cosmographical and other ideas of Homer were those of his age, the sub-Mycenaean. He knew nothing of written constitutions or laws, still less of any such thing as democracy. His gods and goddesses are larger, stronger and swifter men and women, with more acute senses than ours and far greater powers of all kinds, but neither passionless, immaterial, nor morally perfect. This did not fit the theology of later times, still less the developed ethics of the philosophers. His earth is flat, having under it the realm of Hades the death-god and under that again the depths of Tartaros, the prison of rebels against the gods. This obviously did not agree with the discoveries of later times, which not only realized the spherical shape of our planet but measured its size with fair accuracy. But as it was an article of faith with many that all wisdom was to be found in 'the Poet' (as he is often called, without mentioning his name), these discrepancies had to be explained somehow. Apart from a few outspoken critics who accused Homer of attributing all manner of unworthy actions to his gods, making his heroes but poor examples of morality, and so forth, the most usual approach was to find some hidden meaning in the poems, in the form of theological or ethical allegories, riddling descriptions of physical phenomena, and so on. This was perhaps made easier because there really are a few passages in which the poet uses highly figurative language, as when old Phoinix, one of the embassy to Achilles, tries to move him by saying that Prayers are daughters of Zeus, who come slowly after Infatuation and try to undo the harm she has wrought.[1] But the interpreters went far beyond anything that any composer of Epic had for a moment dreamed of. It was the beginning of a remarkable attitude towards any text held in high veneration. In time to come, Vergil was to be subjected to the like treatment, and from about the first century A.D. onwards Biblical passages were made the objects of most elaborate

[1] *Iliad* ix, 502 ff.

allegorization. In all these cases the underlying idea was the same. The text, being ancient and full of wisdom, must be right, i.e. in accordance with the interpreters' doctrines, scientific, philosophical or theological. Therefore, if it seemed to contradict them, and thus to speak falsely, this must be due to a too literal acceptance of its mere words, and the more enlightened reader would seek for a hidden meaning.

Apart from these aberrations, Homer became in later times the subject of much honest philological research, to the results of which we owe much of our understanding of him, for naturally his Greek had become quite obsolete by the age of the classical Attic writers who, with their followers in later times, form the bulk of our Greek literature. More will be said (see pp. 124 ff.) of this work and the manner in which some part of it has reached us. For the present, we are concerned with a remarkable early result of Epic activities.

After Homer, there was available to everyone who had opportunity to acquire it an effective and eloquent means of expression, and there was at least one able man, though not a literary genius of the calibre of Homer, who saw that this need not be limited to narratives of the ancient doings of gods and heroes. This man was Hesiod (*Hesiodos*), a member of a poor family which had migrated from Asia Minor to the wretched little town of Askra in Boiotia, and there got its living by farming a small estate. The father of the family dying, there remained the two sons, Hesiod and Perses, where-of the latter seems to have cheated his brother out of some part of his share of the estate. Hesiod's reply was made in a notable work, the first didactic poem in any European language. We know it generally as the *Works and Days*, since it is largely concerned with the 'works' necessary on a farm, and concludes with a curious section, suspected by many modern critics of being a later insertion, concerning the lucky and unlucky days of the lunar month. Digressions abound, and are of an ethical character for the most part, enforcing repeatedly

Hesiod's fundamental principle, that justice is or should be the characteristic of mankind, and has the active support of Zeus, who will sooner or later punish the unjust. By the most probable dating, Hesiod is of the eighth century B.C., and so roughly contemporary with the prophet Amos, whom he resembles in his passion for justice, if in nothing else. Another work of the same author is the *Generation of the Gods* (*Theogonia*), the first systematic account of the deities worshipped by all or most Greeks and of sundry other powers (we should call them abstractions, but it is far from certain that that is how Hesiod regarded them), whom the poet conceives as having their share in the government of the universe and of mankind. The arrangement follows the only kind of classification then available, that of genealogy. In the beginning came the Void (*Chaos*), then Earth, which produced Heaven, mated with him, and became the mother of a numerous and strange offspring, from whom descended the gods of Greek cult, Zeus, Hera, Poseidon and the rest. These powers did not create either the world or man; man was already there when Zeus came into power by overthrowing his father Kronos (the story has its oriental parallels and may well be of non-Greek origin). Many parts of the universe are the children of one or another of the primaeval figures, but a creation-myth like those of the Semitic peoples is not to be found.

It is plain that Hesiod had meditated much on the world and its government, and by no means all he says is poetical in flavour, despite the generally Homeric language. He used Epic verse and dialect for a cogent reason; no other literary form for works on a large scale then existed. Prose, in Greece as elsewhere, was a later development, to which we shall come in due course. We may perhaps describe his works as natural didactic poetry, as Homer is, at least by comparison with later writers, natural Epic. In many respects he was a forerunner of the scientists and philosophers (the two were not at first distinguished) who came in the following centuries, seeing imaginatively and embodying in his verses more than a little of what they arrived at by reasoning. The immediate result of his activities was the formation of a whole school of poetry, unfortunately lost to us save for fragments and other derivatives, which concerned itself with ethical and other themes, and also with a sort of history, or at least organized mythology. One of the most famous products was the *Catalogue of Women*, also known as the *Ehoiai*, because each section began with the words *e hoie*, 'or such (a woman) as (was) . . .' Apparently the poem was in form one enormous sentence, to this effect: 'In old times there were many famous women, who mated with gods and bore great heroes; such a one as . . . or such . . .' and so forth, section after section. Besides various scraps of the work, we have an enlargement, as it seems to be, of one portion in the poem, known as the *Shield of Herakles*. It begins in the manner just described, 'Or such as was Alkmene, who left her home and her native land and followed warlike Amphitryon to Thebes.' Then follow the birth of Herakles and his encounter with Kyknos, son of Ares, with a description of the champions meeting in fight, special attention being paid to Herakles' shield and its elaborate ornament, in patent imitation of the shield of Achilles in the *Iliad*.

Thus we find the Epic technique and language (for not only Homeric words but Homeric phrases abound in all that we have of the Hesiodic school) used to set forth, one might almost say to codify, both the learning and the ethical aspirations of the age. Incidentally, it is in Hesiod that we first find the personality of the poet emerging. Homer scarcely mentions himself, and that only to ask the Muse to inform him or to say that he could not tell all the tale, for instance the total numbers of the Achaian host, 'even though I had ten tongues, ten mouths and an unwearying voice'.[1]

[1] Invocation of the Muse, e.g. at the beginnings of both epics; need of

Hesiod has comparatively much to say, especially in the *Works and Days,* of himself, his family history, his grievances, and his calling by the Muses, of whom he claims to have had a vision.[1]

Thus the Hesiodic school stands at the beginning of several developments of poetical literature, none of them unimportant. There is of course the obvious one, didactic poetry, which did not cease to be a serious means of communication for many years after Hesiod, since we find philosophers using it as the only vehicle for their written teachings as late as the fifth century B.C. It was not till long after that its more artificial forms, which will be handled later, developed, to last well into modern times. There is also the personal poem, whose author, whatever else he may treat of, tells us something, often much, of what he thinks and feels. It is true that the most obvious form of this is the personal lyric poem, in one of its many varieties, but a very short acquaintance with our own literature is enough to make it clear that this is by no means the only way in which a poet puts himself into the forefront of his work. There was also the first known vehicle for what was most characteristic of Greece, orderly arrangement at not immoderate length of available matter, historical or other; a tendency which never departed throughout the creative periods of Greek literature and Greek thought. Works, however full of other admirable qualities, which lack form and unity are not Greek in spirit, nor as a general rule consonant with European taste. It is not for nothing that Aristotle was to find in Homer examples of his own ideals of constructing a work of literature; the Hesiodic school, for all

---

multiple tongues, etc., *Iliad* ii, 489-90, a famous figure, taken up for instance by Vergil, whose Sibyl (*Aen.* vi, 625-7) could not describe all the torments of Hell nor the sins which have deserved them with ten times Homer's equipment, and the poet himself would be equally unable to tell all that belongs to agriculture, *Georg.* ii, 43-4.

[1] *Theog.* 22 ff. It would be rash to assume that this is mere poetical convention; the author is a pious man in a believing age, and such men on occasion see visions.

its difference of subject, kept to Homer's most fundamental principle of construction, unity in diversity. The classical shape of literature had already established itself.

However, rich and varied though they were, the Epic language and metre could not alone satisfy the needs of a changing age, and the following centuries saw new and important forms, which must now be dealt with.

II

Elegiac, Iambic and Lyric Poetry

SO FAR, WE HAVE BEEN DEALING WITH POEMS
written, or at least composed, in hexameters. This metre,
while flexible and suited to a large variety of themes, has
an innate stateliness which is wasted on the more trivial
matters, such as the personal feelings or opinions of one
individual. Moreover, it does not appear that it ever was
associated with any music which would at the time be regarded as elaborate, or suited for solo or choral production.
The rhapsodes certainly were said to 'sing' their poems, but it
is probable that they delivered them to a kind of recitative,
with some simple accompaniment on their strings. Hesiod
had attempted to treat of personal matters in what was probably the only developed metre of his day, but it was as an
episode in a longer work, not in an independent composition.
In the centuries which succeeded him, full as they were of
revolutionary changes in the political and economic spheres
alike, old ties loosened, and in consequence the individual
became more self-conscious and claimed more importance for
what he, as an individual and not as a carrier of poetic or
other tradition, had to say. The prose speech was not yet a
part of literature, still less the prose pamphlet, for as yet there
was next to no reading public; remained the expression in
verse such as could be readily remembered and published by
being recited or sung to any who chose to listen. And this new
demand on verse brought with it the invention or adoption of
metres which, so far as we know, had hitherto not been used
by professional poets, if at all.

One of the earliest novelties, for we have snatches of it from

the first half of the seventh century B.C., is the elegiac couplet.
To understand this kind of poetry, it is necessary first to get
rid of the modern connotation of the words 'elegy' and
'elegiac'. To the ancients it need not be a poem of reflective
or pensive content at all. It is true that some in later times[1]
thought of it as rather mournful, and there was current a
fantastic etymology which derived the very word *elegos* from
e e legein, 'to say, alas, alas'. But the fact is that it was used from
the beginning for all manner of compositions which had not
the sweep of Epic narrative nor the necessary length of a didactic work. The earliest writer we hear of was one Kallinos,
of Smyrna in Asia Minor, and what little is left of his
poems consists of references to the Kimmerian invasion of the
country and calls for vigorous resistance to the aggressors.
Somewhere about the same time, Tyrtaios of Sparta was composing warlike poems to rouse the Spartans to greater efforts
against their enemies of Messenia, and giving them advice as to
their behaviour among themselves, especially in war. Between
these two comes Mimnermos of Kolophon, whose subjects
were amatory; later (sixth century) are Solon of Athens and
Theognis of Megara, writing mostly on political matters. Yet
all use the elegiac metre, which is a modification of the hexameter, corresponding to it somewhat as the English heroic
couplet does to English blank verse. Every odd-numbered
line in this metre is a hexameter, but the even-numbered
verses consist each of the first half of a hexameter repeated, the
second half consisting always of two dactyls and one syllable
over, while the first allows spondees. Between the two halves
there is always a diaeresis, that is to say the first ends with the
end of a word. An English imitation might run thus:

> *Trumpets from our camp/call me to battle again,*

Or:

> *Galloping into the straight/racer on racer appears.*

---

[1] For instance, Ovid in Latin and Plutarch in Greek.

Clearly, this imposes more or less of a pause at the end of every second verse. Again like the English heroic couplet, this might almost be ignored, compare the 'run-on' couplets of Keats' *Endymion*, or decidedly marked, as in Pope's verses. But in either case, the broad and varying sweep of Epic hexameters disappears, and by that alone the tone becomes less impressive and less suited to narrative on the grand scale. The resulting rhythm is easily adapted to all manner of topics, including those which a modern critic might call elegiac. If Gray's native tongue had been sixth-century Greek instead of English of twenty-four centuries later, he might have made his Elegy an elegy in the metrical sense also, without changing its gently melancholy tone in the least. But equally, any one of a number of peoms of moderate length, from Shakesperian sonnets to Gilbert's Bab Ballads, might in like case have used that very metre, to move, amuse, or advise.

One use that was made of this metre from fairly early times was the epigram, and here again our modern acceptation of the word is misleading for the student of ancient literature. An *epigramma* is originally simply something which is 'written on' a suitable material, generally stone or metal, since it was intended as a permanent record of something. From about the fifth century B.C. onwards, though a few examples are earlier, it was a very common thing to record such events as a death, especially casualties in war, or to mark a public monument of some kind, for instance an object dedicated in a temple, with a brief inscription in verse. Often a single hexameter sufficed, but if something a little longer was needed, the elegiac couplet readily suggested itself and was very often used. Generally, the early examples of this practice are lapidary indeed; their language, while poetical, is simple, concise, giving nothing but the necessary facts. Thus, early in the time of the Athenian democracy, i.e. about the beginning of the fifth century, a grandson of the tyrant Peisistratos held an elective office, that of archon (one of nine annual magistrates

charged with important governmental functions), and recorded it on an altar which he dedicated. The inscription, a
single couplet, may be rendered 'As a memorial of his archon-
ship, Peisistratos son of Hippias placed this in the precinct of
Pythian Apollo.' Not a word is wasted; the reason for the
dedication is given, the god is called by his appropriate title
(he had many), and the dedicator leaves the names to speak
for themselves; he was named after his grandfather, a common Greek fashion, and everyone knew that Hippias, son of
the tyrant, had carried on the tyranny for another generation.
In a more wordy age, much might have been said about the
broad-mindedness of the democracy in electing a man of such
ancestry, or about the younger Peisistratos' own salutary change
of heart, or the like. A lady of the same family married abroad
and died in Lampsakos, where her husband was despot. Her
amiable character called for recognition, in the opinion of the
survivors, and her epitaph ran 'This dust hides Archedike,
daughter of Hippias, the foremost man of his time in Greece.
Her father, her husband, her brothers and her sons were
tyrants, but she lifted not up her heart to frowardness.'[1]
Neither in these nor in many other examples of about the
same date or not very much later is there anything which we
should call epigrammatic. The inscriptions are content to
give the necessary facts with elegant brevity. Of course the
best-known example, which is also perhaps the most excellent
of this period, is the inscription on the three hundred Spartans
who fell fighting when the Persians under Xerxes forced the
pass of Thermopylai in 480 B.C. 'Stranger, tell them at Sparta
that we lie here in obedience to their words.' Again, the
reader is left to draw his own conclusions, that if they ask a
casual passing stranger to carry word to Sparta, it is because
none of them has survived, and that their death resulted from
their orders to hold the pass at all costs. But no translation can

[1] Both these epigrams are preserved by Thucydides, the former in vi, 55, 7,
the latter a little further on, vi, 59, 3.

convey the simple charm of the language of the original. How 'epigram' got its modern meaning will become clearer when we reach the Alexandrians (pp. 140 ff.) and Martial (pp. 254 ff.).

The same age saw a further adaptation of verse to new uses. The natural rhythm of Greek is the iambic, that is to say the alternation of a short syllable with a long one, or less commonly with two more shorts, as was noticed by Aristotle (pp. 99 ff.).[1] In this it has a parallel in English, the accent of which is very apt to fall on alternate syllables, so that a writer in prose, if not careful, may often produce an unintended 'heroic' line. Therefore a metre based on such alternation, while remaining verse, is close enough in sound to ordinary speech to be very well fitted to a slightly heightened representation of it. The first to recognize this was a remarkable man, Archilochos, the loss of most of whose poetry is one of our most serious deficiencies, for those who were able to read him almost without exception praise him highly. He was the illegitimate great-grandson of one of the original settlers of the island of Thasos, adventurers from Paros in the Aegean Sea, and his date was sometime in the seventh century B.C. Even the miserable scraps we have left of his verse are enough to show that one of his main subjects was himself. We catch a reference to a certain Lykambes, who refused to let the poet marry his daughter (sundry late authors tell us that Archilochos so lampooned him and her that they hanged themselves); we hear of fighting in which he seems to have taken no very illustrious part; we learn that he used beast-fables to illustrate something; and so on, from topic to topic, of very different kinds, but practically all personal. The metre varies also. The iambic rhythms are prominent, but not always the same kind of iambic line; thus, we may get a trimeter (six iambi, or their allowed equivalents; the shorter feet were commonly counted by *metra*, that is to say groups of two), followed by a dimeter

[1] *Rhetoric* iii, 1404a31, 1408b33; *Poetics* 1449a24–27, 1459a11.

(four iambi), or again, hexameters or parts of hexameters mingling with iambic lines; or trochees, which are iambi reversed, the long syllable coming before the short, and to a Greek ear had a hurried effect; and various other combinations. All this, so far as we know, was quite new, and meant that future poets had their choice of rhythms further from or nearer to the cadences of ordinary speech, to suit their choice of subjects more or less exalted, or imaginative, or abstract, as they pleased. They seem not to have been slow to learn the lesson. Archilochos himself used the elegiac couplet, as well as his own innovations, for various purposes. One relic of his compositions in this metre, if indeed it is his, is a single couplet pretty evidently written to order, whether for pay or to oblige a friend; it states simply that someone called Alkibie has dedicated her head-covering to Hera on the occasion of her marriage, a common sort of offering, whether a token of gratitude for past favours from the goddess or, what is perhaps more likely, to keep as it were a part of herself in contact with the deity, who could thus continue to bless her worshipper.

Archilochos had a contemporary, one Semonides (not Simonides, with whom his name is often confused), who like him wrote in iambics and used fables on occasion. One remnant of his work is a poem of some length explaining that women are all made out of one or another of the lower animals, and generally have all their undesirable features, the sow-woman being sluttish, the mare-woman too fine and expensive, and so on, only the bee-woman being really laudable and a good wife. On the whole, he ungallantly concludes, women are the worst plague Zeus has inflicted on unhappy mankind.

He also had an imitator, a certain Hipponax, whose fragments and some much later imitations of his manner show extraordinary features. He seems to have belonged to, or at least to have known, the lowest classes of his native city

Klazomenai. His vocabulary includes words which are not Greek at all and others which, although Greek, seem to have been remarkably mispronounced. His subjects included personal affairs, his relations with a woman called Arete, his quarrel with men named Bupalos and Athenis, who were sculptors and allegedly caricatured him (unlikely, at that date, about a century later than Archilochos), and the disgusting habits and actions of sundry people. His favourite metre was apparently his own invention, the scazon or limping iambic line, which ended with a spondee, producing a strange dragging effect, alien to the rapid movement of iambic metres generally. After him and Archilochos there was no doubt as to the correct kind of verse for lampoons; they should be either in ordinary iambic verses or in scazons. This, however, did not mean that such verses could not be used for other purposes; we shall see that the iambic trimeter especially had a great future.

No people seems to be without songs of some kind, and certainly the earliest Greeks of whom we know anything were not. Homer for instance mentions hymns and other songs quite apart from the performances of bards. Some of these are solos, some choruses; hence there was the material for two highly important kinds of lyric composition, only awaiting someone of sufficient talent to give it permanent form and sufficient variety. A poet such as Archilochos might be called upon to lead off one very popular kind, the dithyramb or hymn to Dionysos the great god of the fertility of nature, who in Greece tended to specialize into a god of wine and vine-dressing. No doubt he would improvise some kind of short stanza and the rest would join in with a refrain, perhaps simply one of the traditional ritual cries. This was hardly literature as yet, but there is at least one trace of a kind of metre, meant definitely for singing, which did not follow exactly the same basic principles as those used hitherto by the regular poets. They, it will be remembered (p. 1), followed a convention by which one long syllable was equal to and could often replace or be replaced by two short ones. But we find among lyric metres some which have a fixed number of syllables to the verse, but not absolute determination of the number of times or beats, for some of them begin with what is called the Aiolic base, two syllables whose quantity apparently did not matter, though in practice one of them at least was generally long, at all events in the specimens which, being written, survive to our time. There is a parallel to this in the Sanskrit *sloka*, which has a definite number of syllables, but no more than a tendency for longs and shorts to occur at given points.

The honour of bringing songs into regular literature belongs to the island of Lesbos and to two of its inhabitants; at least we hear of no more. The dialect spoken there was the Aiolic, which differed in many respects from the Ionic used by Archilochos and Hipponax. Somewhere about the middle of the seventh century B.C. there was born Sappho, in her own dialect Psappho,[1] a lady of good family belonging to the city of Mytilene. She was of a strange temperament, having a strong leaning to sexual inversion, attested by the note of amorous passion which is often found in her addresses to other women. Her life seems to have been normal enough, for she was married and had a daughter. She also had sufficient leisure to form about her a sort of literary circle or *salon*, composed largely of young women. It is possible that it was nominally a cult-association, perhaps for the worship of Aphrodite, goddess of love and marriage, but clearly its chief interest was cultural. To judge by the scanty remnants of her poems, Sappho very frequently though not always addressed the other members of this group, not least one whom she calls Atthis ('the girl from Attica', 'the Athenian'), and it would seem that when one of them left to be married a

---

[1] These are the correct forms, sundry ancient mispellings being ignored. The name seems not to be Greek, but rather Asianic.

marriage-song (*epithalamion*) was composed for her, perhaps
not always by Sappho herself, for some of the fragments
which we have appear not to be in the dialect of Lesbos but
to contain traces of foreign speech. Be that as it may, Sappho's
poetry is of a very high order, not equalled by the compositions of any other woman in the whole history of literature.
It is the more to be regretted that we have nothing like a
complete copy of her works, few poems having come down
entire, or nearly enough entire for modern scholarship to
restore them, and most of what is left being scanty fragments, largely papyrus scraps,[1] many of them too small for
even a complete sentence to be recoverable.[2] Her subjects
are always personal, her own feelings, her relations to other
women and to her brother, who caused her no little anxiety,
and similar intimate matters, with here and there a charming
description of something in nature.

Contemporary and acquainted with Sappho lived another
poet of somewhat similar style, Alkaios (Alcaeus in Latin).
Like her, he wrote on matters which concerned him personally, such as the politics of the time (he was an aristocrat and
so the sworn foe of any tyrant who sprang up in those
disturbed years, when the old order was passing and the new,
more or less democratic, constitutions were not yet born),
wine-drinking, for he was a hearty drinker and produced a
number of good reasons for indulging, love, fighting (often

[1] Papyrus is a water-plant very common in the marshy region of the Nile
delta. From its stem was manufactured the commonest sort of paper used in
antiquity (indeed 'paper' is a corruption of the word 'papyrus'). This paper,
although sensitive to damp, will last indefinitely in a dry climate like that of
Egypt, but becomes very friable. From rubbish-heaps on which ancient towns
dumped their waste paper, including old, worn-out books, modern archaeologists have recovered thousands of written papyri, ranging from long documents to fragments containing a letter or two. The great majority of these are
non-literary, but others include welcome, if imperfect, portions of lost classics.

[2] As much sentimental nonsense has been written about Sappho, it is a
pleasure to mention a recent well-informed and sane work, *Sappho and
Alcaeus*, by Professor D. L. Page (Oxford, 1955). It can be used with profit
even by those who cannot read these poets in the original; perhaps it somewhat undervalues the poetic worth of Sappho.

an incident to the political happenings), and hymns to various deities, for he seems to have been pious after his fashion, whereas Sappho's worship tended to be directed mostly to Aphrodite. Of him again we have nothing but fragments, not one complete poem having come down to us; but the testimonies of later authors are enough to prove that he was held in high esteem in antiquity, and what little we can read of his work does not contradict this.

Both these poets used a fairly wide range of metres, all, however, apparently intended to be sung and that generally, if not always, as solos. Many of the verses, but by no means all, have the Aiolic base already mentioned (p. 33), and apart from this one of their most characteristic rhythms is the choriambus, that is to say one long syllable, two short and another long. The best-known forms, to us, for they have been to some extent naturalized in modern languages, are the Sapphic and the Alcaic stanzas, named after their inventors. The former is used, for instance, by Swinburne, appropriately, for a poem put into Sappho's own mouth, 'All the night sleep came not upon mine eyelids', and burlesqued in the *Anti-Jacobin* in the famous parody of would-be classical style and humanitarian sentiment, 'Needy knife-grinder, whither are you going?' The latter is less familiar, but a specimen of it forms one of Tennyson's metrical experiments, 'O mighty-mouthed inventor of harmonies'.

Yet another poet is represented mostly by fragments, but was well known for some centuries for poems which he never wrote. This was Anakreon of Teos in Ionia, afterwards of Abdera, who lived and wrote in the sixth century. Ionia had developed a civilization in some ways more advanced than that of mainland Greece, but was fast losing political importance and becoming subjugated to the Persian empire, then rapidly expanding. One side of its development was the creation of what others called the Ionian way of life, one of refinement, pleasure and literary interests, not degraded but

D

not involving much effort, physical or mental, although in the same age a few choice spirits were beginning the great series of philosophers who were the fathers of European thought and at least the theoretical side of European science. Anakreon was obviously a lover of pleasure, and as obviously a man of refined tastes. His skill in poetry brought him invitations to two foreign courts, that of Polykrates tyrant of the island of Samos and then that of Hipparchos brother of Hippias the tyrant of Athens. His style was limpidly simple, his metres not very much different from those of the two Aiolians, but not identical with theirs; plainly his compositions again are mostly solo songs, and the subjects are generally personal, often amorous.

Centuries after he was dead, there arose a fashion for composing little poems in an imitation of his manner and subject-matter and in one of his favourite metres. There is a collection of these poems, which include some very pretty specimens, dating from late antiquity and at least beginning to be mistaken for genuine Anakreon by the second century of our era. They are generally called the Anacreontea by modern scholars, but for a considerable time they were still regarded as the real productions of the poet by moderns. It is to these which seventeenth- and eighteenth-century writers, for instance, refer to when they speak of Anakreon, and it was these which Thomas Moore translated. In this curiously indirect way the Ionian gave suggestions to writers of future times, not only poets but, for instance, Hans Christian Andersen, whose pretty little apologue about the old poet who gave shelter to Cupid is founded upon one of the Anacreontea.[1]

Indirect also, of necessity, is most of the influence of Sappho and Alkaios upon moderns, for obviously no one can imitate

---

[1] *Anacreontea* 31 Bergk, in his *Poetae lyrici Graeci*, at the end of the genuine remains of Anakreon. Cupid is of course Eros in the original; the Romans had no love-god of their own and adopted the Greek one, translating his name, rather for literary purposes than for cult.

poems which he has never seen or heard. There are indeed to be found occasional translations of scraps of Sappho especially, produced by writers who either understood enough Greek to make out the originals or had read prose versions in one edition or another; but these are not of much importance. But Catullus and Horace (pp. 180, 211) had read and studied both, and their influence, which will be dealt with later, carried on something of the inspiration of the ancient lyrics to later times. In addition, a life of Sappho was current in antiquity, containing a wholly fabulous element, the story of her love for a certain Phaon, really not a man at all but a minor deity attendant upon Aphrodite. This made its way to later times principally through Ovid (p. 223), and furnished materials for several modern writers. To take one example out of many, Addison uses it for No. 233 of *The Spectator* (Nov. 27, 1711), and adds an episode of his own invention, introducing Alkaios. More important than these direct and conscious imitations of ancient tradition was the fact that the two Lesbian poets, more perhaps than any others, made it known that an individual's loves and hates, hopes and fears, were a proper subject for poetry of a high order. This lesson Greece quickly learned, passed it on to Rome, and so made it known to all Europe. Personal poetry had come to stay.

Singing was part of the education of young Greeks in all ages when anything like schools existed, and consequently there was no lack of recruits for choirs when these were needed for religious or other occasions. In one way it was perhaps easier to train them than it is with us, for nothing like part-singing existed till long after the classical epoch; in another it was more complicated, for singing and dancing were regularly connected, and ancient dancing was not simply a movement of the legs but of the whole body, perhaps especially of the arms, and regularly had a definite significance and was not merely a social amusement; in other words, it was nearer our ballet than our ballroom dancing.

For some reason, the art of choral singing was developed
especially among the Dorians, in other respects rather a backward section culturally of the Greek race, and consequently
choral lyric was generally either in the Doric dialect or in
some approximation to it, subject always to the pervading
influence of the Homeric or Epic forms (cf. p. 17). Doric was
spoken in historical times especially in two regions, the
Peloponnesos and Sicily (largely colonized by Dorians),
though it was not the exclusive speech of either; hence it is
largely, but not entirely, here that we find choral lyric
developing.

Omitting three famous early names, those of Terpandros of
Lesbos, who apparently composed sometimes in Sparta, Arion
of Corinth, and the Sicilian Stesichoros, because little or nothing
remains of their works, we may begin with a famous Spartan
(originally a native of Sardis in Lydia, but apparently naturalized
in the city where he composed his works), namely Alkman.
He lived fairly early in the seventh century, at which time
Sparta was not yet the mere armed camp it came to be later,
but something of a cultural and artistic centre, despite its
frequent wars. We have, besides smaller fragments, a considerable portion of a long poem of his, a *partheneion*, i.e. a
song to be performed by a chorus of girls. It is a charming
composition, despite the difficulties which it has for us, who
read it from a battered papyrus and have but an imperfect
knowledge of Spartan Doric of that date. Although it is
choral and contains, or rather contained, for at this point it is
too much damaged to yield complete sense, a mythological
theme taken from the adventurous life of Herakles, a large
part of it is intensely personal. The girls exchange compli-
ments with one another; evidently a good part of the poem
was not sung by the full chorus, but by parts of it, or even by
single voices. The tone is joyous and light-hearted, even
jocular. Other specimens of Alkman's work, although quite
short and fragmentary, again are personal, often dealing with

his own experiences and feelings. We do not know whether these belong to choral or solo poems; some are distinctly amatory, and indeed in later times some considered him the originator of love-poems. Others, including one very delightful fragment which is not in Doric at all but rather in Epic, show an exquisite feeling for nature. The *partheneion*, however,[1] shows that this branch of poetry had already some of the characteristics of its later and more developed form, the myth and the personal element. It has not as yet the characteristic metrical form, for it is simply in stanzas which agree with one another in metre, in other words can all be sung to the same tune. The later and more elaborate works of this kind generally, though not always, have a structure said to have been invented by Stesichoros, the triad. This consists of two stanzas agreeing exactly with one another in scansion, followed by a third which may be in a similar metre, but never in the same. This triad is then repeated as often as the author pleases till the end of the poem. We find Ibykos using this structure in the sixth century, and also departing from the simple and straightforward language of Alkman for something much more elaborate and gorgeous.[2] We find it again in what we have of Simonides of Keos, later in the same century, who although an Ionian conformed to the tradition of the *genre* and wrote his choral lyrics in Doric. It is much to be regretted that we have no complete poem of his, except some epigrams (quite a number reputedly by him have come down to us, but some cannot possibly be his, others are highly doubtful), for his was one of the great names of lyric poetry, according to the universal testimony of later writers. He was moreover definitely a professional poet, writing for pay. His task was much more elaborate than that of a modern who furnishes

[1] There is a good critical edition, containing also a translation and discussion of the many difficulties, by D. L. Page, *Alcman: the Partheneion* (Oxford, 1957).

[2] This is the Ibykos whose murder was revealed by the cranes to which he appealed when dying, as told in Schiller's well-known poem, drawing on classical tradition.

the libretto for some musical work such as an opera, for a composer of choral lyric invariably, so far as we know, composed the music, arranged the dancing, and trained the chorus, or at least superintended its training. He may also in many cases, perhaps in most, have conducted the actual performance.

However, we possess a large proportion, perhaps about a quarter, of the work of the most famous poet of this kind, Pindar (*Pindaros*) of Thebes. There survive to us almost complete his four books of epinikian odes, that is to say compositions performed in celebration of someone's victory in one of the events of the numerous athletic contests which made up a conspicuous part of many Greek festivals, and particularly in the four 'holy' or 'garlanded' contests, at Olympia, Delphoi, Nemea and the Isthmus of Corinth, in honour respectively of Zeus, Apollo, Zeus again and Poseidon. Unlike most contests, these four offered no prizes of material value, but only garlands of various materials, appropriate to the deities honoured. To win in racing, wrestling or any other event was considered a very great distinction, not only for the athlete or chariot-driver in question but for his city, and to win at Olympia was the greatest distinction of all. It was therefore no wonder that among a people fond alike of music and of sport a celebration of the event should mark his return home and include the singing of an appropriate ode composed for the occasion. It might seem that the subject of such odes was limited and unpromising; but in the hands of Pindar, no doubt in those of Simonides, and to no small extent as dealt with by Bakchylides (see p. 45) excellent poems resulted; Pindar in particular was a poet of the first order and created masterpieces out of the commemoration of what, to us, were rather commonplace affairs, the winning for instance of a boxing-match by a boy or a young man. Perhaps we may get some idea of the importance of such victories to contemporary feeling if we imagine that we seriously believed that to win the Derby or some other famous horse-race, to become champion of a country in boxing or wrestling, or to be a member of the victorious football or baseball team was a signal mark of divine favour. For some such belief seems to have been current in classical Greece, before their sport degenerated into the performances of professionals, and not of amateurs who had found time for the long period of training necessary.

With this background, therefore, Pindar and the others went to work. How they constructed their poems will perhaps be most clearly seen if we analyse one ode of Pindar. The eighth Olympian ode will serve as well as another. It commemorates the victory in the boys' wrestling-match of a young Aiginetan, by name Alkimedon, a member of a family of some distinction, especially for athletic prowess. Pindar begins with an address to Olympia, the 'mother of golden-garlanded contests' and 'mistress of truth', that is the seat of the most important athletic contests, 'golden' because they are glorious and perhaps also because of their religious associations, and 'truth' in reference to certain divinatory practices which the poet, an intensely religious man, evidently held in great esteem. He then passes to the victor's kinsmen, who had won events at other games, including the Nemean, and to the victor himself, and so to his native country with its high reputation for justice to strangers (it was an important trading-place and seems to have had good courts for settling disputes between native and foreign merchants), next to a favourite topic, the heroic traditions of the island. Legend made its first ruler the righteous king Aiakos, father of a line of heroes who include Achilles and the greater Aias; Pindar tells how Apollo and Poseidon made him their fellow-worker when they built the walls of Troy, and how a portent showed that the city would be taken at the point where his mortal hands had raised the fortifications. Here we have a regular element of all the longer odes, the myth, which is oftener than not a local one, as might indeed be expected. Now, returning to the event which is the occasion of the ode, he digresses to praise Melesias, the boy's Athenian trainer, to whom, although his city was Aigina's bitter enemy, a share of credit for the success is due; but he had good material to train, for this is the thirtieth victory a pupil of his has won. Young Alkimedon's combination of good fortune and courage sheds new lustre on the whole family; doubtless even their dead will hear of it and tell one another in the underworld.

It will be seen that the whole ode holds together, with the myth as its central feature and the rest leading up to and away from it, like the lines of a good picture. The transitions from one part of an ode to another are not always as easy to follow as in this one, but always intelligible, at least to Pindar's audience, which knew small details concerning family history and local traditions now lost to us. The metre is of the kind already described, the group of three stanzas (known technically as strophe, antistrophe and epode, that is to say turn, counter-turn and after-song) being repeated with strict adherence to the metre of the first triad, only the smallest departures being allowed (as we occasionally allow two notes to be sung in the time of one, or a rest to take up part of a beat, in a song which uses the same air for more than one stanza). Nothing more unlike the 'Pindaric' odes of our literature could well be imagined, and the reason is not very far to seek. Pindar's metrical systems are not easy to follow without considerable knowledge of the technique of ancient poetry and careful study of his and his fellow-poets' odes. Horace in an unguarded moment[1] said of his dithyrambs that they move in 'rhythms free from law', which is not true even of them; he meant probably no more than to contrast them with the simple metres he himself employed. Moderns, knowing much less than Horace did of Pindar, seem to have grasped at this statement, and concluded that in odes like his one might take any metrical licence and vary the metre from line to

---

[1] Horace, *Odes* iv, 2, 11-12.

line as much as one chose, to say nothing of the subject-matter.

Besides the epinikians, we have from various sources considerable remnants of other poems by this great master, paeans and dithyrambs, that is respectively hymns in honour of Apollo and of Dionysos, *partheneia* (see p. 38), encomia, or poems in praise of various persons, dirges, presumably to be sung at funerals, and so forth. All alike use a most gorgeous and complicated style, full of metaphors, similes and other figurative kinds of language, by no means always easy to understand and impossible to translate adequately into any other tongue, though many attempts have been made, some of them very meritorious. An accidental difficulty for us is that we know but little of the people for whom he wrote, though remnants of a good ancient commentary preserve some information about them. It may be doubted if his audiences always caught his full meaning, even with their local knowledge and the expressive gestures of the chorus to help them.

We know something of his life. Born in Thebes, probably in 522 B.C., possibly in 518, he went while still a young man to Athens, where good training in the difficult and complicated art of poetry was to be had. There he seems to have made the acquaintance of Aeschylus (see p. 56) and formed a friendship with him. Afterwards events took place which must greatly have saddened him. Athens and Thebes became enemies in 480, when the Thebans were allies of the invading Persians while the Athenians were the foremost champions of the Greek cause. Pindar therefore saw the crushing defeat of his native place, without the consolation of knowing that his countrymen had espoused a righteous cause, for there is little doubt that his sympathies were with Greece. In or about 476 he went to the court of Hieron, king or tyrant of Syracuse, and was for a while on friendly terms with both him and Theron tyrant of Akragas (Agrigentum). Before long, however, Simonides and his nephew (see p. 44) ousted him from

Hieron's favour, for they were better and more supple courtiers than Pindar, who, proud in the consciousness of his genius, spoke even to the highest as equal to equal, king of poets to kings of men. Returning to Thebes, he before long had fresh griefs, for Athenian expansion brought about the ruin of Aigina, a land which he loved, it seems, next to his own, since it was Dorian and aristocratic, and Pindar was an old-fashioned gentleman, a lover of Dorian ways, which he repeatedly praises, with no great affection for anything democratic. But he was fair-minded enough to praise Athens when he felt her deserving of praise, thus incurring some hostility at home. He seems to have lived comfortably, getting a good income from his poetry (an anecdote or two accuses him, as others do Simonides, of avarice; in other words, both were good men of business). Certainly he lived piously, conservative in this as in other things, for he speaks contemptuously of the philosophy which was growing up in his time, and always reverently of the traditional gods, re-fusing to believe myths derogatory of them. His especial zeal was for Apollo; Thebes is not far from the site of the Delphic oracle. That he believed he occasionally had visions of deities or at least of heroes (venerated ghosts of the great men of old days) is indicated not only by stories told of him in later times but by his own statement that the hero Alkmeon once appeared to him on the road to Delphoi, for that is the plain meaning of the eighth Pythian Ode, line 62. He also was interested, as two or three compositions of his show, in certain eschatological doctrines of the day which painted a less gloomy and empty picture of the life after death than that generally accepted in current Greek belief. He died when about eighty years old.

Bakchylides, Simonides' nephew, was a mere name to us until 1897, when a lucky papyrus find restored a considerable portion of his work, which was quickly published and has since been studied and commented on by a number of good scholars. He was some dozen years or a little more younger than Pindar, and outlived him, perhaps till about 430 B.C. His epinikians are of the Pindaric pattern, which clearly was not peculiar to any one poet, but the regular form of the time. Never so good as the Theban's work, they are none the less of no small merit. We have also what for some unknown reason are described as dithyrambs, which they are not, but narrative poems of no great length, good in style and interesting in content. He hardly deserves the contempt with which Pindar seems to speak of him.[1]

There were other lyric poets; ancient critics had a 'canon' or authorized list of nine names in all. But those of whom we know most have been dealt with. If we look for their influence on modern literature, it is to be found especially in the longer and more elaborate odes. Setting aside wretched compositions made to order for royal birthdays and the like by very minor poets laureate, we have abundance of these by good hands, some for a special occasion, as Dryden's *Alexander's Feast; | or The Power of Musique. | An Ode In Honour of | St Cecilia's Day: 1697* – to give it its full original title. This really has some likeness to a Pindaric ode, for its central feature is the story of how the music of Timotheos[2] roused various emotions in Alexander the Great, at Persepolis.

[1] It is generally accepted that when he mentions 'a pair of noisy learners who chatter ineffectually, like crows, against the divine bird of Zeus' (i.e. the eagle, meaning himself) he alludes to Simonides and Bakchylides, *Olympians* ii, 94 ff.

[2] This Timotheos was a real person, popular in his own day (he was born about the middle of the fifth century B.C. and died about 360, wherefore he could not possibly have been with Alexander; Dryden's chronology is not so good as his poetry). Besides a number of fragments, we have a large portion of one of his lyric poems, *The Persians*, preserved on a papyrus. He was a modernist in music and in other things; a fragment of one of his works says that he does not sing old strains, for the new is always better, so the old Muse (=poetry and music) may go away (fgt. 7 Diehl). 'The new' is certainly not better in the surviving poem, though it has an excellent theme, Xerxes' defeat at Salamis. The metres are jerky and peculiar, the style wantonly obscure without being in the least impressive, and the author's taste execrable; for instance, this being supposedly serious lyric, he introduces a Persian prisoner begging for mercy in broken Greek, as if it were a scene of Comedy. A quaint feature of the work is that he never mentions the Athenians, who were the chief actors throughout the real battle and provided most of the Greek ships engaged. No doubt he wrote after the Peloponnesian War had broken the power of Athens.

Another honourable exception to the general rule that 'Pindaric' odes by moderns are very unlike Pindar is furnished by Thomas Gray. It is well known that he twice (in *The Bard* and *The Progress of Poesy*) tried his hand at this sort of composition and, although his themes are hardly what a Greek choral lyricist would have chosen, at least he had been to considerable trouble to discover the form of the ancient compositions. On March 17, 1747, he writes to Wharton that he is 'now in Pindar and Lysias: for I take verse and prose together like bread and cheese'. Nearly eight years later, on March 9, 1755, he is disputing with the same correspondent on the proper management of 'strophe and antistrophe', and maintaining that they should not be more than nine lines long at most, for if longer 'methinks it has little or no effect upon the ear, which scarce perceives the regular return of metres, at so great a distance from one another'. This is a just observation from the point of view of one to whom verse was a thing to be read aloud; Gray perhaps did not know that in Pindar's time the whole composition was not only sung but danced, so that the metrical correspondences were given a threefold emphasis; in any case, this was irrelevant to him, for he had no intention of having his works set to music and danced out. The fundamental fact about the structure he had grasped adequately, and we have Mason's unexceptionable testimony that 'there was nothing he more disliked than that chain of irregular stanzas which Cowley introduced, and falsely called Pindaric'.[1]

When some moderns write odes to personifications or abstractions, they again have classical precedent. If Wordsworth composed an *Ode to Duty*, Aristotle has left us one *To Virtue* (or Excellence, *arete*), though he was a better philosopher

[1] The passages quoted may perhaps be found most conveniently in *Poems and Letters by Thomas Gray* (ed. John Drinkwater, Everyman Library), pp. 155 and 184-5. Another honourable exception to the un-Pindaric metres of English 'Pindaric' odes is James Beattie, whose *Ode to Hope* is written in perfectly correct triads, corresponding strictly with one another, and so forming a laudable metrical exercise, though not a great poem.

than poet, and Pindar would have quite understood the Englishman's beginning 'Stern daughter of the voice of God', seeing that he greeted Quiet in the eighth Pythian Ode and Youthful Beauty in the eighth Nemean in like style. Such works as Shelley's *Skylark* and *Cloud* have less direct classical authority, but birds, especially nightingales, are a common incidental subject of ancient poetry and clouds have a little mythology of their own. Compositions in praise of sundry non-human objects, some of them highly unlikely, are among the most characteristic performances of ancient rhetoricians, from Gorgias and Isokrates (pp. 106, 108) on; but whereas they used ornate and elaborate prose, the moderns have generally brought such subjects back to poetry.

With the death of Bakchylides, the great age of Greek lyric poetry as a separate art, not as part of another kind of literature, came to an end. It would have done so in any case, sooner or later, for it seems to be the invariable rule in literature that every form it takes rises to its greatest height and then, slowly or quickly, declines. Music and the accompanying words continued to be popular, and we shall see in the next chapter that they were important for some time in drama, but great poetry was not produced in this form outside drama, so far as our evidence goes, from the fifth century to the end of antiquity. Such specimens of it as we have are merely showy, like the work of Timotheos (see p. 45, n. 2), or commonplace, such as almost anyone who had had the necessary technical training could turn out, and many no doubt did, to satisfy the continuing demand for performances by choirs at festivals. But there never was another Pindar nor another Simonides. Something of the kind is to be seen in modern literature; poetry of various sorts continues to be composed, and some of it is good, but I know of no one who is likely, in any European language, to attempt another *Alexander's Feast*, or *Skylark*, or *Intimations of Immortality*.

It is worth while to reckon up the technical procedures

available to Greek poets by about the beginning of the fifth century. They had metres (the iambic and trochaic) suitable for imitating straightforward narrative and ordinary speech, whether calm or emotional. They had the traditional metre (the hexameter) for lofty and dignified narration, description or instruction. To lower the tone, without becoming in the least prosaic, they had the elegiac couplet. Finally, to express any of a variety of emotions, they possessed the lyric metres. As to language, they had precedent for using any one of three, Ionic, Aiolic and Doric, besides the old, artificial Epic speech. Now a fourth dialect and a new centre of literary activity appeared.

III

Attic Drama

LIVING AS THEY DID IN COMMUNITIES OF NO
great size, separated from one another by the more
hilly and unfertile parts of their country, and never
forming a single nation, the Greeks naturally varied in their
speech from one place to another. Modern linguists distinguish
some ten dialects of classical Greek, but of these only four
ever were of literary importance. Three have already been
mentioned (see p. 48), we have now to deal with a fourth,
and also with a fourth people. The inhabitants of Attica
(properly *Attike*), the territory of which Athens was the
capital and seat of government, spoke a dialect somewhat
like Ionic, claimed to be the ancestors of the Ionians, and kept
up fairly close relations with them from early times. Till the
advent of the enlightened tyrant[1] Peisistratos (in power
560–527, with some interruptions), Athens was of no great
importance, politically or otherwise. He did much to expand
her trade and to encourage literature and art, and his sons
followed his policy in this respect till the fall of the tyranny
and establishment of a republican constitution in 510. Twenty
years later the State gained great prestige by defeating a
Persian raiding force at Marathon, and in 480 and the following years Athens was the primary force behind the successful
Greek resistance to the large-scale invasion of Xerxes. The
fifth century was the time of Athenian expansion, and also

[1] A Greek tyrant (*tyrannos*, simply an Asianic word for 'king') was what
modern journalism absurdly calls a dictator, one who got and held power by
unconstitutional means. The strong Greek respect for law led sooner or later
to the replacement of the tyrants, however moderate and popular, by constitutional governments, democratic or other.

of Athenian poetry, prose being rather the product of the following century. The greatest contribution so far as compositions in verse were concerned was a new literary form, the drama, tragic and comic.

Exactly how Tragedy originated is a problem perhaps never to be solved, for we lack documentary evidence of its early stages. But, as we invariably find it associated with a religious festival (in Attica, always with one of the festivals of Dionysos), it is highly likely that its origin was religious. There is no lack of evidence from other parts of the world that dramatic performances are part of religious rites. To take one example recently published, the Marind-anim of Dutch New Guinea believe in the existence of certain superhuman beings which they call *demas*, and credit them, not indeed with the creation of the world, but with originating the outstanding features of it as they now are. But the power which brought about these partial creations is apt to become exhausted and needs renewing from time to time. This is done by acting out certain myths concerning the *demas* and their activities, which must be done with the most minute accuracy, else the world would become imperfect.[1] There is no sufficient evidence that Greek myths ever were used in this manner, but it remains quite possible that something of the kind was customary among the pre-Greek inhabitants of the country, at all events of Attica, in connexion with the worship of certain local gods, whose cult may have been swallowed up by that of Dionysos when his religion was established in Greece (about the seventh century B.C., as is usually supposed). If anything of the kind did exist and was taken over by the Greeks on their arrival (a thing not at all improbable, for polytheists are generally very hospitable to strange cults, especially those of a land in which they mean to settle), we have a reasonable origin for Tragedy, the more so as gods of the fertility of nature often

[1] H. Nevermann, *Söhne des tötenden Vaters* (Kassel, Erich Röth, 1957) pp. 12 f.

are thought of as dying and coming to life again, and in a tragedy someone usually dies, or at least is in great danger of death. However, all this is hypothetical to the last degree, and other suggestions which have been made ever since the days of Aristotle (who supposed that Tragedy developed out of the dithyramb) are also without solid proof. It is indeed more than likely that the earliest tragedies were never preserved, in the public archives or otherwise, not impossible that they never were written down. Hence no good evidence of their nature could be available to Aristotle, and certainly none is to be had now.

Traditionally, the first man to produce anything like regular tragedies, i.e. plays having an acting-part as well as the songs of the chorus, was a certain Thespis of the deme[1] Ikaria. He is alleged to have invented the 'answerer' (*hypokrites*), i.e. the actor who 'answered' the questions or other utterances of the chorus. This person had a tent or marquee (*skene*) into which he could retire, and there make any change of costume which was necessary and so act several parts, provided only one person was on the stage at a time.[2] About 536 B.C. this innovator is said to have produced, or as the Greeks put it 'taught', some of his plays, which probably means that he received official recognition, presumably from Peisistratos, and henceforth Tragedy was part of the State festivals of Dionysos. But Thespis remains a very vague figure, and none of his work survives; a few fragments attributed to him have long been recognized as forgeries, of much later date than the sixth century. Practically, the history of the stage begins with

---

[1] Attica was divided into a number of demes, *demoi*, roughly corresponding to our parishes, each of which had its own local cults and a certain amount of self-government in local affairs. Ikaria had a cult of Dionysos, and possibly before his arrival of some other power of fertility or of viticulture, perhaps the 'hero' Ikaros.

[2] By 'stage' is meant simply that part of the theatre which the actor or actors used. Whether it was raised or otherwise marked off from the orchestra (see below) is a disputed point and of small importance from the purely literary point of view.

E

Phrynichos, who is first heard of in 511 and was celebrated in later times especially for the beauty of his lyrics. The earliest author of whom we have anything more than a few short quotations is the great Aeschylus.

Before attempting to sketch the careers of him and his fellow-poets, it is well to realize how the plays were produced. The occasion (apart from some performances of no great importance up and down the countryside, the Rural Dionysia) was either the Lenaia, in the month Gamelion (about January–February) or the Great, or Urban, Dionysia, in Elaphebolion, about two months later.[1] The place was the precinct of Dionysos on the south-east slope of the Akropolis, the rocky hill which was the most ancient part of Athens and remained its citadel and the site of its most important temples. Here, at the foot of the hill, was traced out the *orchestra*, the dancing-floor, a great circle, used by whatever choruses, dramatic or other, might be performing. On the side towards the hill was the place for the spectators, who in early times were accommodated on a sort of temporary grandstand of wood, later on more and more elaborate and permanent seats. At the opposite side were the stage-buildings, the *skene*, at first hardly more than a wooden partition with entrances cut through it for the actors, the chorus coming in around the ends by the passages known variously as *eisodoi* (ways in) or *parodoi* (ways beside). Through the principal entrance there could be rolled a platform large enough for two or three persons to stand on; this was the conventional way of showing the inside of a building which the *skene* represented. Later constructions made the stage-buildings more elaborate and permanent, stone instead of wood, but there continued to be no curtain,

[1] No Greek month corresponds exactly to one of ours, for their calendars were soli-lunar, months coinciding, at least theoretically, with lunations and an extra month being intercalated from time to time; see the art. *Calendar* in any classical dictionary. Hence any Greek date shifts about as much as that of Easter when equated with the Julian calendar. For details of the dramatic festivals, see the excellent works of Sir A. W. Pickard-Cambridge.

no realistic scenery, and no possibility of lighting effects, for
the whole performance took place in broad daylight; if it was
supposed to be night, someone, actor, chorus, or chorus-
leader, mentioned it, as when required one of them told the
audience where the action was supposed to take place, and
now and then even what expression was on the face of one
of the characters; for the actors were masked, and so no play
of features was possible, even if in so large an auditorium (the
Theatre of Dionysos could hold several thousands) it could
have been seen had the actor worn no mask. The play consisted of a prologue, that is to say everything which took place
before the chorus entered (if they did not, as in some dramas,
come on at the very beginning) followed by as many scenes,
epeisodia, as the poet chose, separated by odes, *stasima*, sung by
the chorus. During one of these, as much time might elapse
as the author wished, for no Greek had ever heard of the
notorious Unity of Time, an invention of post-Renaissance
critics misinterpreting Aristotle, nor for that matter of Unity
of Place, as several changes of scene in the surviving plays
prove. It is, however, a fact that with the typical Greek fond-
ness for simple, concentrated effects in art or literature, the
action of a play is usually all in one place and the time supposed to elapse not more than about a day. According to
tradition, Aeschylus first introduced a second actor, Sophokles
a third, and there are a very few scenes in which a fourth
would be needed for some few lines. The poet seems to have
been regularly his own stage-manager.

The chorus consisted originally of twelve persons, later of
fifteen. Their songs, in keeping with the tradition of choral
lyric, had a sort of Doric flavour, certain inflexions belonging
to that dialect being commonly used, and some few Doric
forms occurring sporadically even in the spoken dialogue;
but the language in general was Attic, with the usual poetical
freedom of using archaic forms and words, and a general
stateliness of style which raised the tone of the play above the

commonplace. This naturally differed from one poet to another, being most marked in Aeschylus, least in Euripides, but it is never absent altogether and prose is nowhere used except for a few passages in Comedy, and in those for some special reason. The proportion of sung to spoken parts varies, getting gradually less as Tragedy develops; the earlier plays were more like our operas than our ordinary dramas. The importance of the chorus also varies very much, its members being anything from the principal characters, as in the *Suppliants* of Aeschylus, to casual spectators, as in the *Iphigeneia in Aulis* of Euripides. Its members were amateurs, furnished by one or another of the twelve tribes into which the Athenian citizens were divided. The actors were regularly professionals, and must have been highly trained and in possession of very good voices, to make themselves clearly heard (though the acoustic properties of the theatre were excellent), and also to sing on occasion elaborate solos, or take part in sung scenes with the chorus.

A minor puzzle, never yet satisfactorily solved, is why the performance was called a goat-song, for that is what Tragedy (*tragoidia*) properly means. The ancient explanation is that in the days of Thespis the best performance was rewarded with the prize of a he-goat, an animal often sacrificed to Dionysos; but it is more than likely that this is simply some etymologizer's guess. It cannot be said that any suggestion put forward by a modern is much more plausible.

These then were the conditions under which Aeschylus (properly *Aischylos*) and his contemporaries competed, for there was regularly a competition between three tragedians, each of whom seems to have put on a group of three tragedies, which might or might not be connected in subject so as to tell successive parts of the same story, followed by a play of lighter tone, generally a satyr-drama, that is to say one whose chorus was composed of satyrs (*satyroi*, lustful beings of grotesque but quasi-human shape, with horses' tails, attendant on

Dionysos) and the plot treated in a more or less burlesque fashion.[1] This, at all events, was the normal arrangement in Aeschylus' time, from quite early in his career; his *Suppliants*, for instance (see below), was the first of three plays which told the story of the daughters of Danaos and was followed by another which treated of one of them, Amymone, and her adventure with a satyr; but we do not know how old it was. The plays having been performed, a jury or committee of citizens (*kritai*, literally choosers, hence the words 'critic' and 'criticism') gave their opinion as to who had done best, and a prize was accordingly awarded him. The plots of all the plays were generally mythological, but historical subjects were occasionally used. Phrynichos for instance composed at least two dealing with recent events, the *Phoenicians* and the *Sack of Miletos*, and we have one such by Aeschylus, the *Persians* (see p. 57).

Aeschylus was born in Eleusis, the site of the famous Mysteries, about 525 B.C., and died near Gela in Sicily in 456/55.[2] He is said to have begun to exhibit plays between

---

[1] We have but one complete specimen of a satyr-play, the *Cyclops* of Euripides, a large portion of another, the *Trackers* (*Ichneutai*) of Sophokles and fragments of others. Pratinas, a somewhat older contemporary of Aeschylus, is said to have composed more satyr-plays than any other, thirty-two out of a total of fifty, which certainly seems as if it was not yet the rule in his time that but one play out of every four should be of this sort. For a long time after the Revival of Letters the accidental resemblance between *satyros* and Latin *satura* led to the wrong idea that these plays were satirical in tone, dealing with the vices and absurdities of mankind. This for instance is assumed by Sidney in his *Apologie for Poetry*. It was put right by the great scholar Isaac Casaubon in his treatise *De Satyrica et Satira* (Paris, 1595), but needless to say the half-educated continued in the error for long after; it was one of the many blunders which Bentley lashed in Boyle's silly book on the Epistles of Phalaris (*Dissertation upon Phalaris*, pp. 287, 306, Wagner). As to the plots of Tragedy in general, it is asserted by some ancient authorities that they all dealt originally with the adventures of Dionysos, and in support a common proverb is quoted 'nothing to do with Dionysos', meaning that something is quite off the point. Such facts as we have concerning the earliest known plays do not confirm this, but it may have been true in the times of Thespis. Myths concerning the god naturally could be and were used as well as any others, by those poets of whom we know anything definite.

[2] Besides the difficulty of the months, explained in note 1, p. 52, Greek years did not begin at the same time in all places. At Athens, whose years form part of

500 and 497 and to have won the first prize for the first time in 484. He composed about ninety plays in all, of which we have seven, a selection made at some unknown date, but long after his death. He spent most of his life in Athens, save for two visits to Sicily, one at the invitation of Hieron of Syracuse, between 472 and 468, the other after 458. In temperament he was deeply religious, more than a little of a prophet as well as a poet, and intensely interested in theological and moral problems. As already mentioned (p. 43), he probably was acquainted with Pindar, and certainly the two poets knew each other's work and were somewhat influenced by one another. The surviving plays are the following.

The Suppliants (*Hiketides*), the earliest Greek play left to us,[1] though its precise date is unknown. It has come down in one manuscript, itself evidently copied from a copy damaged and illegible in places, and hence its text is often uncertain or even past recovery. But the structure and the greater part of the text are plain enough. As already mentioned, it deals with the fortunes of the daughters of Danaos (cf. p. 54). They with their attendant maids form the chorus; their father accompanies them. They arrive in Argos and take refuge in a holy place where several statues or emblems of the gods are to be seen. In a long series of lyric utterances,[2] they explain their condition; they are descendants of Zeus' love, the Argive

---

the basis of our chronology, the year began with the first new moon after the summer solstice (Longest Day). Hence, unless we know in what Athenian month, or at least in which half of the year, an event took place, we are obliged to equate one Athenian year with two of ours, seeing that the first half, approximately, was in one and the second in the other.

[1] Some doubt has been thrown on this by a papyrus scrap (Oxyrhynchus Papyri No. 2256, 3) which records the performance of two plays of this tetralogy along with others known to be comparatively late. But in my opinion this can refer only to a 'revival', some time after Aeschylus' death.

[2] 175 lines, counting the opening passage, which is in anapaests (two short syllables followed by one long, or an equivalent of this). For the story of Danaos and his quarrel with his brother, see Rose, *Handbook of Greek Mythology*, p. 272; for Io, ibid., 271 f. Exactly how the rest of the story was handled in the remaining plays we do not know; they were entitled *Egyptians* and *Daughters of Danaos* respectively.

priestess Io, and have fled to their ancestors' land for refuge from their cousins, the sons of their father's brother Aigyptos, who would force them into marriage. Their father now tells them that he sees troops coming, and presently the King of Argos arrives and asks their business. They convince him that, despite their foreign dress and complexion, they are true Argives, and ask for protection against their cousins. He, on their threatening to hang themselves in the holy place, thus polluting it unspeakably, compromises by putting the question to an assembly of his people, and Danaos goes with him to state his daughters' case, for women could not appear before such a public body in person. Returning, after a long ode which tells of Io's wanderings and glorifies the power of Zeus, Danaos announces that the citizens have unanimously voted to protect them. Shortly afterwards the sons of Aigyptos arrive by ship and their herald tries to remove the daughters of Danaos by force. The King, fetched by Danaos, arrives in time to drive him away, and the members of the chorus leave the theatre, after invoking blessings on Argos and discussing their own future, to safe quarters in the city. In almost no scene of this play, except that in which the King rebukes the Herald, is a second actor absolutely necessary; the choral part, not counting the scenes in which the leader of the chorus speaks and does not sing, amounts to some 560 lines out of about 1,075, besides some short solos from the Herald. We are not very far from what we may suppose the technique of Phrynichos to have been.

In 472 Aeschylus produced the second play which we have, the *Persians* (*Persai*), rehandling the theme already treated by Phrynichos (p. 55). The chorus is composed of the elders of Xerxes' royal council, who anxiously await news from the front. Queen Atossa, Xerxes' mother, enters and tells them of a disquieting dream which bodes ill for her son. They advise propitiatory ceremonies and answer her questions concerning Athens. Enter a Messenger, bringing news of the defeat of the

Persian navy at Salamis and the disastrous retreat of the army. On the advice of the elders, Atossa and they summon the ghost of Dareios, who blames Xerxes' rashness for the ill-fortune, which, however, was to have come sooner or later on Persia. The ghost disappears, and Xerxes enters, alone and in rags. His and the chorus's laments conclude the play. Again the choral part is large, but in the central scenes two actors are definitely needed and used with some skill, first for the Messenger's report and Atossa's horrified comments, next for her dialogue with the spirit of her dead husband. A remarkable feature, considering how short a time intervened between the end of the war and the composition of the play, is that the Persians are neither ridiculous nor undignified and there is no cheap exultation over them.

Next, in 467, came the *Seven against Thebes*, a magnificent play with further advances in stage technique. The interest lies in the central character, king Eteokles, who has the opening speech, while the chorus of Theban girls, instead of marching in to anapaests as the choruses of the two earlier plays do, run in, singing in a rhythm denoting strong emotion, in this case fear. The city is being attacked by the Argive army supporting Polyneikes, Eteokles' brother.[1] Eteokles, kept informed of the enemy's dispositions by a scout, proceeds to detail, one after another, appropriate defenders of the city's seven gates against the Argive champions who are to attack them. Last comes the gate he himself means to defend, and now he learns that the assailant is his own brother. He accepts what he considers his abandonment by the gods, goes out to the unnatural conflict, and a messenger brings word that the Argive army is defeated, but the two brothers have killed each other. With the lamentations over their bodies the play ends.[2] The rest of the trilogy, of which this is the

[1] For the legend, see Rose, op. cit., pp. 187-92.
[2] That is, the play as Aeschylus wrote it. Our manuscripts label the leaders of the two halves of the chorus Antigone and Ismene, the two sisters of Eteokles and Polyneikes, and add an extra scene imitated from the *Antigone*

third play, told the earlier parts of the story, from the sin of Laios to the misfortunes of Oidipus and his curse on his sons.

Here the interest is entirely in the character of Eteokles, a courageous and resolute man, but haunted by apprehension of the results which the past sins of his family may bring about. He is in no way the helpless puppet of fate, an idea quite foreign to Greek tragedy, but influenced for ill by the actions of his father and grandfather, or rather by his own brooding on them. The psychology, for Aeschylus was a great psychologist, is typical of the poet.

Next in order of time comes the poet's greatest work, the Trilogy, sometimes known in antiquity as the *Oresteia*, or work concerning Orestes. Its three plays, for the satyr-play which completed the tetralogy is lost, are the *Agamemnon*, *Choephoroe* (Libation-Bearers) and *Eumenides*. It is the only trilogy we have, and tells a continued story, covering the events of something like a decade. In the first play, beacon-signals announce to Argos that Troy has fallen, and Klytai-mestra, Agamemnon's queen and secretly his implacable enemy, because he had sacrificed their daughter Iphigeneia to get favourable winds for the fleet on its way to Troy, passes the news on to the chorus. This is 'about the setting of the Pleiads', that is to say about the beginning of November. After a long choral ode, one of the several magnificent lyrics of the play, a Herald comes in, bedaubed with summer dust and incidentally mentioning the date, the tenth day of the year, i.e. about the beginning of July. He announces the arrival of Agamemnon, but on further enquiry tells the chorus that most of the fleet has been wrecked or scattered by a violent storm, and no one knows whether Agamemnon's brother Menelaos is alive or dead. Klytaimestra welcomes her

---

of Sophokles (see below, p. 63). This was no doubt intended for a revival of the play, not earlier than the concluding years of the fifth century and probably later.

husband with a great show of affection and, having beguiled him into the palace, murders him in his bath. His captive, the prophetess Kassandra, in a most impressive scene, foresees the murder and vainly tries to warn the chorus. The queen's lover Aigisthos now enters, full of swaggering bravado and telling at length the tale of the wrongs done to his father Thyestes by Atreus father of Agamemnon. The chorus and he, when on the point of fighting, are separated by Klytaimestra. The *Choephoroe* begins with the entrance of Orestes, son of Agamemnon, who was a child at the time of the earlier play. He is now a young man, returned from the home of a family friend whose son, Pylades, is his faithful companion, and charged by Apollo with the duty of avenging his father. Getting entrance to the palace with a false tale of Orestes' death, the young men set upon and kill Aigisthos, Orestes then, after some natural hesitation, putting Klytaimestra to death. In the last scene, supposed to be the morning after the slayings, he begins to be haunted by the Erinyes, the powers which avenge the spilling of kindred blood. The title of this play refers to the sending by Klytaimestra of offerings to her husband's grave, in a vain attempt to undo the evil omen of a dream she has had. The *Eumenides* begins at Delphoi, whither Orestes has gone for purification and deliverance from his pursuers. Apollo sends him on to Athens, whither he has arrived in the next scene, but without throwing off the Erinyes, who have been roused by the ghost of Klytaimestra from a sleep into which they had fallen. Athena, appealed to by Orestes, enters and institutes the court of the Areios Pagos (Hill of Ares, near the Akropolis), the traditional tribunal at Athens for cases of homicide. The Erinyes plead their own cause, Apollo appears as Orestes' advocate, and the votes of the jury are equally divided. Athena, presiding, gives her casting-vote in Orestes' favour, thus establishing the principle that an equal vote was tantamount to acquittal. Orestes departs with expressions of warm gratitude; Athena after a long debate succeeds in calming the rage of the Erinyes, who now become the Eumenides (Kindly Ones; goddesses locally worshipped at the foot of the Areios Pagos), and are escorted by the citizens of Athens to their new shrine.

The *Prometheus Bound*, a very fine play, is also the most puzzling of the surviving works of Aeschylus. In structure it resembles the *Seven*, for its whole action consists of the varying effects on one central figure (there Eteokles and here Prometheus) of encounters with a series of other characters, first the sympathetic chorus of ocean-nymphs, then their father Okeanos, next Io daughter of Inachos, whom we have already heard of in the *Suppliants*, lastly Hermes. At the beginning of the play, Hephaistos unwillingly fastens Prometheus (represented by a large wooden figure) to a cliff on a mountain-top. His offence has been that after foiling an alleged plan of Zeus to destroy mankind he refuses to reveal a secret which if not discovered in time will bring about the god's fall. In addition, he has stolen fire from some celestial source and given it to mankind, along with much instruction in the arts. To the chorus he tells the whole story of his helpfulness to Zeus in his struggle for supremacy with the Titans under Kronos, and of the god's ingratitude, also of his own gifts to man. Okeanos, a very human figure, well meaning but platitudinous and timid, gets but scanty courtesy from him; Io, a victim of the lust of Zeus as Prometheus is of his hostility, is treated with tenderness, forewarned of the wanderings which yet await her, and comforted with the assurance that a remote descendant of hers (Herakles) shall deliver Prometheus. Hermes comes with an ultimatum. Prometheus must reveal his secret at once, or further torments shall be added to him. The secret is that Thetis the sea-goddess, whom both Zeus and his brother Poseidon love, is destined to bear a son mightier than his father and, therefore, if Zeus is the father, strong enough to bring about yet another change in the government of the universe. Prometheus defies and insults the divine messenger, and the play closes with an earthquake which swallows him and the chorus.

It is a play full of difficulties. The archaic structure is flatly contradicted by certain metrical features belonging to the end of Aeschylus' poetical career, also by the comparatively small and insignificant choral part. Furthermore, the chorus, against all precedent, never are in the orchestra, but remain grouped about the figure of Prometheus. Finally, it is impossible to reconstruct the tetralogy, or group of four plays, to which this one belongs, for although we know of three other plays dealing with Prometheus, only one of them, the lost *Prometheus Unbound*, is available, the other two belonging to other tetralogies. The one allusion to a historical event (the eruption of Etna in 479/8) helps us but little. The only reasonable solution, in my opinion, is that the play was composed for performance in Sicily during Aeschylus' second visit, when he was writing for one of the new republics (perhaps Gela), and so was not bound by Athenian rules. Certain features of the text also lead to the suspicion that he died before he quite finished his work.

A greater problem is the treatment of Zeus, who appears as a harsh and unjust tyrant, whereas Aeschylus elsewhere treats him with immense reverence as the all-wise and all-just ruler of the universe. How much this strange view of him was modified in the sequel, we cannot know; so far no convincing explanation has been put forward.

It is clear that Aeschylus, besides his admirable qualities as a poet, led the art of composing plays a long way towards perfection. In his maturest work we have the interplay of contrasting characters, the element of contest and struggle which is so characteristic of serious drama, and the loftiness of style which befits lofty themes, all brought to a high degree of development. There was still something to do, however, and by common consent it was done by the next great poet in this kind, Sophokles.

Traditionally, Aeschylus fought at Salamis (479 B.C.), Sophokles led a choir of boys who sang a hymn of thanksgiving for the victory, and Euripides was born during the fighting. This gives their respective dates nearly enough; Sophokles was born early in the first decade of the fifth century and died, over ninety years old, in 406/5. He seems to have had ambitions to become an actor, and appeared in some of his own early plays, but his voice was not strong enough, and he devoted himself to composing tragedies, in the intervals of a fairly active life in which he occasionally held important public office. Of all the Tragic poets he was the most popular in his own day, winning the first prize something over twenty times. Like Aeschylus, he is represented for us by a selection from his works, seven plays, which range in date over a large part of his career.

Perhaps the earliest is the *Aiax* (Latin form of Aias; Greek works are often called by Latin or Latinized titles). Aias son of Telamon, the second-greatest of the Achaian heroes before Troy, has claimed the divine arms of Achilles after the death of the latter, but they have instead been awarded to Odysseus. Aias goes mad with rage and disappointment, and in his frenzy vents his anger upon sheep, taking them for his enemies, the other chieftains. Recovering his senses, he determines on suicide and, making an excuse to leave his followers, he falls on his sword. Agamemnon decrees that his body shall be left unburied, so depriving him of the right of entry to the underworld and leaving a lasting stain on his memory. Teukros, Aias' half-brother, defies Agamemnon and all who side with him, but the quarrel is settled by a generous gesture on the part of Odysseus, who secures an honourable funeral for his would-be murderer.

One of the most famous and best plays is the *Antigone*, which takes up the story of Thebes from where Aeschylus (p. 59) left off. After the defeat of the Argives, Kreon, uncle of the two dead princes and now king of Thebes, forbids the body of Polyneikes to be buried. His sister Antigone sets his edict at defiance and contrives to give her brother formal burial by sprinkling dust over his corpse. She is captured when making a second visit to the spot to offer a libation, and Kreon has her shut up in a tomb to starve to death, despite the protests of his son Haimon, who is betrothed to her. When the prophet Teiresias warns him of the impiety of his decree, he is slowly brought to see the error of his ways, but his repentance comes too late. Antigone has hanged herself by the time he arrives at the tomb to free her, Haimon stabs himself over her body, and Kreon's queen commits suicide. The play ends with his despairing lamentations and a few sage comments of the chorus of Theban elders on the value of wisdom and modesty.

This play continues to be imitated by sundry authors in various languages, because it illustrates superbly a recurrent problem, the relative claims of personal, or family, duty and of loyalty to the State. It has no villain; Kreon is honest and patriotic according to his very defective lights, but his narrow insistence on the supremacy of the State makes him a tyrant. Antigone is noble but, as the chorus say, she shows herself the ferocious daughter of a ferocious father (471), being needlessly harsh to her amiable but timid sister Ismene and unable to see anything but the imperative need of giving her dead brother due burial. Like several Sophoklean heroes and heroines, she finds herself isolated in the hour of trial and feels this so intensely that she takes well-meant attempts at consolation by the chorus as mere mockery (839).[1]

Sophokles' most famous play, which served Aristotle (p. 100) as a model for the ideal tragedy, is the *Oedipus Tyrannus*, or *Rex*, *Oidipus the King*. We do not know its date, but it certainly is the product of the poet's ripest powers. Oidipus,

---

[1] For very interesting analyses of the poet's chief characters, see G. Méautis, *Sophocle, essai sur le héros tragique* (Paris, 1957). For the story of Oidipus, see Rose, *Handbook of Greek Mythology*, pp. 187 ff.

son of Laios king of Thebes, exposed in infancy by his father and brought up by Polybos king of Corinth, whom he supposes to be his real father, has been warned by the Delphic oracle that he is to kill his father and marry his mother. Coming to Thebes, after a casual quarrel in which he has killed an unknown elderly man, he delivers the city from the Sphinx and is rewarded with the throne and the hand of the queen, Iokaste (usually Jocasta in English), Laios having been reported killed by brigands. When the play opens, the city is ravaged by an epidemic, and the Delphic oracle declares that it will cease only if the slayer of Laios is driven out. Oidipus, who all this time has thought himself safe so long as he avoids Corinth and his supposed parents there, now discovers by stages that the unknown man he killed was Laios and Iokaste is his own mother. In despair he blinds himself; Iokaste has already taken her own life. The play ends with Oidipus' farewell to his two little daughters and his retirement till the oracle has advised what to do with him. The merits of this great work need not be dwelt on; it has been acted, in its original form, in translations and in modern adaptations, again and again on many European and American stages. Its thrilling suspense and wonderful character-drawing fully outweigh its initial improbability, that Oidipus, now for several years king of Thebes, has as yet taken no steps to find out who was guilty of the death of his predecessor.

The *Electra*, again famous by reason of modern adaptations, covers the same ground as Aeschylus' *Choephoroe* (p. 60), but with more prominence given to the character of Elektra, Orestes' elder sister. There are no Erinyes and no hint that Orestes' deed is other than wholly praiseworthy; Sophokles has recaptured the atmosphere of Homer's telling of the story, or rather his references to it, in several passages of the *Odyssey*. Like Antigone, Elektra, who hates her mother concentratedly, has a softer-tempered sister, Chrysothemis, who serves as a foil to her. Again the date of the play is unknown.

Of unknown date also is the *Trachiniae* (*Maidens of Trachis*; the play is named from its chorus) a very fine drama, centring around the character of a woman who perfectly embodies the conventional Greek idea of a good wife, Deianeira, wife of the great Herakles. She is anxiously awaiting news of her long-absent husband; tidings come, firstly, that he is returning victorious, having taken the town of Oichalia and killed its king, Eurytos, but next, that among the captives he has sent ahead of him is his latest mistress, Iole, Eurytos' daughter. Deianeira has accepted his frequent infidelities abroad, but to have a rival, and that a woman younger and more attractive than herself, actually under her roof is more than she can be expected to endure. She therefore feels justified in using a charm to regain Herakles' affection. Years before, a Centaur, Nessos, had tried to rape her and was shot down by Herakles. Dying, he bade her keep the blood from his wound, assuring her that it was a potent love-charm. In her innocence of magic and of poisons she has done so, and now smears it on a new garment which she sends to her husband. Actually, it is mixed with the venom of the Hydra from Herakles' arrow and is a deadly poison. Word is brought that Herakles is dying in great pain; their son Hyllos curses her for a murderess and, quietly departing, she laments her loneliness[1] and kills herself. Herakles is carried in, learns the truth, recognizes that this is his destined end (it had been foretold that a dead man should kill him, 1160-1), and gives directions for his funeral. The play ends with the departure of him and his attendants to Mount Oite (Oeta), where the hero was traditionally burned, his immortal part joining the gods.

Another very fine play, this time of known date, 408 B.C., shows clearly the influence of Euripides, of which indeed not

---

[1] Still conventionally good, she can think of no independent existence for a woman. Now her marriage has separated her from her father's family, she has unwittingly killed her husband, and her son has cursed her. If she can be neither daughter, wife nor mother, there is nothing left for her to be in this world, which she therefore quits.

a little is to be found in the *Trachiniae*. It is the *Philoctetes*, and the man after whom it is named is one of the Achaian chieftains of the Trojan War. A snake-bite has given him an offensive and incurable hurt, which at times causes acute pain; his comrades have left him on Lemnos, which is assumed to be a desert island. It being known that Troy can be taken only by the bow and arrows of Herakles, which are in his possession, Odysseus and Neoptolemos, son of Achilles, are sent to bring him and them by any means. Odysseus induces Neoptolemos to help in a plan to get them by deceit; Neoptolemos is reluctant, but contrives to win the confidence of Philoktetes and get hold of the bow. But Philoktetes' agony when he finds that he has been cheated so touches him that he hands the weapon back, and the decision of the hero to refuse to go to Troy is overcome by the glorified spirit of Herakles, who assures him that he will find healing as well as victory there.

Once more we have a moral conflict, between Philoktetes' justifiable anger at his heartless treatment and his patriotic feelings, and also between Neoptolemos' native honesty and the duty he owes to the common cause. The most Euripidean feature is perhaps the appearance of Herakles to solve the human problem, a common device in his dramas, the famous *deus ex machina* (the 'machine' being a contrivance by which an actor could be raised some distance in the air and so be represented as flying, descending from heaven, etc.). The subject was a favourite one in antiquity, all three tragedians writing plays on it, besides some of the Latins, while several artists portrayed it. In contrast to the *Antigone*, it has found but few modern imitators, and those of little importance.[1]

Towards the end of his life Sophokles composed one of his noblest works, the *Oedipus Coloneus* (*Oidipus at Kolonos* [*Hippios*], the birthplace of Sophokles, near Athens). Several places claimed to possess the bones of so famous a man, not for sentimental reasons but because it was thought to bring

---

[1] See the introduction to Sir R. Jebb's edition (Cambridge, 1890), p. xxxvi

F

the protection of his powerful ghost. Oidipus enters, a blind beggar guided and tended by his daughter Antigone. Unwittingly, he trespasses on a sacred precinct, and recognizes that he has come to the spot where he must die. The inhabitants of the place, on hearing who he is, are horrified, but he justifies himself to them, pointing out that he has been the victim rather than the wrong-doer. At his urgent request they send for king Theseus, who arrives, Ismene having in the meantime joined her father and sister. Theseus promises Oidipus leave to stay, and protection against the Thebans, who want him to return to somewhere near their territory. After his departure, Kreon, whose character in this play is wholly unlovely, enters and tries to force Oidipus to submit to him by kidnapping his daughters. The girls, however, are rescued by Theseus and his men. Now Oidipus has an interview with Polyneikes, who vainly seeks his support and is cursed by him. After his departure, Oidipus again urgently sends for Theseus; they leave the stage together, and a messenger brings word of Oidipus' mysterious disappearance, the secret of the actual spot being known only to the king and his successors. The play ends with the laments of the two daughters and their departure for Thebes.

This most lovely play seems to have had little or no direct influence on modern literature. Analogies have been noted between the characters of Oidipus and Antigone and those of Lear and Cordelia, for instance, but there is no evidence that Shakespere in any way imitated Sophokles, or even that he knew the *Oedipus Coloneus* directly or otherwise. The figures of a father in distress attended by a faithful daughter are not peculiar to Greek or any other literature, nor indeed to literature proper, for they occur in the popular traditions of many countries. Perhaps the very beauty of the play has deterred some, but more to the point is the nature of the central theme, which is no longer a current problem. Oidipus is a great sinner by the older conception of law, especially sacral law, for he has indeed killed his father and mated with his mother; but by more modern conceptions, such as are embodied in both Greek and Roman jurisprudence, he is the victim of circumstances, having killed an unknown man in a quarrel not brought about by himself and wedded a woman whom, to the best of his knowledge, he had never seen before. There was no intention (*animus*) of committing any offence, although no doubt his own hasty temper was to blame for letting the quarrel be fatal.

One outstanding difference between the Sophoklean and Aeschylean plays must be noted. Sophokles' chorus, although it always has a part in the action, never is the centre of interest, and its lyric comments on the situation, while always apt, do not embody such profound reflections as we generally find in Aeschylus. Sophokles' attention was not primarily directed to theological matters, although he was a decorously pious man, but to human character. Hence the actors have the most to say and the choral part is regularly shorter than in the older dramatist, excepting his abnormal *Prometheus Bound* (see p. 61). Lyric solos from an actor are fairly common. It must be said that the odes, choral or other, are regularly of great beauty.

Last of the three great tragedians was Euripides. His supposed birth-date, which in any case is not far wrong, has been mentioned (p. 63). He died about a year before Sophokles, being then in Macedonia, whose king, Archelaos, took an interest in Greek culture, claimed Greek ancestry and liked to have Greek men of letters about him. Euripides is a product of perhaps the most remarkable movement of his age, that of the Sophists. Under this general name are included a number of men, of varying ability and character, who concerned themselves with what we now know as higher education, and gave training, often for large fees, in the new art of rhetoric, in literary criticism, and in philosophic questions, ethical and other. At the same time Ionian thinkers were laying the foundations of science. The results of such teaching and research were very disturbing to the more conservative of the Greeks, for criticism was directed against all manner of things, including the received ideas of ethics and of what we may roughly call theology. Several sophists were even accused of atheism, by which a Greek regularly meant, not denial of the existence of any kind of deity, but more or less hostile examination of the claims of various traditional gods and goddesses to be such. Thought was on the whole remarkably free, but to maintain the established cults was part of a citizen's duty, and to neglect them or try to bring about any radical change in them was at best impiety, an indictable offence. Rhetoric again involved disputations for and against all manner of propositions, and so it is not surprising that the sophists were accused of teaching their pupils to make the worse case appear the better.[1] The effect of all this speculation, as yet not countered by a positive and thoroughly critical philosophy such as resulted later from the efforts of Sokrates and Plato, was to cause much unrest in a sensitive and receptive mind, and such a mind Euripides had. He was moreover at once a man of humane instincts, full of pity for human distress, and at the same time, a curious investigator of the human mind, especially its reactions to strong impulses, such as desire, hate, jealousy, grief and pain. This is one reason why so many of his leading figures are women, as being more emotional than men and more given, at least by Greek ideas, to expression of their feelings. To make him a woman-hater, as the comedians of his time did, is absurd; it is almost as absurd to represent him as a feminist. Women, good and bad, interested him as a psychological dramatist.

[1] Milton's Belial (*P.L.* Bk. ii) is a thorough sophist, who 'could make the worse appear the better reason'. Hence also the skill with which other hellish characters, notably Satan himself, plead their cause. It is of course well known that Milton had had a good rhetorical and philosophical training, and that he was a bold and original thinker, not shrinking from theological and other heresies. It is no accident that he had studied Euripides carefully, as his copy (in the Bodleian Library) witnesses.

Since we have eighteen[1] plays of his, no complete analysis can be attempted in a book of this size, and I merely draw attention to a few of the most characteristic. In general it may be said that their construction varies from almost Sophoklean artistry to the loosest stringing together of scenes. The importance of the chorus, except as the singer of very fine lyrics between the episodes, has dwindled, and its members vary from sympathetic or hostile spectators, much as in Sophokles, to a mere encumbrance to the action, of which the poet obviously would gladly be rid if the conventions of his art did not compel him to have it. Outstanding features are the rhetorical debate which very commonly occurs between two of the principal characters, the long and elaborate speeches of messengers describing what has happened behind the scenes, and the frequency with which an apparently impossible situation is resolved by the appearance of a deity who explains what has happened or tells the characters what they must do. The play regularly opens with a prologue in which someone explains who he or she is, where the action is supposed to take place, what has led up to the initial situation and what is to happen. None of these features is entirely new, for we find them all in one or the other of the earlier tragedians, but they are commoner in Euripides than in either of the other two.

The first surviving play of Euripides, and already characteristic of him, is the *Alcestis*, the fourth play of his tetralogy of 438, and so taking the place of the usual satyr-drama. When it was acted he had been before the public for seventeen years. Its foundation was a folktale already handled by Phrynichos. Apollo, condemned to temporary expulsion from heaven for killing the Kyklopes who had forged the thunderbolt that killed his son Asklepios, became the herdsman of

---

[1] Seventeen tragedies and one satyr-play, not counting the fragmentary *Hypsipyle* nor the *Phaethon*, which can be largely reconstructed. The *Rhesus*, which has come down under Euripides' name, is spurious, being the work of some unknown writer, probably of the fourth century.

king Admetos of Pherai in Thessaly, and was treated by him with all kindness. In return, discovering that Admetos had not long to live, he beguiled the Moirai (the Destinies; what the Latins called *Parcae* or *Fata*) into agreeing that he should have a longer life if someone would consent to die for him. No one would do so except his wife, Alkestis daughter of Pelias. Either the powers of the underworld were so impressed by her wifely devotion that they sent her back to earth, or Herakles rescued her by wrestling with Death (*Thanatos*) and compelling him to let his prey go. The latter is the version Euripides follows; but his originality consists in emphasizing the baseness of Admetos in accepting his wife's sacrifice, a point which apparently had struck no one earlier. Admetos, as the play progresses, realizes his despicable conduct and is genuinely repentant; Herakles, a half-comic character, brings all to a happy ending by restoring Alkestis to him. The debate is between Admetos and his father Pheres, who is assailed by his son for not being willing to die and defends himself stoutly; Herakles supplies the necessary divine intervention in a way, though he is not yet a god.

This play has its established place in English literature, for it is the one which the heroine of *Balaustion's Adventure* recites at Syracuse. But apart from that, it has been translated and imitated often enough. Euripides handles the old tale after his own fashion. He is willing to assume, for literary purposes, that the extraordinary things related in the legends really happened. Granted this, what would the feelings of those concerned be? In this instance, what sort of human beings would Admetos and his family, Alkestis herself, and Herakles be, and how would they react to the remarkable circumstances in which they found themselves?

Some twenty years later (the exact date is unknown), he was still interested in Herakles, this time under stress of a horrible and quite undeserved misfortune. The hero has just returned from the underworld, where he has accomplished his last and most terrible Labour,[1] the bringing up of Kerberos, and incidentally the rescue of Theseus, who had been held prisoner there. He is just in time to rescue his wife, children and putative father, Amphitryon, from death at the hands of Lykos king of Thebes. Now Hera, spiteful as ever, sends Madness in person (*Lyssa*) to drive him violently insane, and in this state he murders his wife and children. Regaining his senses, he falls into black despair, from which he is rescued by Theseus, apparently representing the reasonable, civilized man, perhaps especially the civilized and enlightened Athenian, who points out to him that although most unfortunate he is not, save in a purely ceremonial sense, the polluted creature he imagines himself to be, and so wins him from his intention of suicide and persuades him to accept the hospitality and welcome of Athens. The title of the play is properly *Herakles*, but moderns generally call it by the Latinized name of *Hercules furens*. The author's rationalism shows itself here and there in odd ways, such as the denunciation, by Herakles son of Zeus, of stories of the amours of the gods and of myths in general.

Quite an early work (it was produced in 428) is also one of Euripides' best-constructed and most famous, the *Medea*, which has been often translated into modern languages, not for reading only but for the stage. Medeia daughter of Aietes king of Kolchis, having fled from her native land with Jason (properly *Iason* or *Ieson*) chief of the Argonauts, has been married to him for some years. They are living in Corinth; he now proposes to put her away and marry the daughter of Kreon, the local king,[2] thereby improving his fortunes and his social position. Medea, who has saved his life and sacrificed everything for him, contemptuously rejects his arguments

---

[1] For the Labours, see my *Handbook of Greek Mythology*, pp. 211–16.

[2] *Kreon* means simply 'prince' or 'ruler' and occurs many times as the stop-gap name of a character of legend who is really nameless; i.e. 'this or that befell Kreon' means no more than 'once there was a king to whom such-and-such things happened'.

when they meet, and plans revenge, using her knowledge, not so much of witchcraft as of poisons. She sends the intended bride a robe imbued with some drug which burns her to death, and also her father, when he tries to save her. She then nerves herself to kill her children, thus leaving Jason sonless. His attempts to take revenge on her are frustrated by the appearance of a flying chariot, sent by her grandfather the Sun-god (Helios). In this she departs for Athens, where king Aigeus, in return for promised help to the begetting of off-spring, has agreed to shelter her.

The plot disagrees in so many respects from other legends of Medeia which we have that it is quite probable that Euripides modified them to suit his own requirements. The result is a powerful and moving study of jealousy at its most deadly, embodied in a thrillingly exciting play. The story was told and retold by various later authors in antiquity, to say nothing of the moderns.

The *Hippolytus*, produced three years later, centres around two characters, both somewhat abnormal, both virtuous, and brought to ruin by their virtue. Hippolytos is a son of Theseus; his mother is dead and his father is married a second time, to Phaidra, a Cretan princess. She is strongly sexed; he, although healthy and athletic, is disgusted by what he has heard of physical passion, and is a chaste votary of Artemis, the virgin huntress-goddess. In the absence of her husband, Phaidra falls desperately in love with him; mythically, this is expressed as a passion sent by Aphrodite (who speaks the prologue of the play), in revenge for Hippolytos' failure to honour her. When her duenna reveals Phaidra's desires to Hippolytos, under pledge of secrecy, he is horrified and at first threatens to betray all to Theseus, despite his oath to the contrary. But he is too honourable to do so, and when Phaidra hangs herself, leaving behind a letter falsely accusing Hippolytos of an attempt on her, he defends himself against his father's anger only by denials, which Theseus will not believe, and prays his father Poseidon to bring about Hippolytos' death. This is done by sending a sea-monster to frighten the young man's chariot-team, who throw and drag him, inflicting deadly injuries. Artemis now appears and reveals the truth to Theseus, to whom Hippolytos is reconciled before he dies.

The great merit of the play is the character of Phaidra, who is not an unchaste woman, but one of strong moral principles, and therefore struggles against overwhelming desire till she nearly dies of the effort, besides being so overcome with shame when her passion is made known to Hippolytos that she kills herself. In Racine's *Phèdre* we have one of the most direct cases of influence of the ancient poet on a great modern dramatist. There is no comparable work in English, although Browning's *Artemis Prologises*, dealing with an off-shoot of the same legend, is a noble fragment, and the story, a very old folktale appearing among many peoples, of the false accusation has been used often enough from the compilation of the Book of Genesis to recent times.

The grief of a terribly wronged mother changing to vengeful fury is the central interest of the *Hecuba*, which was produced perhaps about 425. Hekabe (Hecuba in Latin), queen of Troy, is shown at the beginning of the play overwhelmed with sorrow at the fall of the city and the deaths of her husband and most of her children. Her grief is aggravated by the sacrifice at the tomb of Achilles of her daughter Polyxene. She now learns that her one remaining hope, her young son Polydoros, has been murdered by the Thracian prince Polymestor to whom he had been entrusted to keep him from the dangers of war. Using as a lever Agamemnon's love for her daughter Kassandra, who is his slave-concubine, she gets permission to deal with Polymestor. She and her women beguile him into her tent, where he is seized, his children killed before his eyes, and he is then blinded. The play ends with his banishment to a desert island and Hekabe's departure to bury her dead.

To Euripides, the behaviour of Orestes and Elektra as depicted by Aeschylus and Sophokles seems to have been unintelligible save on the assumption that they were a sort of monomaniacs. It is the characteristic weakness of many rationalists, who seem often to lack all historical sense or sympathy with any who follow another code of morals and live under another system of law than theirs. Certainly an Athenian of the fifth century who murdered his mother because of some crime she had committed would have been abnormal; even Euthyphron, in Plato's dialogue of that title, who indicts his father for causing the death of a slave by ill-treatment, is shown as a fanatic. But Orestes, supposing him to have been a real person of the twelfth century B.C., lived in an age when blood-revenge was a sacred duty and the women of a family were under the governance of their men and of no one else. Thus in the *Electra* (about 413) and the *Orestes* (408) the names and scene are traditional, but the atmosphere is of Euripides' own day, when practically our ideas of the proper procedure in cases of homicide and of the relations between members of the same family were prevalent. In the former play Elektra has been married to a decent peasant, who knows that she has been given to him simply to prevent her bearing any but peasant children, who would have no concern with the quarrels of a royal house, and so has never consummated the marriage. Orestes arriving and making himself known, she plays upon Klytaimestra's maternal feelings by sending word that she has borne a child and asking her to come. On arriving, full of concern for her daughter and the supposed grandchild, the queen, after a debate in which she defends her own conduct quite moderately, is induced to enter Elektra's house and there set upon and killed, Aigisthos having already been attacked and struck down at a sacrifice. Once the deed is done, Orestes and Elektra fall into hysterical remorse, until quieted by the appearance of Kastor and Polydeukes, who direct her to marry Pylades and him to quit Argos and go to Athens. In the *Orestes*, the scene is in Argos just after the killing of Klytaimestra and Aigisthos. Orestes, who is subject to fits of madness in which he sees phantasmal Erinyes, is tenderly watched by his sister until it is time for him to be tried before an assembly of the people. The brother and sister are condemned to death, but given permission to kill themselves. They get possession of Helen's daughter Hermione, to force her father Menelaos to intervene on their behalf. The main action of the play ends with the palace on fire, Orestes with his knife at Hermione's throat, Helen mysteriously vanished, and Menelaos shouting for help. A most unconvincing Apollo now appears, directs Orestes to marry Hermione instead of killing her, and reconciles everyone.

From such painful themes as these Euripides on occasion took refuge in romantic drama, as the *Iphigenia in Tauris*. He follows the version of the legend according to which Iphigeneia was not sacrificed, but miraculously rescued by Artemis and conveyed to the land of the Taurians (the Crimea), a savage people who worshipped her with human sacrifices, the victims being strangers. Orestes has been ordered, as a final act of purification, to bring her image from the Taurian temple to Attica. He and Pylades are captured by the natives and taken to the shrine, where Iphigeneia is priestess. She and her brother recognize each other, and she now tells the barbarian king, Thoas, that the image has been polluted by Orestes' touch and he and it must be taken down to the sea and bathed. They thus get free and board their ship, but are driven back on the shore by huge waves. Now Athena appears, and directs Thoas not only to refrain from pursuing the fugitives but to send the chorus, which consists of Greek women, back to Greece. He at once obeys.

This play is founded on the legend of the shrine of Artemis at Halai in Attica. There was an old cult of Artemis there, at which a pretence was made of human sacrifice. It was alleged that the cult-image had been brought from the land of the Tauroi and that the rite was in memory of real human sacrifices which the goddess had received in their country. This is one of several dramas which we either have or hear of in which the poet allowed his abundant fancy to wander into a sort of fairyland where unbelief could be suspended and all manner of wonderful happenings accepted. Thus in a way Euripides may be thought of as the ancestor of romantic drama in general. He also introduced more realism than most of the tragedians, his characters often being shown in utter misery, dressed in rags, or again of humble origin but (like the peasant in the *Electra*) with a nobility of character above their station. This last feature was due partly no doubt to the poet's own deeply humane character, but also to sophistic teaching, for it was a favourite doctrine of theirs that many established institutions, including social distinctions, did not exist by nature (*physis*) but resulted purely from custom or convention, *nomos*.

With Euripides, the great age of Tragedy ends, and it is obvious that at times he found its conventions burdensome and was feeling for some new form of expression. After him no tragedian of comparable merit is heard of, and gradually, although plays continued to be performed at Athens and elsewhere, it became not uncommon to compose dramas which were tragedies in form, but in content merely literary, often vehicles for setting forth some philosophic doctrine in popular shape. A continuation of this will be found when we come to discuss Latin literature, and modern examples are not wanting of works imitating Tragedy or Comedy in outward appearance, but purely for reading (like Milton's *Samson Agonistes* or Matthew Arnold's *Merope*, though the former has on occasion been acted), sometimes disguised political satires, like Shelley's *Swellfoot the Tyrant*, with its chorus of swine reminiscent of Aristophanes' chorus of frogs.

Coming now to Comedy (*komoidia*, the song of the *komos*,

i.e. band of revellers), we again have a literary form originating in a popular religious rite. The origins are obscure, but amusing performances connected with the worship of Dionysos and containing elements of social and personal satire are heard of in several parts of Greece, including Megara in the Peloponnesos and Syracuse in Sicily, where indeed at least one writer of eminence, Epicharmos, arose as the author of a number of plays on various themes, including funny or burlesqued episodes from mythology. None survives and not much is known of them, except that they do not appear to have been either long or elaborate and that the prevailing metre was the trochaic tetrameter catalectic, the Latin *uersus quadratus*, which has come down through the centuries, adapted itself to the accentual scansion of sundry modern languages, and appears for instance in Tennyson's *Locksley Hall*. But the important development was Attic, where allegedly Comedy was 'given a chorus', that is to say recognized as a regular public performance, in Thespis' deme of Ikaria early in the sixth century, and Athens itself received it about 487, when a certain Chionides was given the prize, presumably at the Great Dionysia. Of several other early comedians we know the names, approximate dates, and here and there a little of what they wrote, preserved mostly in quotations by later authors; but more definite knowledge begins further down the century. In 453, Kratinos first put on a play, and of him we know that he supported Kimon and attacked Perikles, in other words that his political sympathies were with the more conservative statesmen of his day; also we have, besides sundry fragments, a prose outline of one of his plays, the *Dionysalexandros*, that is to say Alexandros (Paris), son of Priam, combined with Dionysos. It was a burlesque of the legend of the Choice of Paris, which told how he, as the handsomest of men, was called upon to decide which of three goddesses, Hera, Athena and Aphrodite, was the most beautiful, and awarded the prize to Aphrodite, who

had bribed him with the promise of the most beautiful of
women for his wife. In the play he apparently ran away when
the goddesses appeared, and Dionysos took his place and shape,
gave the judgement, and then went to Greece and carried off
Helen, the most beautiful woman of that day. Now, as in the
orthodox story, the Greeks proceeded to invade Troy;
Dionysos disguised Helen as a goose and himself as a ram, was
detected by the real Paris, and the play ended with a compromise; the Trojans kept Helen, but Dionysos and the chorus
(which consisted of satyrs) were handed over to the Greeks.

It is known that there were political allusions in this play,
which must have been very funny if at all adequately acted,
but the most surprising thing to a modern is that the god in
whose honour the festival was held played such an undignified
part. It seems to be the native European instinct to be rather
free with the objects of worship, although they may be
venerated quite sincerely and feared on occasion. This is true
even of that religion which has in the end displaced all the rest,
Christianity; witness the occurrence of figures so august as
God Himself, Christ, and St Peter as comic or half-comic
characters in sundry medieval ballads and other popular productions. Gods, to our ancestors, seem to have been thought
of as powerful beings, helpful when rightly approached, but
once their favour had been gained by proper ritual, good-
natured to the extent of not minding harmless jokes directed
against themselves. This certainly is true of Attic Comedy, as
we shall see presently in another striking instance or two.

For us, Old Comedy, as it is called, is embodied in the
works of one author, Aristophanes, eleven of whose plays
have come down to us, together with some fragments of the
others. Every one turns on a farcically topsy-turvy situation,
brought about by the fantastic scheme of one of the characters.
In the earliest, the *Acharnians* (425), the hero, Dikaiopolis,
wearies of the discomforts of the Peloponnesian War, then
in its sixth year, and employs a minor god who comes con-

veniently to hand as his go-between to arrange a separate
peace for him with the Spartans and their allies. This concluded, he opens a market, which is attended by various comic
foreigners, and enjoys a triumph over one of the principal
military men of the day, Lamachos. The play gets its name
from the chorus, inhabitants of one of the most populous
districts of Attica, who furiously oppose Dikaiopolis at first,
but are persuaded that he is right in a scene parodied from
Euripides. In this, Dikaiopolis puts on the ragged costume
worn by a Euripidean hero, Telephos, in a famous tragedy
now unfortunately lost, and like him convinces a hostile
audience which at first is barely persuaded to listen to him.
The action ends with Dikaiopolis returning merrily drunk
from a feast, while Lamachos staggers home wounded from a
skirmish. The *Knights*, produced the next year, again is
named from its chorus, composed of young men of good
families who served in the cavalry. Demos, i.e. the sovran
people, has a rascally foreign steward who makes the other
slaves' lives a burden to them. Two of his fellows conspire
against him (they are plainly the well-known officers Nikias
and Demosthenes, the steward being the able demagogue
Kleon), and steal from him an oracle which instructs them
that the way to be rid of their enemy is to find an even viler
character to supplant him. They discover a seller of haggises
or black-puddings (*allantes*), whose one handicap to a political
career is that he can read and write a little; he possesses all the
other requirements for success, low birth, shamelessness, dis-
honesty and a loud voice. With these accomplishments he
quite outdoes the steward in gross flattery of Demos, is given
his place, and then turns out to be really a most respectable
person, who boils Demos in a magic cauldron and turns him
into an old-fashioned Athenian gentleman, and therefore a
determined enemy of extreme democracy and a supporter of
a policy of peace, especially with Sparta. It is to be remembered that the Athenian conservatives were throughout in

favour of such a policy, for they had the most to lose, being comparatively large land-owners, from the continual raids on Attica which were a regular accompaniment of war, whereas the poorer people favoured enterprising, Imperialistic and warlike activities, which meant among other things chances of well-paid work as rowers in the war-fleet (no galley-slaves were employed by Athens), and further prospects of a share in captured lands or other spoils of war if all went well.

A year later Aristophanes took a non-political target and met with failure, though his play, to judge by the partly revised edition which we have, was an excellent one. The butt this time is Sokrates, chosen as the typical sophist.[1] A certain Strepsiades is heavily in debt and would gladly argue himself out of paying. Failing to absorb the new learning himself at the Phrontisterion (Reflectory), Sokrates' school, he manages to induce his son to go there. The young man emerges a perfect pupil of Sokrates, puts off creditors with fallacious arguments, and then proves to his father that he owes him no duties and is quite justified in beating him if so inclined. This is too much for Strepsiades, who ends the play by burning the Phrontisterion down. In 422 another new target was adopted, this time the jury system of Athens. It was the custom to try cases before much larger juries than ours, often numbering several hundreds, with no official corresponding to our judges, the jurymen being the sole arbiters of fact and law also, and the sole assessors of the penalty to be inflicted in case of conviction. A small fee, apparently a minimum living wage, was paid to them out of the State funds. The central characters are an old juror, Philokleon

---

[1] It is a commonplace that the caricature of Sokrates in this play is utterly unlike the portrait drawn of him by Plato, Xenophon and others; but it is sometimes forgotten that over twenty years intervene between the *Clouds*, as the comedy is called, and the earliest of the philosophers' works. In any case, Aristophanes was no philosopher and not likely to make much distinction between one critic and another of traditional ideas in ethics and other matters.

('Love-Kleon') and his son Bdelykleon ('Blast-Kleon'), who tries to win him from his fanatical devotion to his work in the courts. After sundry farcical scenes, he induces him to substitute a private court in his own house, where a dog is put on trial for stealing a cheese (there is a political allusion here; the dog is called Labes, 'Grabber', and the cheese is of Sicilian make; a prominent contemporary, Laches, was accused of peculation in Sicily). Philokleon, unintentionally and for the first time in his life, votes for acquittal, and faints from shock. His son induces him to dine out in high society, and he ends the play by returning very drunk and dancing wildly. The outline of the play is familiar to anyone who has the least acquaintance with classical French literature, for it gave Racine the idea for *Les Plaideurs*, and that in turn was imitated by Wycherley in *The Plain Dealer*. The fact that the former play is completely French, the latter robustly, if not very delicately English, does nothing to rob Aristophanes of the credit of first making too much zeal for legal procedure a subject of broad farce. His title was *Wasps*.

The year 421 saw an uneasy break in the hostilities, in the form of the Peace of Nikias, and Aristophanes welcomed the prospect of a lasting truce with an appropriate play, the *Peace* (*Eirene*). A worthy countryman, Trygaios (approximately 'Vintager'), flies up to heaven on an enormous beetle, learns from Hermes where Peace is buried, and digs her up with the help of the chorus. A series of comical scenes ends with his marriage to Opora ('Fruit'), one of the attendants of Peace. By 414 war had recommenced, the ill-fated Sicilian Expedition was under way, and the comedian gave vent to his dislike of too ambitious schemes in the *Birds*. Two Athenian adventurers persuade the birds to build a city, Nephelokokkygia ('Cloud-cuckoo-ville'), in mid-air. This cuts off the gods from the earth, and having no fumes of sacrifice to nourish them, they soon are forced to make peace on the adventurers' own terms, which include Zeus resigning the lordship of the

G

universe to one of them, Peisetairos (about equivalent in meaning to Bunyan's Plausible). Three more years of war, and Aristophanes brought out his masterpiece, *Lysistrata* ('Breaker-up of armies', i.e. Madame Demobilizer). The women of Greece join in a great conspiracy to accept no advances from husband or lover until peace is established. Before long, distressed-looking representatives of Sparta appear on the scene; the Athenians very readily welcome them and the play ends in feasting and the singing of songs in Attic and in Spartan Doric. Translations and adaptations of the work on the modern stage have had such success as to prove that the fun, with its marked undertone of seriousness, has by no means evaporated, certainly not for the present generation with its long experience of devastating warfare and uneasy peace. That same year saw a slighter play; Euripides tries to spy on the women during the Thesmophoria, a very ancient festival celebrated by women only, hence the title of the play, *Thesmophoriazousai*, 'women keeping the Thesmophoria'. Afraid to go himself, he persuades a kinsman, Mnesilochos, to disguise himself as a woman and go in his stead. Mnesilochos is soon detected, partly because he pleads the cause of Euripides the woman-hater with too much eloquence and knowledge, and attached to a plank, a sort of crucifixion inflicted on particularly vile criminals, who were left to die of hunger and exhaustion. After vain attempts at rescue in the manner of sundry heroes of his own romantic plays, Euripides makes his peace with the women, beguiles the Scythian watchman who is guarding the plank and releases Mnesilochos.

Old Comedy, with its farcical plots, free attacks on real persons, casual treatment of the very gods, and large lyric element, may be said to have died with the ruin of Athens when at last the war ended in 404. The last play we have is the famous *Frogs*, produced in the year before the final collapse, and so rich in fun as to be still very amusing when played in one of its many translations, despite the fact that much of its humour 'dates', turning on contemporary literary disputes. Dionysos finds himself without a respectable poet, now that Euripides and Sophokles are dead and Agathon[1] gone to Macedonia. He decides to go to the underworld and bring Euripides back. Arrived there, after sundry ridiculous adventures, he finds a hot contest going on between Euripides and Aeschylus, the former having the backing of all the rascals among the dead. Aeschylus has been given the seat of honour reserved for the best tragedian, and Euripides now claims it. Dionysos is asked to judge between them, and they proceed to criticize and parody each other's works most amusingly. The simple-minded god is quite incapable of following much of what they say, but at last decides that it is really Aeschylus whom he wants. Accordingly he departs with him, leaving Sophokles to occupy the tragic throne for the time being.

In all these plays, a prominent character under various names (Dionysos himself is one of them) is the ordinary man, at least the ordinary Athenian, as Aristophanes saw him. He is regularly shown as lustful, stupid and cowardly, yet somehow lovable and never such a rascal as the demagogues, sophists and others who mislead him. A prominent formal element in all the plays is what is known as the *parabasis*. This occurs about the middle of the play, and in it the chorus, dropping to some extent their dramatic rôle, turn to the audience and offer advice, fundamentally serious despite the fantastic forms in which it may be couched, on various matters, including contemporary politics. The *Frogs* in particular contains a strong plea for unity in view of the desperate condition of the State, now nearing the end of a long and disastrous war.

What has been known ever since the time of Hadrian (Publius Aelius Hadrianus, Emperor of Rome A.D. 117–38) as Middle Comedy may be said to begin with the two latest

---

[1] A tragedian, apparently of merit, whose first victory was in 416. He left his native Athens for Macedonia in 407. His works are lost.

surviving plays of Aristophanes. The *Ecclesiazusae* (*Ekklesiazousai*, female members of the Assembly) was acted some ten years after the beginning of the fourth century B.C. Formally, it shows great degeneration of the part of the chorus, which is no longer in the position of an important actor. Materially, it criticizes an idea rather than attacking any individual. Legislation may have had something to do with this, for we hear rather vaguely of a law being passed to forbid comedians attacking anyone by name. Be that as it may, the butt of the poet's wit is certain political speculations, some of which were later to find expression in Plato's *Republic*. The women of Athens disguise themselves as men, pack a meeting of the Assembly, and pass a decree entrusting the women with government, as being the only true conservatives. Once in power, they establish a communist state, and the rest of the play depicts life under the new order. Aristophanes' last surviving work, a revised edition of one originally produced in 408, is the *Plutos* (Wealth) acted in 388. A decent poor man, Chremylos, finds Wealth, who is blind and in miserable plight, gets his sight restored in the temple of Asklepios, the physician-god, and thereafter only the honest are visited by him, to their great content and the dismay of the rascals, also of the other gods, whom no one worships any more, so that Hermes is reduced to taking a subordinate place in Chremylos' household.

Old Comedy has found no precise imitators in modern literature, for its form is too closely bound up with Athenian customs, especially religious, to be adopted as it stands into any country now existing. Translations have indeed been numerous, but they are for the most part meant simply to be read, not acted, although there are exceptions, particularly for the *Lysistrata* and *Frogs* (see p. 84). But one department of English literature has caught not a little of the spirit, though not the form, of Aristophanes, and that is ballad opera, as handled by John Gay in the eighteenth century and Sir

W. S. Gilbert in the nineteenth. Naturally, neither of these authors has ventured to echo the familiar attitude of the ancient comedians towards the objects of their worship, which indeed continues to shock some modern readers of Greek; nor are public men attacked by name, the nearest approach thereto being the traditional 'business' with which the 'gaps' are filled by the singer who renders 'They never would be missed' in *The Mikado*. But there is keen social satire under the merriment of *The Beggar's Opera* and even in its more sentimental and far less felicitous sequel, *Polly*, and criticism of contemporary England abounds in the long and famous series for which Sullivan supplied the music. The absurdities of plot are there also, and the abundant musical interludes, comic or sentimental, have a good deal of the tone of Old Comedy. One feature is absent. Aristophanes is often broadly obscene, for the excellent reason that Dionysos is a god of fertility, and obscenity is a well-known fertility-rite, an accepted means of frightening off or overpowering the forces which make against increase. No doubt the same feature was to be found in the work of Kratinos and the other comedians of that time. But it was acceptable neither to the general taste nor to the laws of Victorian England, at any rate. We shall see (pp. 151 ff.) that something of the broad fun of Aristophanes and his rivals flashed again in Plautus.

For the best part of half a century after the death of Aristophanes we have nothing to record except names and fairly numerous fragments, which sometimes throw a little light on the development of Comedy. There is nothing to suggest that literature is very much poorer for the loss of these writers, and certainly their influence on later drama is negligible, or nearly so. For us, the story recommences with the age of Menander (*Menandros*), whose dates are approximately 343/2–292/1. By that time, it would seem that certain conventional plots had come into general use for comedians – it is not known what part, if any, he had in bringing the convention about. His subject was human nature as observed by him in contemporary Athens, by that time a place of little political importance, but still a cultural centre and respected for her glorious past. One of the common elements of his plots was furnished by the practice of exposure. It was lawful, if a newborn child was for any reason (such as the poverty of the parents) not wanted, to leave the infant somewhere out of doors, clothed, enclosed in some kind of receptacle, and, to judge from Comedy, regularly having about it some small ornaments or trinkets by which it could be recognized later. Anyone who liked might take possession of the child, to be reared in any way, as free or unfree; but if at any later time the parents recognized their offspring, they might reclaim it, the foster-parent having apparently no claim for any kind of compensation. How common this practice was is a disputed point, but it is a stock feature of New Comedy, as the plays of this period are called. The central plot usually turns on the love of a young man of respectable Athenian family for a girl whom he wants as his wife or mistress, but in the former case she is supposedly an alien, and therefore not capable of being his legal wife, or is simply poor and dowerless, and therefore inacceptable to his family; in the latter, she is the property of a slave-dealer who wants an exorbitant price for her. By some means, often the machinations of a cunning slave, the necessary money is got in the one case, or the marriage somehow brought about in the other, when commonly the girl is recognized as the exposed daughter of a prosperous citizen, who reclaims her and gives the pair his blessing. Obviously, the modifications of this type of plot are fairly numerous and the tone of the play capable of much variation. In Menander's hands the character-drawing seems regularly to have been very good, the dialogue lively, in verse (generally iambic) not very different from the ordinary spoken Attic of the time, and the sung parts almost if not quite absent. The chorus was by this time reduced to a band of what we should call music-hall performers, who gave a 'turn' in pauses of the action, indicated in our texts simply by a marginal direction *chorou*, i.e. '(Dance) by the chorus', which is found here and there also in the last works of Aristophanes and some post-Euripidean fragments of Tragedy. The author evidently did not trouble to write words for whatever songs were sung. Absent also are the broad farce and the occasional obscenities of Old Comedy. If a superhuman figure appears, it is, so far as we can see, merely to explain something which the human characters do not know, and often it is not one of the traditional gods but an abstraction.

An illustration of this, which will also give an idea of a Menandrian play, is to be found in a rather famous work of this author, the *Perikeiromene* (approximately 'Shaven and Shorn'), of which we have a considerable part. It is a remarkable fact, considering the immense posthumous reputation of Menander, that not one of his plays has come down to us complete, and until 1907 we had nothing but small though numerous fragments of him. In that year was published the famous Cairo papyrus, on which were preserved three plays, not indeed complete but nearly enough for us to taste their quality and reconstruct them to some extent, while another was represented by its opening scene and a synopsis of the action. There has since been an important discovery, soon to be published in a critical edition. An almost complete copy of Menander's *Dyskolos* ('The Ill-natured Man') has come to light, and is promised for publication towards the end of the current year (1958).[1] The *Perikeiromene* concerns the adventures of exposed twins, brother and sister. The brother, Moschion, has been adopted by a wealthy woman, who at the time when the play begins is married to a man named Pataikos. The sister, Glykera, has been brought up by a poor woman, and is now the mistress of a soldier, Polemon. Moschion is ignorant

[1] It appeared in March 1959, while this book was in proof.

of the relationship, Glykera knows it. He steals a kiss from her; Polemon catches them, supposes Moschion to be Glykera's lover, and cuts her hair off (hence the title of the play). She is deeply offended, and seeks refuge with Pataikos' wife. Now Polemon, who is a good-natured man despite his hasty temper, begs Pataikos to bring about a reconciliation between himself and Glykera. Pataikos consents, and in seeking to do so discovers that Glykera and Moschion are his own children, exposed when he had lost his wife and found himself suddenly poor. The play ends with the marriage of Glykera to Polemon (Pataikos finds her the necessary dowry) and Moschion is also to be married to the daughter of a friend of his newly found father; the play as we have it ends with his surprised exclamation on hearing the news, but it is quite possible that he went on to say that he had long wished to marry her. In any case, by the conventions of New Comedy, he is now to become a respectable married man and give up flirtations with casually met girls. Early in the play, though not precisely at the beginning, comes a long speech by Agnoia (Ignorance, or as Allinson renders it in the Loeb edition, Misapprehension), who explains the whole situation to the audience; it is what is called a deferred prologue, and such a device occurs a time or two in Plautus (p. 151).

Substitute some other way of separating the twins from their father early in their lives, and it is surely clear that we have practically a specimen of Comedy of Manners, or of Humours, in French or English, of date somewhere in the seventeenth or eighteenth century. The scene does not vary and the time supposed to elapse can hardly be more than about a day; the feeble remnant of the chorus apparently can no longer indicate by its performances the passage of any considerable extent of time. To judge by what we know of this kind of drama, the stage represents a street behind which stand two houses (those of Polemon and Pataikos), into which the characters make some of their exits and from which on occasion they enter. This convention is to be found still as late as the earliest works of Molière, though later he, and even more perhaps his imitators, found it convenient to set some at least of their scenes indoors.

More important than this scenic convention is the question how such plots originated. No doubt the authors of Middle Comedy had a share in their development, but beyond and through them we can trace the influence of Euripides. Indeed, we have a whole play of his which might be described as a comedy with its characters transposed into a higher sphere of life than the middle-class Athenians and their households about whom Menander and the rest regularly wrote. In Euripides' *Ion*, the hero, the legendary ancestor of the Ionians, is the exposed child, the offspring of an intrigue of Apollo with an Athenian princess, Kreusa.[1] The infant has been rescued by Hermes, acting as Apollo's emissary, and has become a temple-servant at Delphoi. Mother and son are to be made mutually known, and after exciting scenes in which either attempts to kill the other, the recognition duly takes place. It obviously is not possible for a god to make amends to Kreusa by marrying her, especially as she is married already to a certain Xuthos, but Apollo, whose actions are explained by Athena, arranges matters as best he can. Xuthos is already persuaded that the boy is his own illegitimate child by a chance-met mother, and he is not to be undeceived, but left to accept his wife's irregular, though half-divine, offspring into his family. Thus the play has a 'happy ending', at some cost to a deity of whom Euripides manifestly had a poor opinion, partly perhaps on account of the Delphic oracle's strongly pro-Spartan attitude throughout the Peloponnesian War. Besides this influence on the plots, of which we should certainly know more if so large an amount of Euripides' work were not lost to us, his text is continually put under

---

[1] Cf. note 2, p. 73. Kreusa is the feminine of Kreon and, like it, a stop-gap name. The best-known bearer of it is perhaps Aeneas' first wife in Vergil.

contribution, several characters, even in the little we have left of Menander, referring to plays of his and on occasion quoting verbatim; indeed it is not uncommon to find one later writer attributing a passage which he cites to Euripides while another says it is Menander, both in a sense being right, for the tragedian originated it and one of the comedian's characters quoted it.

Since Menander's plays were completely lost for a long time and are very far from being completely recovered now, his influence on the moderns has of necessity been almost wholly indirect, passing through his Latin imitators. Thus it is that a like indirect influence has been exercised by several of his contemporaries and rivals, including Philemon, who was born in 361, died a very old man in 263, composed about a hundred plays, and often was preferred to Menander on the stage, although after the death of both it was the latter who was more read, admired and quoted. It is noteworthy that this successful dramatist of the Athenian theatre was not an Athenian, but a Syracusan, and two other foreigners, Diphilos of Sinope and Apollodoros of Karystos, were likewise prominent in Menander's time. Drama had become an international art, and practically a branch of literature, not cult, although its nominal connexion with Dionysos never was broken, in Greece at least, and professional actors, organized into gilds (a sort of ancient equivalent of 'Equity'), called themselves his artists (*technitai*). But we need not go into this here.

It follows that most of what is to be said about the connexion between the ancient and the modern stage will find a more appropriate place when we come to discuss Latin drama, whether written for the theatre or the study or recitation-room. For the present, the above brief and incomplete sketch must suffice.

IV

The Development of Prose

TO THE GREEKS, AS TO ALL NATIONS WHICH have a literature, prose was a later development than verse. This naturally does not mean that the people habitually spoke in metre; but prose is not simply absence of metrical form, but has complicated rhythms of its own, also its own vocabulary and other peculiarities which are the product of long evolution. This is why verse continued to be used for purposes to which a modern would not seriously put it, as late as the fifth century B.C. Two notable philosophers of that period, Parmenides (born about 540), who denied the reality of change and plurality, and Empedokles (dates uncertain, born perhaps not long after 500, died between 440 and 430), the author of a remarkable system of cosmology, in which among other things the famous four elements (earth, water, air, fire) and the forces of attraction and repulsion (he called them love and strife) made their appearance, used verse only for their published works; the latter was also a good poet, the former did little more than put his views into hexameters which would scan. However, philosophy took to expressing itself in prose, not formless but already literary to some degree, from the time of the famous Herakleitos, surnamed the Obscure, contemporary with Parmenides. The fragments we have of his work *Concerning Nature* are enough to show that he was designedly not merely concise but as 'obscure' as his stock epithet implies. He did not wish to be understood save by men of high intelligence. Unfortunately, so little is left of one of the greatest of early philosophers, Demokritos, the father of the atomic theory, that not much can be said of his style. Another great name, contemporary with Demokritos (both are said to have been born about 460), is that of Hippokrates, miscalled the Father of Medicine, but certainly the first scientific physician of whom we know anything very definite. There are fifty-three treatises bearing his name, whereof a number are certainly not his composition, and there is much doubt concerning the rest; for they are medical treatises, and as such liable to be revised, added to and subtracted from, by other physicians. They form, it would seem, some part of the library of the Koan school of medicine, of which he was the founder or at any rate one of the earliest and greatest members. Their style is consistently plain, full of technical terms, though less so than modern works would be, for medicine was still forming its specialist vocabulary. In this they resembled the best works of Greek science in all branches, so far as they survive. Ornament is out of place in such compositions, and the excellent native taste of the nation realized this.

All these writers and several others of whom we know a little used the Ionic dialect. We now pass once more to Athens, and meet one of the greatest names in all philosophy, that of Plato (*Platon*, born 427, died 348/7). His master, Sokrates, never wrote anything, but several of his followers composed dialogues in which they represented him as arguing with various interlocutors. Most of these works are unhappily lost, but we have what are no doubt the best, Plato's own. To estimate his services to philosophy, or even to give the barest outline of them, is impossible in a work of this kind. It is no exaggeration to say that every subsequent European philosopher, to say nothing of those of other parts of the world, has been influenced by him, directly or indirectly, espousing his views, modifying them, adapting them to other systems, or opposing them. Here he can be discussed only as a stylist, and in that as in thought he is supreme. He was master of every variety of his rich native language, from the tone of casual friendly conversation to the highest imaginative flights, in which indeed some later critics said that he went beyond the proper limits of prose. The framework of his dialogues, the usual form of his writings, is enough to show that if he had not been a great philosopher he could have been an admirable dramatist, a Menander before Menander. Every speaker lives, drawn from life with a few masterly strokes, which bring out without undue heightening his salient characteristics, modesty, conceit, conventionality, mild fanaticism, dogmatic radicalism, and so through a wide range of traits. This is especially true of Plato's early and middle periods,[1] in which Sokrates is the dominant figure, although as the author's own thought progresses he appears more and more as the exponent of views which are really his great disciple's and not his own. In the later stages Sokrates recedes into the background, even being absent from some works, and the tone becomes more positive and less lively and dramatic.

Besides the dialogues, Plato is credited with the authorship of a collection of letters, thirteen in all, whereof some are certainly spurious. But not less than three, the sixth, seventh and eighth, are almost beyond doubt Plato's own, and others may well be his. They relate to philosophical and political affairs, connected with Plato's two visits to Sicily, about 388, to the court of Dionysios I, tyrant of Syracuse, and some years later to that of his successor, Dionysios II. Plato was intensely interested in politics, and his vision of a model state, embodied in the great *Republic* and modified to suit what he believed might be immediately practicable in his last important work, the *Laws*, was no mere theoretical construction, but the basis of what he hoped might be put into practice, if an enlightened governor and legislator could be found, or, as he put it, if the

---

[1] We have almost no direct evidence of the order in which Plato wrote his dialogues. After much unprofitable speculation, the right method, based on minute stylistic observations, was demonstrated by Prof. Lewis Campbell of St Andrews (1867) and further developed by later writers, notably Lutoslawski (*Origin and Growth of Plato's Logic*, 1897).

philosophers became kings or the kings philosophers.[1] That he failed to convert either of the Sicilian despots into a philosopher-king was their fault, not his; the younger at least did lip-service to philosophy, and Plato, at the cost of much that was disagreeable and not a little that was actively dangerous, had shown the courage of his convictions. Later, his advice and encouragement did much to secure the success of Dion, who overthrew Dionysios II, and he did not cease to urge moderation and wisdom on Dion and Dion's friends.

In addition to the undoubted works, several pieces have come down to us bearing Plato's name. They vary from one, the *Epinomis*, or supplement to the *Laws*, which may be actually his own, to compositions which cannot possibly be by him or even of his age, such as the *Axiochos*, an interesting sketch of certain much later eschatological views, put into the mouth of Sokrates, supposed to be visiting and consoling a sick friend. There are also some epigrams attributed to him, which so far as their style and vocabulary go may well be at all events by an educated Athenian of the fourth century B.C.

No account of Plato would be complete without some mention of his famous myths. A close reasoner, he was far too clear sighted not to perceive that some of his beliefs were incapable of proof, and were matters of feeling quite as much as of analytical thought. These included eschatological speculations, corollaries to the doctrine that the soul is immaterial and immortal, which was of immense importance to Plato and the subject of several attempts at logical proof. But, a stranger thing to our ideas, they included physical and cosmological speculations also, for Greek physics was still far from being the exact science, dealing with measurable matter and calculable forces, which ours is. For these, therefore, he claimed no more than reasonable probability, and as such he sets them forth in the impressive and poetical account of the origin and nature of the universe which forms the subject of

---

[1] *Republic* 473 c, d.

one of his most famous works, the *Timaeus*, the one Platonic dialogue of which the Middle Ages in the West had any accurate knowledge, it being available in the Latin translation of a certain Chalcidius. But the best and greatest of the myths deal with such matters as the nature and destiny of the soul (so in the *Symposium*, which handles its ascent, due to the power of Love,[1] in the *Phaedrus*, where we hear of its limited ability to share the perfect happiness of the gods, and in the *Phaedo*, still more in the *Republic*, which speak of the experiences of man in the other world) or other matters more or less definitely transcendental. It has long been recognized that Plato had been influenced, especially in the matter of his imagery, by Pythagoreanism and also by a movement conventionally known as Orphism, because its writings were regularly attributed to the mythical musician Orpheus or one of his companions. It dates from the sixth century B.C. and taught, not indeed any one consistent doctrine, but a number of strange speculations, generally cast in mythical form and expressed in hexameters strongly influenced by Hesiod and his school, concerning the origin of man and his relations to the supernatural powers.

In this development of his philosophical activities, Plato is the father of a long line of visions and other apocalyptic descriptions of matters which lie outside scientific or other rational investigation. It may be said that but for him and his later imitators (see p. 190 for a remarkable example) such a masterpiece as the *Divine Comedy* would not have been what it is, and this although Dante knew no Greek and could not have studied the Platonic myths for himself. Naturally the later works of this kind are coloured by the religious views

[1] Love (*Eros*), in Plato, differs unrecognizably from the vulgar and etiolated thing known as 'Platonic love' by the ignorant. It begins with the natural attraction exercised by a beautiful body; it then progresses, if it has found a worthy subject, to admiration for and attraction by the beauties of mind and character. Thence it advances to the contemplation of Beauty in general, the Form (*eidos* or *idea*) of Beauty, which is imperfectly mirrored in material objects, and so to the Form of Good, whereof Beauty is only one manifestation.

current when they were written, but these in their turn generally owe more than a little to Platonic influence, direct or indirect.

Contemporary with Plato (his dates are about 430 to after 359) was a man of unphilosophic mind, but possessed of practical ability and a simple, perspicuous style, in which Attic usage is a little corrupted, no doubt by reason of his long sojourns abroad. This was Xenophon, who seems to have been on the extreme fringe of the group of followers and admirers surrounding Sokrates. His *Memorabilia*, as they are generally called, that is to say reminiscences of Sokrates and his teachings, show little grasp of what that great innovator in philosophy really stood for; he appears rather as a sound moralist, who argues with and confutes holders of wrong views. The general effect is dull, although there is useful information in the work and it serves as a check on the very different portrait drawn by Plato. The question of the extent to which the historic Sokrates is to be found in either writer cannot be gone into here. Xenophon also wrote several shorter works of a more or less philosophic kind, the most interesting being the Banquet (*Symposium*; it has only the title in common with the Platonic dialogue of the same name), in which a charming sketch is given us of a supposed occasion when Sokrates and some friends met socially and chatted on a variety of topics. Another is the *Oeconomicus*, i.e. the treatise on domestic economy, which is an account by a husband of how he trained his very young and inexperienced wife to be a good housekeeper. In telling his story he says much that throws light on Greek private life of the time.

A much longer work of Xenophon, which is on the border between his philosophic compositions and his historical writings (see p. 121), is the earliest historical romance in any European language. Its title is *The Education of Cyrus* (*Cyropaedia*, i.e. *Kyrou paideia*; like many Greek works it is named from the subject first treated in it). This gives, in the form of a largely fictitious life of Cyrus the Great, its author's notion of the ideal ruler and how he should be trained and developed; for Xenophon was sufficiently in touch with the political thought of his time to be something of a monarchist, democracy by then having lost such prestige as it ever had had in the minds of the more intelligent. On the whole, the work is dull, but enlivened here and there by battle-scenes, which Xenophon, having been a soldier himself, could describe with a certain vividness, and a really pretty love story, the tale of the barbarian prince Abradatas and his faithful wife Pantheia.

The *Cyropaedia* enjoyed wide popularity for many generations, its admiring readers including such different characters as Scipio Africanus the Younger and his circle and the immortal Mr Shandy, whose *Tristropaedia* borrowed its title from it.

Plato had many pupils, most of whom are of little interest from a purely literary point of view; but the most celebrated was Aristotle (Aristoteles) of Stageiros (the form Stageira is later) in Thrace. Son of a physician, he may have inherited an interest in biology from his father, but he lost his parents while still young, was brought up by one Proxenos, came to Athens when seventeen years old (in 367, his birth-date being 384), studied under Plato for some twenty years, spent some time abroad after the older philosopher's death, and came back to Athens in 335/4, where, like Plato, he founded a school, or rather a sort of college, the Lykeion (more familiar to us under its Latinized form Lyceum), which, like Plato's Academy,[1] had a regular course of instruction, besides much research. Of his enormous services to logic[2] and metaphysics, ethics and politics, and many other departments of philosophy

---

[1] Plato began to teach in the precinct of the hero Akademos, or more correctly Hekademos; Aristotle, in that of Apollo Lykeios (one of the god's best-known titles, 'Lord of Wolves'), near Athens. Thus both made use of a sacred spot. There is a certain analogy with the growth of some of our schools and universities around churches or monasteries.

[2] Faustus, in Marlowe's play, thinks for a moment of devoting his life to Aristotelian logic, 'Sweet Analytics [title of Aristotle's four books on the subject], 'tis thou hast ravished me'. It says little for the intelligence of some

H

and science, this is not the place to speak, although he has
left his mark on every one of them, even to the terminology
we use. But one of his subjects of study and instruction was
literature, and we still have two important works dealing
with it. The shorter is the *Poetics*, which seems from its form,
or rather almost formlessness, to be someone's lecture notes,
or at best Aristotle's own outline of what he was going to say.
In any case, it is defective, for one sentence begins 'As to
Epic poetry' and gets no further, clearly proving that something has been lost, and a further loss is the section on Comedy
which it once obviously contained. Yet with all its defects, it
is a magnificent piece of criticism, containing also interesting
remarks on the history and origin of Tragedy, and giving the
famous description of its purpose, 'the purging through pity
and fear of the corresponding emotions', which apparently
means that the spectator, beholding the sufferings of an
Oidipus, for instance, is lifted above merely selfish fears and
griefs into something nobler.[1] It also contains the account of
the ideal Tragic hero, a person of noble character, marred by
some fault (*hamartia*; the word was later to mean 'sin', but
had no such sense in Aristotle's time), which proves his downfall. It is not the author's fault that this work was made, by
critics after the Revival of Letters, the basis for the notorious
'three Unities', of Time, Place and Action. Of these, only the
third is Aristotelian, and means that the plot should be
organically connected, every incident arising necessarily or at
least probably from what has gone before, and should have a
definite beginning, middle and end, not a mere aimless
sequence of events. Concerning Time, he remarks that the

---

early editors of the play that the nonsensical words 'Bid Economy farewell and
Galen come' are presently put into his mouth. Marlowe of course wrote 'Leave
to on kai me on', i.e. 'is' and 'is not'.

[1] *Poetics* 1449b27. For a discussion of this and other matters, the most convenient book is the edition by S. H. Butcher, title *Aristotle's Theory of Poetry
and Fine Art*, ed. 4, London, 1932 (re-issued 1951), which has a very good
English translation opposite the Greek text.

later plays regularly occupied no more than twenty-four hours for their action, a simple statement of fact, and of Place he has nothing whatever to tell us. The longer work is the *Rhetoric*, which is not a handbook of the subject for the would-be writer or speaker to learn rules from, although it contains some practical advice, but a study of what oratory is and how it persuades.

Aristotle's style was praised by Cicero,[1] and that of the surviving works is universally found crabbed and difficult by moderns. The explanation is simple however. By a series of accidents we have lost all Aristotle's 'exoteric' works, that is those which he wrote for 'outsiders', in other words non-specialists, containing popular discussions of philosophical questions, an exhortation to the study of philosophy, and other matters, so treated as to be intelligible to any educated reader without preliminary training in the subject. But we have the 'esoteric' writings, or at least a large number of them, i.e. works intended for the use of 'those inside' – his own students, who had had the preliminary instruction, from him or another, and therefore could follow even highly technical discussions. We have also a not inconsiderable bulk of writings which are certainly not his, some of them being manifestly much later than his time. Neglecting these, we find in the 'esoteric' writings manifest signs that they are notes for lectures rather than books intended for publication as they stand. Not only are there repetitions and other signs of a work composed over a long period and here and there revised as the lecturer changed his views, but the style is often, especially at really important points, so condensed as to be scarcely in-telligible unless the reader is thoroughly accustomed to Aristotle's manner. One gathers that Aristotle was not a very ready speaker except on matters concerning which he had thought deeply and felt intensely; this would for instance

[1] Cicero, *Prior Academics* ii, 119, 'Aristotle, pouring as it were a golden river of speech'.

explain why in his great treatise on Ethics, the so-called
Ethica Nicomachea, he devotes far more space to (i.e. had
written out more fully) a number of comparatively trivial
matters than to such things as his important and searching
criticism of certain Platonic views. All this is perfectly in-
telligible to anyone who has himself had experience in
lecturing, whether to students or to a wider public.

After Aristotle, we need hardly mention any philosopher
save his pupil and successor Theophrastos, of whose
voluminous writings there survive, besides two botanical
treatises, the first we have on this important branch of science,
a brief work on metaphysics, hardly less crabbed in style than
the writings of his master, some short essays or excerpts on
various topics, and one little masterpiece which has had a long
line of imitators. This is the *Characteres*, literally distinguishing-
marks, and contains, besides a preface written for it by some
Byzantine many centuries later, thirty masterly sketches of the
absurdities and minor vices of such men as one was likely to
meet on the streets and in the public places of Athens. He says
nothing, except incidentally, of women, for respectable
women kept mostly to their own houses and, if they had to go
abroad, did not talk freely to men who were not of their own
kin. His minor sinners and fools include the Flatterer (No. 2),
the Chatterer (No. 3), the Rumour-mongerer (No. 8), the
Absent-minded Man (No. 14), the Pietist (No. 16; it is a
mistake to label him superstitious, as many do, for his actions
are silly exaggerations of normal religious practices; e.g. most
contemporaries believed in omens, but he sees an omen in
every trifle), the Suspicious Man (No. 18), the Pettily
Ambitious (No. 21), the Boaster (No. 23) and other such.
All are portrayed in the same manner: the petty vice is first
defined, and then, 'The . . . is the sort of person who' (follows
a string of characteristic sayings and actions). Whether the
work was always independent or is a number of extracts from
some larger treatise on ethics is uncertain, and not of much

importance, for it has come down to us as a complete and self-contained book, and was handled as such by its many modern imitators. By the late sixteenth century it was becoming known in England, and in 1592 Casaubon published a Latin version of it, followed by a commentary in 1599, welcome helps to an age which had more enthusiasm for Greek learning than skill in it, and for the comprehension of a work which is not without its difficulties. At all events, the best-known imitations are later than Casaubon's two contributions, Hall's *Characteristics of Vertues and Vices* in 1606, Overbury's *Characters or Witty Descriptions of the Properties of Sundry Persons* in 1614, and in France the most famous of all, La Bruyère's *Les Caractères, ou les Mœurs de ce Siècle*, 1688. Farther down than this we need not trace Theophrastos. He was not an author of the first rank, and consequently his imitators, especially La Bruyère, had little difficulty in equalling or outdoing him, but the credit of hitting on the fruitful idea remains his.[1]

Concerning the later philosophies, Stoicism and Epicureanism, not much need be said, for they produced no great writers in Greece, at all events from the literary point of view. Both were consistently materialistic systems, denying the existence of anything but matter, however refined and tenuous some forms of it might be. Stoicism was not of pure Greek origin, for its first founder, Zenon, was a native of Kition in Cyprus, where the population was partly Phoenician, and neither Zenon himself nor his most celebrated follower Chrysippos seems to have had any merit as a stylist. As to Epicureanism, its founder Epicurus (*Epikouros*) despised all ornaments of language and sought only after clarity. Here and there we find a Stoic work of some literary interest, the best-known and the one which makes the nearest approach to eloquence being the famous *Hymn to Zeus* of Kleanthes,

---

[1] See (Sir) R. C. Jebb and J. E. Sandys' edition of the *Characters* (London, 1909), Introduction, pp. 22–32.

one of Zenon's immediate disciples; it is in hexameters of
very fair quality, and sets forth a popular account of the lofty
Stoic conception of the nature of deity, the mythological
name here meaning simply 'God'. The first eloquent Epicurean was also a poet, and a much greater one, Lucretius
(see pp. 174 ff.). To the credit of the Stoics, however, must be
put an intelligent interest in grammar, a needful accessory to the
logic in which they delighted. Much of their terminology is
still in use, generally in Latin translations adopted into modern
languages.

Two minor schools, the Cynics and the Skeptics, produced
compositions of no great importance in themselves but noteworthy as forming part of the antecedents of Roman satire.
The Cynics were, so to speak, the popular preachers of their
day, perhaps more than any other school, and the subject of
their harangues, addressed apparently to any who would
listen, was morals. One of them, by name Kerkidas, who
seems to have written about the middle of the third century
B.C., varied this means of influencing the public by putting
what he had to say into verse – lyric in metre, so perhaps
meant to be sung – and a papyrus has preserved part of his
work.[1] In this, one passage in particular reads almost as if
Horace had translated it, and others treat of matters with which
he too deals. Of the same century were a few other writers,
as Bion of Borysthenes, Teles, and, perhaps the best-known
name, Menippos, who seems to have criticized life freely, in
a mixture of prose and verse, and given his remarks quaint
settings, one at least being placed in the other world. How
close a parody this was of the descent of Odysseus into the
land of the dead, in the *Odyssey*, we do not know, but certainly
Menippos influenced not only Varro (see p. 198) but also
Lucian (p. 280), from whom we can gather something of his
manner, enough to make us regret that hardly anything of

---

[1] It is the Oxyrhynchos papyrus No. 1082. The passage referred to is col. 5,
lines 13 ff., with which compare Horace, *Sat.* i, 2, 121–6.

his own work remains. One of the Skeptics, Timon of Phleius (not to be confused with Timon of Athens, the misanthrope), wrote a mock-heroic work in hexameters, in which he made fun of all philosophers save those of his own school or something like it. He called his poems *Silloi*, literally squint-eyed, that is to say laughing or mocking pieces.

When Aristotle and others of his time or earlier wrote on rhetoric, they were supplying a want, particularly those who produced manuals for the guidance of would-be speakers. Political life was very lively in the numerous city-states, especially of course those with a democratic government, such as Athens and the republics which grew up in Sicily after the fall of the great tyrants, or kings as they naturally preferred to be called, that is to say after about the middle of the sixties of the fifth century B.C. As there was then nothing corresponding to our popular press, and reading matter of any kind was comparatively scarce and dear, the spoken word was the usual form of propaganda and persuasion, the more so as the public to be reached was small (the population of one of our larger cities is greater than that of the average city-state) and concentrated within an area of not many square miles. Hence to speak persuasively and forcefully was the obvious means of political advancement. Moreover, the Greeks, and not least the Athenians, were a litigious people, and their courts consisted of large juries, sometimes several hundred in number, meeting with a presiding magistrate whose business was to keep order, not to instruct the jurors concerning law, of which, as of fact, they alone were judges. Therefore a man's fortunes, his very life, might at any time depend on his being able to persuade the majority of the court that he was not guilty of one of the numerous offences recognized by law, and in theory at least he must be his own advocate, nothing corresponding to our barristers existing. So even quiet citizens with no ambition to be prominent in public affairs had an excellent reason for learning to express themselves well, although the legal requirement was often circumvented by the litigant delivering a speech composed for him by some more able hand. Such speech-writers, *logographoi* in Greek, were fairly numerous, at all events in Athens, and a number of specimens of their work have come down to us, many by the foremost orators. The earliest writers on rhetoric of whom we hear were two Sicilians, Korax and Teisias, and the most famous teacher of the subject was the great sophist Gorgias, whose long life extended through most of the fifth century. He is remembered chiefly for the figures of speech called after him Gorgian. These consisted essentially of arranging the subject-matter in a series of antitheses, emphasized by their elaborate balance (*parisosis*, the grouping of the words so that each half of the antithesis was of the same length) and further by what is strange to our ears but was a valued ornament of prose in and after Gorgias' time, *paromoiosis*, in other words rime. Once the novelty of these devices had worn off, the best writers and speakers were wary enough to use them sparingly, for occasional effect, not, as Gorgias himself seems to have done, as the staple of their style, but they continued in use down to the very end of antiquity. With zealous study of the lessons of Gorgias, supplemented by such things as the principles of rhythm laid down by other prominent teachers, such as Thrasymachos, the famous sophist who is confuted by Sokrates in the first book of Plato's *Republic*, it is no wonder that men of ability quickly developed, not a prose style, but several styles, suited to different types of composition. Later theorists distinguished three main classes, the simple, the middle (or florid) and the grand (or elevated). All these can be easily illustrated from the Attic orators, of whom the Alexandrians (see p. 126) chose out ten to form their canon. They were Antiphon, Andokides, Lysias, Isokrates, Isaios, Demosthenes, Aischines, Lykurgos (a fourth-century politician, having only his name in common with the half-mythical framer of the Spartan constitution), Hypereides and

Deinarchos. Several of these are but of minor importance, at least to us, because not much of their work has survived; I therefore attempt to sketch the careers only of a few.

Antiphon, a native of the deme Rhamnus, was of the fifth century, being executed for treason in the troubles of the year 411. Of his speeches, written for other men's trials, we have three, all dealing with cases of homicide; i.e. there has come down to us one section, or part of a section, of some classified edition of his works. We have lost, save for a few scraps on a papyrus, his famous defence against the charge which cost him his life. He was a teacher of rhetoric, and attributed to him (the matter is somewhat uncertain) are a series of model speeches, the *Tetralogies*, i.e. groups of four speeches each, two for the prosecution and two for the defence, all in imaginary trials for homicide. These are the first surviving examples of a long-continued class of compositions, rhetorical exercises on sundry subjects, of which we shall hear more later.

Lysias was born about the middle of the century, perhaps in 445, and lived well into the fourth. His family were not citizens of Athens, but resident aliens (*metoikoi*, metics), originally from Syracuse. He had the citizenship for a brief period after the restoration of the republic in 403, but the decree under which he enjoyed it was soon revoked. Therefore, except for the short time in which he was an Athenian and could appear personally in court, he composed nothing but speeches for other litigants and some show-pieces, elaborate rhetorical exercises, such as were then very common and much liked; Plato's dialogue *Phaedrus* opens with a meeting between Sokrates and a young acquaintance, Phaidros, who has got hold of one of these performances of Lysias and is walking in the country to con it over. As a speech-writer for the courts he was unequalled in his own manner, the 'simple' style, owing to his remarkable power of identifying himself with the character as well as the interests of his client. His regular attitude is that the speaker is a peaceful man, unaccustomed to forensic strife, but forced by the villainy of his opponents to state a few facts which the jury ought to know and rebut the shallow arguments of the other party. The purity of Lysias' Attic suggests that he and his family had quite lost their original Syracusan speech; as to his effectiveness, that excellent critic Dionysios of Halikarnassos (see p. 231) says that whereas Isaios and Demosthenes are so obviously masters of rhetorical devices that they seem suspect even when they have a good case, Lysias and Isokrates arouse no such suspicions, even if they have a bad one.[1]

This Isokrates (436–338), Milton's 'old man eloquent', who by the way did not die of shock on hearing of the crushing Athenian defeat by Philip II at Chaironeia, had more influence, direct or through his pupils and other imitators, on subsequent European style than any other single writer. He produced fewer but longer works than Lysias, to judge by what we have of them both. The former was credited with no less than 425 speeches of various kinds, of which the best critics adjudged 233 to be really his, but the latter, with only sixty, not more than twenty-eight being certainly genuine, in the opinion of the same critics. We therefore have most of what he wrote, for there survive thirty works bearing his name, nine letters, a little work of advice on conduct addressed to someone named Demonikos, and twenty speeches. One of the letters and the address to Demonikos are spurious or doubtful, so that at least we have about twenty-eight specimens of his composition, several of them long and elaborate. His is the 'middle' style, suitable for all works not intended to move hearers or readers very strongly, but to persuade or inform them pleasantly. The author was not himself an orator, for he was shy and had a weak voice, but he had a measure of success as a *logographos* and was famous as a teacher of rhetoric of the highest class, using no cut-and-dried system and writing no textbook, taking into account the natural capabilities of

[1] Dion. Hal., *de Isaeo*, 4.

each pupil, but having certain principles, adherence to which was insisted upon. He would not allow strange or poetical words, but only the vocabulary of ordinary life, properly chosen and arranged. As Thrasymachos had done before him, he recommended the use of the period, the long complex sentence whose full meaning is revealed only when it is read or heard entire; but he would use it in moderation. A random example will illustrate this. If we look at sections 14–18 inclusive of the eighth speech in a modern edition, that *On the Peace*, we find first three periods, occupying respectively ten, eight and nine lines of the printed page, but two of them with a decided break in the middle, allowing the speaker to draw breath or the reader to gather a sufficient sense, though not all the author has to say at the moment. Then comes a short sentence, less than two printed lines. Now follows a long period, twelve lines, once more with a break in the middle, the result of one conditional sentence ending and another beginning ('If I stop here . . . but if you listen to me till the end . . .'), and then two short sentences, one two and the other three lines long. The general effect is exactly what Isokrates is aiming at; his argument is expressed weightily and impressively, but without ponderous monotony nor in a manner difficult to follow, given reasonably intelligent hearers or readers. Another rule which found great favour with all subsequent writers on literary and political topics was to avoid hiatus, that is the ending of one word and the beginning of the next with a vowel or diphthong which could not be elided, that is to say more or less completely dropped in pronunciation. It is a rule to be neglected at their peril by some of our own writers, in both verse and prose, for it is as true now as when Pope wrote it that 'oft the ear the open vowels tire'.[1]

As to Isokrates' subjects, they naturally vary, but the most interesting are perhaps those essays (speeches in form) which

---

[1] Pope, *Essay on Criticism*, 344.

are in reality political pamphlets. The most celebrated is the
Panegyricus, No. 4 in modern editions. Its title does not signify
what we mean by a panegyric, but simply a composition
somehow connected with (in this case, meant to be recited
at) a *panegyris*, that is to say a festival, namely the Olympic
Games of 380 B.C. It is said that he spent ten years in composing
it. This may or may not be founded on fact, but certainly
it embodies his political ideal in its earlier form. He urges his
hearers to cease from the endless internal squabbles which, as
he rightly held, were weakening and ruining Greece, and unite
under the headship of Athens against the natural enemy,
Persia. Later in life, when Macedonia had become the pre-
dominant power and the vision of Athens as head of a pan-
Hellenic confederacy had faded, he still urged action against
Persia, but led by Philip II of Macedonia, the ablest politician
and greatest general of the day. The ideal became something
of a reality after Philip's death, with the conquests of his son,
Alexander the Great. The seventh, *Areopagaticus*, which gave
Milton the title of his most famous prose work,[1] deals with
a very different topic, a plea for the restoration of the old
powers of the Council of the Areios Pagos, which, according
to the orator, had in early times exercised a most wholesome
influence over the conduct, public and private, of the citizens.
It cannot be said that Isokrates' excursions into history, here
or elsewhere, are marked by much accuracy; he seems rather
to echo the popular ideas of what had happened in the past,
and certainly he had made no profound researches himself,
being interested chiefly in the moral lessons to be drawn. For
he was a moralist, who fancied, quite mistakenly, that he was
also a philosopher.

The net result of his activities was that henceforth there
was a way opened for the man of some, though not first-rate,

---

[1] The reason why Milton changes the gender to *Areopagitica* is presumably
that he was thinking of the Latin *oratio*, which is feminine, whereas the Greek
title understands the Greek word for a speech, *logos*, a masculine noun.

literary ability, who was willing to study and practise along
the lines laid down by Isokrates and followed by his pupils.
Given diligence and a moderate talent, he might be sure of
achieving a style which, if not particularly distinguished, was
pleasing, dignified and suitable to serious topics not involving
strong appeals to the emotions. Such a style was well adapted
to the sort of historical and political compositions which were
and for a long while remained most in vogue. For example,
there are clear traces of Isokratean influence in the latest work
of Plato, who avoids hiatus in the *Laws*. The moralizing tone
was to be found in history after history, to judge from what
has survived in Greek and from the Latin historians, especially
Livy. With this sound basis, the occasional man of real
literary genius, or first-rate oratorical abilities, had something
from which he could advance along his own lines, to make a
respectable means of serious expression into a great one.

When Isokrates was in his fifties, in the year 384, the
greatest of all Greek orators, Demosthenes, was born. It is
said that he was a pupil of Isaios, who in turn is said to have
been taught by Isokrates himself and certainly was a *logographos* of ability, to judge from the specimens (all written for
cases dealing with wills and successions) which survive. Whatever the source of his training, Demosthenes by the age of
twenty was a finished speaker, and successfully sued his
guardians, who had been filling their pockets at his expense
ever since he lost his father at the age of seven. Becoming
a *logographos*, like his alleged teacher (for he was never a rich
man, most of his patrimony being apparently irrecoverable,
and his political ambitions involved him in considerable expense), he produced a number of speeches, effective and
regularly couched in a tone of moral earnestness, though they
lack the subtlety and elasticity of Lysias. But he was at his best
in the 'grand' style, and for this his political career gave
abundant scope. He was clear-sighted enough to realize early
that Philip of Macedonia was aiming at the mastery of Greece,

and it was his constant aim to frustrate this design and bring Athens once more to her old status as the leading power in the Hellenic world. What he seems never to have realized was that the material for such an achievement no longer existed. Not only was the State chronically short of funds, but the morale of her citizens was lowered by generations of continual and often disastrous conflicts, and she was no longer the head of a confederacy whereof the other members were in everything but name her tributary vassals, nor was it in the least likely that she could regain any such position. But national pride and a feeling of superiority to barbarous Macedonians remained, and with these Demosthenes did probably more than anyone else could have done. He missed no opportunity of addressing the Assembly (which, it is to be remembered, was not a representative body but a meeting at which all citizens had a right and indeed a duty to be present if they could), and turning whatever was under discussion into warnings against the ambitions of Philip and exhortations to vigorous action and to personal service, not to what was common at the time, the hiring of mercenaries under Athenian generals to fight the people's battles. Another method of propagating his views was through the courts of law, in the form of impeachments and defences respectively of members of the party favouring Macedonia and his own faction, whereof he was the leading spirit, but there were associated with him several other men of eminence, including the orators Hypereides and Lykurgos. The earlier political speeches mostly advocate such reasonable things as keeping up the strength of the Athenians' great arm, the navy, and sound financial policies; but in 351 begin the direct attacks on and warnings against Philip. From a series of these speeches we get the term 'philippic'[1] (cf. p. 187) with its connotation of violent and personal denunciation; for personalities were of the order of the day in contemporary politics, and neither Demosthenes nor his opponents hesitated

---

[1] *Logoi Philippikoi*, speeches concerning Philip.

to use every weapon, including aspersions on character. With these goes a group of speeches, the Olynthiacs, dealing with the attack by the Macedonians on the town of Olynthos, which lay some little distance southwards from their territory. A peace, in 346, brought about a pause in hostilities, and Demosthenes and his associates attacked members of the opposite faction, not least Aischines, who was apparently their most effective speaker; naturally counter-attacks were delivered, and impeachments by one side or the other were rife. After the renewal of hostilities in 340 and the defeat of the confederacy which the efforts of Demosthenes had had a great share in forming at the battle of Chaironeia in 338, the war of accusations still went on, for Philip's triumph still left Athens an independent State, and her internal affairs were little, if at all, interfered with by him or by Alexander. A certain Ktesiphon brought forward, in 336, a motion to 'garland' Demosthenes, that is formally to present him publicly with a golden wreath. It was the Athenian equivalent of admission to one of the great orders of knighthood, or elevation to the peerage, in recognition of public services. The immediate occasion was his efficient conduct of certain necessary measures to make Athens itself more defensible after the defeat at Chaironeia and the subsequent peace. Aischines caught at a legal informality in the decree, and indicted Ktesiphon for unconstitutional legislation. After long delays, the matter was brought to trial, and the accuser put forward his case with great eloquence, only to be answered by Demosthenes, appearing as an interested party on Ktesiphon's behalf (of course the whole process was really directed at him), with the greatest of all Greek orations, the speech *Concerning the Garland* (*De corona* is its traditional Latin title).[1] Besides a scathing attack on Aischines, his parentage, his upbringing, his occupations, and especially his public career, the orator reviewed

---

[1] The usual English rendering 'On the Crown' is misleading; a garland (*stephanos* in Greek, *corona* in Latin) was not a mark of royal or other rank.

the history of his party, justifying its and his measures and laying the blame of the final defeat on ill-fortune and on treachery. His highest point is perhaps the famous apostrophe to his countrymen, 'You were not mistaken, men of Athens, who faced danger for the freedom and safety of all; no, by those ancestors of yours who risked their lives at Marathon, who stood in their ranks at Plataiai, who fought at sea off Artemision and at Salamis.'[1] We have no later oration of Demosthenes; eight years later he died, by his own hand, to escape a worse fate at the hands of the Macedonian regent Antipatros, when the final revolt of Athens against the new power was crushed at the battle of Krannon, 322 B.C.

After Demosthenes there were no Athenian orators of the first rank, though clever speakers abounded. The ultimate reason was that there was no longer any great subject for oratory; Athens was no longer a great power, or even a State independent in more than name. Oratory may still be good, but cannot be deeply impressive, on such subjects as lawsuits between undistinguished persons, discussions of local politics, rhetorical displays, or speeches of compliment to visiting notabilities.

Before leaving the subject of oratory, I give two instances of famous sayings which found their imitators in ancient and modern times. Gorgias ventured on the bold expression 'animated sepulchres' in speaking of vultures. Many centuries after his death, Shakespere put into Macbeth's mouth the phrase 'our Monuments Shall be the Mawes of Kytes' (*Macb.* iii, 2, 72–3). Demosthenes, who seldom used metaphor in his speeches (it was sparingly employed by all the great orators, perhaps as being an ornament rather of poetry) said of a decree moved by him, 'This decree made the danger which threatened the State pass like a cloud'. One of very many references to this famous passage is found in a speech of St Ambrose of Milan, who says of his memories of his dead

---

[1] *De corona* (speech No. xviii in our editions), section 208.

brother, 'But they remain and shall always be; they never pass like a (cloud)-shadow.' (Dem. xviii, 188; Ambrose, *de excessu fratris* i, 63). Modern echoes might be quoted for whole pages; the reader will doubtless be able to make his own list. And these are but two noteworthy phrases, torn from their context.

As to actual imitation of the Attic orators in modern times, it is not very apparent. There is a native elegance about the Attic dialect which enabled those who used it skilfully to be at once simple and effective; perhaps the nearest approach to this happy combination is found in good French prose. Neither Latin nor the majority of modern European idioms can match the tongue of Athens in this respect, and therefore are apt, if simple, to be bald and unimpressive, if more elaborate, to be too florid and artificial. Demosthenes, ever since his own time, has remained the unrivalled ideal of great oratory, and borrowings from him (including of course an occasional parody) are to be found commonly enough in the later classical literature. But on the whole it was from the Latins that moderns learned to compose an effective speech.

With history we once more visit Ionia, for the word itself is Ionic for enquiry or research into anything (*historie*), including past events. Appropriately, therefore, we find Ionian names among the earliest recorded narrators of the history, as we now call it, of their people or of the world generally. Since generally they are names only, with some few quotations from their works or statements about them, they may be left to the attention of specialists; to us the first writer is the Father of History, as Cicero called him,[1] Herodotos of Halikarnassos. He was born probably in the second decade of the fifth century and lived long enough to see the beginning of the Peloponnesian War, that is till after 431; he left his native country sometime before the middle of the century and spent the rest of his life on Athenian territory, partly in Athens

---

[1] Cicero, *de legibus* i, 5.

itself and partly at Thurioi in Italy, which was an Athenian colony. His life-work was a history of the Persian Wars, with an account, on a grand scale, of the events leading up to them from mythical times onwards; for he saw Dareios' attack on parts of Greece in 490, which resulted in the Athenian victory at Marathon, and the invasion by Xerxes in 480, as parts of the age-long struggle between Asia and Europe. He was indefatigable in collecting information wherever he could find it, though neglecting several sources which a modern would think indispensable, for he knew no language but Greek, the science of archaeology did not then exist, and not only was there then no regular study of epigraphy, but he refers but seldom to the thousands of inscriptions which must have been easily available. What he wrote is coloured by a naïve mixture of piety and rationalism; thus he now and then tells us that he refrains on religious grounds from mentioning something, but on the other hand when he uses a myth he is apt to explain away its supernatural features. For example, speaking of Io daughter of Inachos (cf. p. 56) he supposes that she was simply kidnapped by Phoenician traders and carried by them to Egypt (Book i, 1, 4), and the local tale that the Vale of Tempe was made by Poseidon is to him an indication that it was formed by a violent earthquake (vii, 129, 4). He is critical after his fashion, often expressing disbelief in what he has been told, or read, but recording it nevertheless, especially if it is a good story, which he never could resist and could tell inimitably. It has repeatedly been a commonplace to accuse him of lying, and many times his supposed falsehoods have been found on further investigation to have at least a substantial foundation in truth. His style is what ancient critics called 'strung together' (*eiromene*), that is without periodic or other elaborate structure, although it is plain enough that, as befitted a contemporary of Gorgias, he was sufficiently acquainted with rhetoric to use his figures where he thought proper. His dialect is Ionic, but not the precise speech of any

one Ionian community; it is a literary language, coloured here
and there by Epic usage. The effect is somewhat naïve on the
whole, and apt to make a careless reader forget that he is
dealing with a very acute intelligence. If such a thing as an
impartial historian exists, he probably is rather dull; Herodotos'
narrative is coloured here and there by enthusiasm for Athens
and for democracy, and is far from dull, but gross partiality
he is never guilty of. As he says in his preface, his aim is to
prevent what has occurred from fading with time, and the
great and wonderful deeds both of Greeks and barbarians[1]
from lacking renown. One feature of his structure, to which
he himself draws attention, is the long digressions on all
manner of topics, geographical and historical especially; his
term for them is *prosthekai*, or additions to the main narrative
(iv, 30, 1). This is partly due no doubt to the shape of ancient
books, written as they were on rolls of papyrus, with no
facilities for exact cross-references, appendices, footnotes and
the rest of our printed apparatus, but mostly to Herodotos'
own tendency to become insatiably inquisitive about whatever
topic he had on hand, and never to rest till he had found out
and set down as much as he could concerning it. Yet the
work as a whole does not lack a certain unity of structure;
Herodotos was too thoroughly Greek for that.

That he never finally revised it is clear from several things,
such as references to fuller treatment of some subject in a part
of the history obviously planned but never written, also from
occasional double handling of a subject; for instance, Book
iv gives us a shorter and a longer account of the geography
and ethnology of Scythia (approximately European Russia).
There is also no formal conclusion to the whole. My belief is
that he continued to work at and enlarge his 'enquiry' till
he died, and would have elaborated it still more had he lived

---

[1] To Herodotos, and Greeks generally, this word means simply foreigners,
non-Greeks, with no implication of inferiority. The radical significance is 'of
unintelligible speech'.

longer. But no synopsis can do him justice; the reader is urged to read him for himself, in a translation if he cannot understand the original.[1]

As he is the first great historian, so he is the last great writer in Ionic. He had no important imitators, though very many readers, friendly or hostile. Henceforth Greek historians used either Attic or the 'common dialect' (*koine dialektos*), which was the lingua franca of the Eastern Mediterranean world after about the death of Alexander, displaced the local dialects, except for artificial revivals, and much later split up in its turn into the many varieties of spoken Modern Greek (*dhimotiki*). Its largest constituent was Attic simplified. Though Herodotos has not been consciously imitated, there have been at least two writers not unlike him in mind and in style, Froissart in French and Sir John Mandeville in English.

The next great name is that of one as unlike Herodotos as any writer well could be, Thucydides (properly *Thoukydides*), son of Oloros, descended from a wealthy family with Thracian connexions (the name Oloros is Thracian). He was born somewhere about the time when Herodotos left Halikarnassos. In 424 he was in command of an Athenian force in Thrace, and was out-generalled by the very able Spartan commander Brasidas. Knowing that the misfortune would be blamed on him, rightly or wrongly, he did not return to Athens until after the war was ended; he had interests in the mines of Thrace, and so was not without means. Thus he saw events as much from the enemy's side as from that of his countrymen. No one seems to have molested him on his travels. He evidently had early formed the resolution of writing a history of the war, and no doubt gathered materials for it during his

[1] There are translations into English, the oldest one by Rawlinson, available in two volumes of the 'Everyman' Library, and the newest by J. E. Powell, (2 vols., Oxford, 1949), which I prefer both for its more modern scholarship and because its language is good seventeenth-century English, which catches the tone of the original better. Between the two in date are a rendering by G. C. Macaulay (London, 1890), praised by Powell as painstaking and accurate, and another by A. D. Godley, in the Loeb series.

exile. Hence his sternly impartial and impersonal tone, broken only by a certain animosity towards Kleon, the vulgar but energetic and patriotic demagogue who came into power after the death of Perikles. He restricts himself to the matter in hand, except for an introduction sketching the earlier history of Greece and an occasional excursus into events prior to the war. He disdains all mythological adornments, in fact everything that does not give his readers the full facts and enable them to draw their conclusions, for their future guidance, in case a like situation should recur. Here he strikes a note echoed in several later historians who survive, and no doubt also in the lost works of others. Thucydides, in his famous reflections on the civil commotions at Kerkyra (Corcyra, the modern Corfu) says[1] 'Faction brought many hardships upon the cities [of Greece], such as occur and will always occur, so long as human nature remains unaltered, but to a greater or a milder degree and in different forms according as circumstances vary. For in peace and prosperity both states and individuals are more reasonable, because they do not fall into unwished-for necessities, but war, robbing them of sufficiency for daily needs, is a stern teacher and adapts the moods of the multitude to the present conditions.' In other words, he who studies the conditions in Kerkyra and elsewhere in Greece then, as he goes on to detail them with his usual force of language, will know what to look for should external and internal disturbances recur in his own lifetime. With this we may compare the opening paragraph of Polybios' history (p. 147): 'If it had happened that the recorders of events who were before me had neglected the praise of history itself, it might be necessary for me to exhort all to acquire and hand on such memorials, since there is no readier road to improvement for mankind than exact knowledge of former doings. But since not only some, or only to some extent, but practically all begin and end by telling us that to learn history is the truest education and

[1] Thucydides iii, 82, 2.

preparation for public actions, and that the most vivid, nay the only teacher of the power to withstand nobly the changes of fortune is the recollection of the reversals that have befallen others, it is clear that no one would think it proper to repeat what has already been well and often said, and certainly I should not.' And Livy, in his celebrated preface to his history, is still of the same opinion (p. 229): 'This is the chief benefit and profit to be gained from historical knowledge, that you [the reader] are shown examples of every kind set forth in a conspicuous memorial, and thence you may seek for yourself and your state something to imitate, thence also learn what to shun, as foul in its beginning and foul in its result.' I have already mentioned (p. 111) that the historians who learned style and manner from Isokrates wrote history with this end in view; Thucydides, though no Isokratean, was of his age and proves clearly enough that the idea was current.

His style is like no other, except that of one or two imitators. It shows here and there the influence of Gorgias (cf. p. 106), as might be expected, but is sterner and rougher than anything he or his immediate pupils produced. Thucydides appears to have had a certain contempt for the minor elegances; later critics mentioned, for instance, that he is at no pains to avoid harsh collocations of words. In narrative he is generally plain and straightforward, though impressive, except when some very exciting scene is to be described, such as the decisive sea-fight in the harbour of Syracuse (vii, 69, 3–72, 4), when the words seem to tumble over one another and clause piles upon clause, keeping pace with the varying fortunes of the battle. In the speeches with which the history is diversified, the difficulty of following his thought is often great, for he packs more into each sentence and phrase than one would have imagined it could be made to contain, witness the difficulty translators have in keeping to anything like the same length as their compressed original. In these speeches, according to his own account (i, 22, 1) he tries to give the substance of what was actually said on each occasion, so far as he can discover it, but does not profess to record the very words. Hence it is, presumably, that he regularly introduces each oration by the formula 'he spoke to the following effect'. As a matter of fact, these speeches serve to embody the historian's own comments on the political and military situation from time to time. In the latter, his experience as a commander enables him to give good tactical descriptions of battles, whereas Herodotos seems always to portray them as they appeared to the rank and file. The plan of the work is annalistic, each year's events being completed before the next is told, with the result that, although the chronology is easy to follow, the account of anything which took more than a year is interrupted, sometimes by the telling of quite petty contemporaneous happenings. The formula which draws attention to the passage of time is of this kind, 'And so this winter ended, and (with it) the third year of this war the history of which Thucydides has written.'

Besides his merits as a stylist, it is not too much to say that Thucydides was the first scientific historian of Europe. For his combination of factual accuracy and skill in presentation he can hardly be said to have been rivalled, despite the introduction since his day of new methods of arriving at the facts.

Thucydides never completed his great work, the eighth and last book ending with hostilities still going on and Athens weakened, but not yet crushed. He found several continuators, one of whom was Xenophon (see p. 98). His *Hellenica* catch something of the vividness and order of his great model for the first two books, which bring down the narrative to the restoration of the democracy under Thrasybulos; but after that the work is disjointed and ill-proportioned. It is, however, on the whole our best source for events down to its end, the death of Epameinondas in 362. A much better work is the famous *Anabasis*, i.e. *The March from the Sea*, for here Xenophon is relating stirring events in which he bore a leading part, the attempt of Cyrus the Younger to dislodge his brother Artaxerxes from the Persian throne, the battle in which Cyrus was killed and all his army, except the Greek mercenaries, scattered, the loss by treachery of all the senior officers of the Greeks, their election of Xenophon to command them, and the means by which he got them through rough country populated by often hostile tribes down to the sea, with their adventures there until the remnant of them were taken up into Thibron's Spartan force. It is our only full account of these events, therefore Xenophon's veracity cannot be checked, but the claims he makes for himself, if untrue, could have been exposed so easily and by so many men who had shared the campaign, also his treatment by the Spartans was so friendly, that we cannot suppose him guilty of more than perhaps a little exaggeration here and there. He indulged in a petty mystification regarding his authorship, referring to the *Anabasis* as composed by a certain 'Themistogenes of Syracuse'.[1]

Over the other historians of that time we need not linger, for they are represented for us only by fragments, and none of them seems to have been of merit in any way comparable to Thucydides, or even to have had any such adventurous career as that of Xenophon, coupled with ability to tell his story.

With the establishment of Attic prose the great age of Greek literature ends. This is not to say that nothing of merit was produced later; indeed, we shall find presently that there was great literary activity in the centuries following the death of Alexander the Great (323), the periods which we designate as Hellenistic and Roman. But no writer emerged of calibre like that of Pindar, Aeschylus, Plato or Demosthenes. What did occur was the formation of new styles and *genres* of writing, which had much influence first on the Latins and later, through them, on the modern world.

[1] Xenophon, *Hellenica* iii, 1, 2.

V

The Alexandrian and Roman Periods

WHEN ALEXANDER DIED, THERE WAS NO HAND strong enough to keep his vast empire together, and it fell apart into a number of independent kingdoms, each much larger than the old city-states of Greece and her colonies. Two of the most important were those of Pergamos in Asia Minor and of Egypt, where Ptolemy son of Lagos, one of Alexander's officers, made himself king and was succeeded by his son, Ptolemy (*Ptolemaios*) Philadelphos, a man of great ability and enlightenment, under whom learning and literature were zealously encouraged. Pergamos and still more Alexandria, the capital of the Ptolemies, were now the centres of the civilized world, and it is after the latter that this age, and especially its literature and scholarship, is generally called, until the final extinction of the dynasty (fall of Alexandria and death of Kleopatra VII, 30 B.C.) gave over Egypt into the hands of the Roman Emperors and the centre of gravity definitely shifted to Rome. The old cities, especially Athens, continued to be of some importance, though their political power dwindled to nothing, but on the whole the ablest men in all branches of activity made their way to one or other of the new centres. Alexandria in particular had its famous library, apparently begun by Ptolemy son of Lagos, otherwise Ptolemy Soter (Preserver, a common complimentary title of Hellenistic[1] kings), and completed by his son. Attached to it was the Museum (*Mouseion*, temple of the

---

[1] 'Hellenistic', a modern coinage, is the adjective used to describe this age, especially in its political aspect. It signifies that though mostly Greek in language and culture, the civilized world and its inhabitants were no longer exclusively Greek.

Muses), which was what we should call a college or academy, having its regular members, salaried by the government, its dining-hall, and its president, a governmental functionary whose official title was Priest of the Muses. The religious colour was nothing new, and certainly connoted no fervent piety on the part of its members. To be associated with the nominal cult of some deity or deities was hardly more than a mark of respectability for any society. As to the occupation of the members of the Museum, let us imagine some such body as the Fellows of All Souls College, Oxford, or those of Harvard University, appointed for life by an enlightened government, well salaried, and given the duty of managing and making useful a Bodleian or a Widener Library hitherto uncatalogued and containing many works on all manner of subjects which are not generally known even to educated people. Let us further imagine that among these Fellows are several who, without being literary geniuses of the first order, still have considerable talent for original composition, especially in verse, as well as for research of all kinds, and that it is their ambition to turn their learning to advantage by presenting the world with some new form of literature. This imaginary picture will be a not unfair representation of the Alexandrian body. Of the most celebrated poets of that age several are known to have held posts in the Library, some as chief librarians. Other Fellows, if we may call them so, were not poets nor composers of original works of literature but scholars pure and simple, and to them is due the establishment of standard texts of many of the older authors, which form the basis of those we now possess.

Homer, as first and greatest of Greek authors, naturally was one of the first texts to be examined, and his first editor was also the first librarian, by name Zenodotos. He examined, it would seem, a number of copies of the epics and put out a text and a commentary, the latter no doubt a separate work, not, as generally with us, attached to the text itself, a thing hardly possible considering the shape of ancient books. He offered a number of emendations, some based on his study of Homeric grammar, an early attempt and not always leading to sound conclusions, some on the grounds of the great Alexandrian canon, *to prepon*, 'that which is proper or fitting' – to the context of the character in question. Thus, he found grave fault with *Iliad* iii, 424, in which Aphrodite, disguised as a servant, sets a chair for Helen, because it is improper, *aprepes*, for a deity to do menial service to a mortal. The weakness of his argument lies not in the canon itself but in his implied expectation of Alexandrian etiquette in sub-Mycenaean Greece. The next editor, better known as a poet (see p. 130) was Rhianos; the next, and better known in scholarship, was Aristophanes of Byzantium, who also invented the critical marks which adorned the margins of Alexandrian texts, and signified that the editor thought certain lines or passages spurious, doubtful, incomplete or somehow calling for elucidation, no doubt supplied in the commentary. Later (he lived under Ptolemy Philometor, 181–146), was the greatest of all Homeric critics, Aristarchos of Samothrace. To him, more than to any other single scholar, was due the creation of a standard text of the poet, got by weeding out the spurious additions and other corruptions which were to be found in many of the common copies then circulating; for ancient books, like modern, were published sometimes in carefully copied, critically examined editions, sometimes in hurriedly made examplars, no doubt sold at a much lower price. His own suggestions as to the true reading, which were numerous, were not inserted in the text itself, but embodied in his very bulky commentary, now lost. Again, this was due at least partly to the shape of an ancient book. If a modern critically edits any text in any language, he is at liberty to print whatever he thinks the author wrote, provided that he attaches an *apparatus criticus*, or brief account of what his authorities actually give and what changes he has made. This was hardly

possible when the text was contained in a series of rolls, with
no guarantee that any copyist would exactly follow the
division into columns of his original. So the text we have often
contains readings which we know Aristarchos personally disagreed with, but did not change because his copies, or the
oldest and best of them, contained them. Lastly Didymos
(about 65 B.C.–A.D. 10), surnamed Chalkenteros, that is to say
Bronze-guts, because of his huge capacity for work, produced
a commentary which gave the opinions of Zenodotos,
Aristophanes and Aristarchos, and added his own. The
scholia, or marginal notes, which we find in several existing
medieval manuscripts of the poet are derived from two series
of excerpts from this commentary, and thus much of the
labours of these learned and industrious Alexandrians has
come down to us. Between them, these and other scholars
edited or at least commented on the dramatists, the lyric poets,
and later on some of the earlier Alexandrians themselves, who
in time attained to the rank of classics, or at least of authors
worthy of serious study. The term 'classic', by the way, itself
descends from Alexandria. *Classis* is the Latin representation
of the technical term *kanon*, properly a ruler or straight-edge,
applied to the lists drawn up by the Library authorities of
those authors whom they held to be the models in their own
departments. The 'canons' of the lyric poets and Attic orators
have already been mentioned (pp. 45, 106). Those of the
dramatists included, for Tragedy, the three great names
already dealt with (pp. 54, 63, 69 ff.), and Agathon (p. 85)
also an obscurer writer, an Eretrian, by name Achaios, and
for Old Comedy, Aristophanes, Kratinos, and four other
Athenians, together with Epicharmos. The historians included
those dealt with in the last chapter, with seven later names,
the best-known to us being Polybios (p. 147). Other branches
of literature had similar lists. Other things for which we have
to thank the Alexandrians are the Greek marks of punctuation,
which differ but little from those in use for modern tongues,

also the written accents, meant to serve as a guide to foreigners towards the correct intonation of the language. Hence it is that at first they were set only over syllables which had something unusual in their pitch, and not, as with us and with copyists and writers of the Middle Ages, over practically every word. Before the Alexandrians, indeed for some time after the beginning of their age, Greek books were written without such helps to reading, even without division of the words, as many early papyri survive to attest.

Turning now from the purely scholarly to the literary activities of the Museum, we have first to notice that there were two schools of thought, which we may conveniently label Kallimachean and Apollonian. Kallimachos of Kyrene, born somewhere about 315–310, began his career as a schoolmaster in Eleusis, a suburb of Alexandria, and rose to be something like a court poet; at any rate we hear of or possess several poems of his which concern the doings of members of the royal house and speak of them in most complimentary, not to say fulsomely flattering terms. His guiding principle was that henceforth poetry should be highly polished and of moderate length; the days of long compositions such as Epic were over. His own work, as we may see from what we have of it (six Hymns complete, five in hexameters and one in elegiacs, a number of epigrams, and fragments, varying from a word or so to considerable remnants, of his other pieces) adheres exactly to these rules. The metres, which are not many in number, use refinements of rhythm unknown to the earlier writers. The length is never great, a few hundred lines at most. The matter is regularly learned (Kallimachos was, as we should say, on the staff of the Library, and brought out what seems to have been a *catalogue raisonné* of its contents), and the vocabulary full of archaic and unusual words, got from a variety of sources, including of course Homer and Hesiod. In his principal work, however, he compromised. It was a long series of short episodes, under the general title of

Aitia, that is 'causes' (historical or legendary; we still speak of
an 'aetiological' myth) alleged to explain various customs,
natural phenomena, etc. A surviving fragment may serve as
an example. Kallimachos is at dinner and there meets a
stranger from the island of Ikos. Kallimachos asks him why
the inhabitants of Ikos so reverence the memory of the hero
Peleus, whose connexions are rather with Thessaly. The
stranger no doubt told an explanatory tale, but what it was
we do not know, for the rest is lost.[1] In this or any one of a
variety of ways each episode would be introduced, making a
series of poems of moderate length into the semblance of one
long composition, and giving room for as much variety as the
author pleased, also for the exhibition of his abundant learning. Other works included the *Iambi*, which were written in
the metres of Archilochos (or some of them) and in scazons
after the manner of Hipponax (pp. 30, 31) and seem to have
dealt with a variety of topics; the dialect was Ionic. Another
famous composition was of the kind which it is the fashion in
modern times to call an *epyllion*, tolerable Greek for 'little
epic'. It is the *Hekale*, and its foundation is an adventure of
Theseus, or rather an incident of that adventure. On his way
to kill the bull which was ravaging the country around
Marathon, he was benighted, and hospitably entertained by
Hekale, a poor old woman. On his return he found her dead
and ordered a cult of her to be instituted. The bulk of the
poem, to judge by what is left of it, dealt with the evening
spent in her house, the stories she told him and the rustic
supper which she gave him. It is assumed that the reader
knows already who Theseus was and has read of his exploits.
This kind of composition has found plenty of modern imitators, to say nothing of its employment by Catullus (p. 180)
and his school in antiquity. Not the worst is Tennyson, in his
Oenone and several other poems, perhaps the best being the

[1] Frags. 178-85 in the latest and fullest edition of the fragments, vol. i of
Pfeiffer's *Callimachus*, Oxford, Clarendon Press, 1949.

original *Mort d'Arthur*, which assumed that the reader knew, presumably from Malory, who Arthur was and how he came to be fighting a desperate battle in which all but one of his followers were killed.

The other school I have named after its best-known member, Apollonios of Rhodes (Apollonius Rhodius),[1] so surnamed because he spent some time in Rhodes. This man was apparently of about the same age as Kallimachos, and he held that it was still possible to write long epics, though perhaps not so long as Homer's masterpieces, which belief he gave form to in his *Argonautica*, a work extending to 5,853 lines, divided into four books. Its subject is of course the story of Jason and his quest for the Golden Fleece, beginning with the setting out and ending with the return to Iolkos. Its style is a kind of modernized Homeric. That is to say, it is founded upon the Homeric dialect and is full of reminiscences of his formulae, though regularly with slight changes. A curious feature is that the poet, who was also a very considerable Homeric scholar, takes occasion to set forth his views on the significance of certain Epic words of disputed meaning, by putting them in contexts where their sense cannot be in doubt. For instance, opinions were divided as to whether when Homer used the word *endios* he meant noon or evening; Apollonios informs us indirectly that he thought it could mean either, for in one passage (iv, 1312), the day was *endion* and the rays of the sun extremely hot; in another (i, 603), Athos is as far from Lemnos as a well-found merchant-ship could run (from morning to) *endion*, obviously evening. The work is interesting enough, but as a whole it lacks unity, being held together by little except that it deals with the varied adventures of one party of mythological heroes. Its longest episode, however, is in itself exempt from this fault,

[1] Names compounded of that of Apollo are so frequent that it is very common to find any well-known person who bears one of them provided with some kind of distinguishing adjective or surname to avoid confusion with another Apollonios, Apollodoros, or the like.

for it tells from beginning to end the story of how Medeia, daughter of the king of Kolchis, where the Fleece was kept, fell in love with Jason through the machinations of Hera and Aphrodite, helped him to perform the tasks imposed by her father, eloped with him, aided him to murder her brother Apsyrtos when he pursued the Argo, and finally wedded him.[1] The influence of Euripides is patent, and the amatory subject characteristic of the Alexandrians, who, in their constant search for unhackneyed subjects to write about, happily lighted on that of romantic love between man and woman.

The two schools attacked each other vehemently, and some remnants of their mutual invectives survive, including an incisive epigram of Apollonios concerning Kallimachos' abilities and work, and a typically learned and obscure assault on Apollonios by Kallimachos in one of the Hymns; but the most famous poem, Kallimachos' *Ibis*, has not survived. It seems to have invoked a number of mythical misfortunes, obscurely alluded to, upon the head of the Rhodian, and was imitated cleverly by Ovid (p. 226). At all events, Apollonios was influential enough to have followers or associates, perhaps the least obscure to us being Rhianos, one of the early editors of Homer, who wrote several epics with titles suggesting that they were of the nature of chronicles, as one of them, the *Messeniaka*, certainly was. It consisted of a highly coloured account of the long struggle of the people of Messenia against Spartan domination. The hero is the Messenian commander, Aristomenes; the work was not less than six books long, and the plot full of exciting episodes. We know something of its contents because Pausanias (p. 279), who apparently took it for sober history, inserted an outline of it in his famous guidebook, but the text is quite lost.

Two important Kallimacheans remain to be discussed. The former was not an Alexandrian by residence, though he was

[1] This part of the Argonautic story is pure folktale, the theme known generally to students of the subject as *Ogre's Daughter*.

one by taste and performance. This was Aratos of Soloi in Kilikia, perhaps the hardest ancient poet for a modern to appreciate, not because of obscurity in his style, for he is generally quite lucid, but because of his enormous popularity in antiquity. He wrote a didactic poem; this in itself was typical of the age, for as already mentioned the Alexandrians were on the lookout for subjects not worn by too frequent handling, and since Hesiod and the earlier philosophers no important didactic poetry had been written. His subject also was characteristic, for this was an age of important studies in astronomy. But his poem consists simply of an account, taken from a handbook by Eudoxos of Rhodes (408–355 B.C.), of the visible heavens and the apparent movements of the stars, followed by a list of weather-signs, probably from an essay on the subject by Theophrastos (p. 102). The title is *Phaenomena*, a regular term for whatever is visible to scientific observers; the style is perhaps best described by Kallimachos, who in a laudatory epigram says it has 'wiped off the most honied part' of Hesiod – but a modernized Hesiod with Alexandrian refinements of metre and language. There is a majestic prologue in honour of Zeus, for Aratos appears to have been a Stoic and a pious man. That is all; most of the work never tries to attain much elevation or impressiveness, and there are but few episodes to relieve the monotony of accounts of this and that constellation, its appearance, position relative to the others, and so on, or of the atmospheric conditions preceding storm or calm. But the work had a huge success, not only in its own day but for many centuries afterwards; Ovid predicted that it would last 'with the sun and moon',[1] and few would have disagreed with him. It was translated by some of the most eminent men in Rome, including Cicero and Germanicus the father of the Emperor Caligula, and exhaustively commented upon not only by philologists but by the great astronomer

---

[1] Ovid, *Amores* i, 15, 16, the poem Ovid is composing at the beginning of Ben Jonson's *Poetaster*.

K

Hipparchos, whose essay, mostly a series of corrections of mistakes in Eudoxos or of Aratos' own, is the one work of his which still survives. This was written about 150 B.C. Of the long list of subsequent poets who had read and admired Aratos, as is shown by their imitations of him, the most famous name is that of Vergil.

Another of the same school, much easier for us to understand, is the poet who was, among other activities, the first to write pastoral. This was Theokritos of Syracuse. He was of an undistinguished family, and seems early in life to have become a professional poet; we have a laudatory address of his to Hieron II (ruler of Syracuse 270-216), and of several very good epigrams from his pen some at least have all the appearance of having been written to order to commemorate real people or events. But he found a better market for his wares in Alexandria, where he attracted the favourable notice of the court and probably also of Kallimachos, whose literary principles he espoused. Again he sought originality, and like a good Alexandrian he found it by combining two existing styles. Hexameter poems had never ceased to be written; in the fifth century B.C., Sophron of Syracuse had put out a number of mimes, that is short pieces in dialogue describing everyday life. The medium was rhythmical prose, not metre of any kind. Theokritos, keeping Sophron's themes, or some of them, and something of his division of the works into 'male' and 'female', according to the sex of the characters, wrote in hexameters. He employed his native dialect, Doric, as Sophron had done, taking however a poet's privilege of using Epic forms when it suited him. Several, but by no means all, of his mimes (or *eidyllia*, as they are called; the word connotes nothing idyllic in our sense, but merely means little sketches) have for their characters country people – shepherds, cattle-men, harvesters – and they converse often in a very realistic manner. But also they sing to one another, which is no poetical fiction, for herdsmen of all kinds had and have, in

Mediterranean countries, music for one of their amusements, though it on occasion serves a practical purpose also, the beasts being trained to follow a particular tune played by their guardian. This enabled Theokritos, whenever he chose, to strike a higher note, as in the first[1] idyll, where a pathetic legend of the Sicilian countryside (as it seems to have been) is beautifully sung by a shepherd to his friend, a goatherd. He also wrote mimes with a city setting, as the second, in which a deserted girl tries to win back her lover by magic, and the delightful fifteenth, in which two good Alexandrian housewives go to the royal palace to see the festival in honour of Adonis and hear the fashionable soloist sing the hymn to him. Not the least admirable feature is the skill with which the stately Epic metre is made to fit the natural chatter of these and similar characters. But Theokritos also wrote epyllia (cf. p. 128), and two of these, one on the loss of Hylas and one on the fight between Polydeukes and Amykos king of the savage Bebrykians, look decidedly like criticisms of Apollonios, who handles both episodes in his *Argonautica*. But the chronology of both authors is too uncertain for us to be sure which came first in either case. One idyll has had a long and glorious literary history. It is the eleventh, in which the Cyclops Polyphemos, a much less formidable monster than in Homer, is in love with Galateia, a sea-nymph, and sings to her in such verses as he can contrive. Vergil knew this poem very well, and imitated one of its most famous passages. The Cyclops describes his sweetheart by comparing her to various country objects; the passage runs thus in Mr Gow's translation:[2]

O white Galatea, why dost thou repulse thy lover—whiter than curd to look on, softer than the lamb, more skittish than the calf, sleeker than the unripe grape.

[1] The numbers of Theokritos' poems are modern and purely conventional, being neither chronologically justified nor in accordance with any known ancient arrangement; but they are the handiest way of citing him.

[2] Theokritos xi, 19 ff.; p. 87 of *Theocritus edited with a translation and commentary* by A. S. F. Gow, vol. i (Cambridge University Press, 1950).

Vergil after his manner used a different set of images, but still
in the same tone and setting; the singer is actually a goatherd,
but singing in the person of the Cyclops, for which again he
had Theokritean precedent:[1]

> Galatea daughter of Nereus, sweeter to me than the
> thyme of Hybla, whiter than swans, more beautiful than
> pale ivy.

Ovid handled it again and, being Ovid, he expanded it:[2]

> Galatea, whiter than the petal of the snowy privet,
> fairer blooming than a meadow, taller than a lofty elm,
> brighter than glass, more playful than a tender kid, smoother
> than shells polished by the ever-washing sea, more welcome
> than winter sun or summer shade, more glorious than a
> palm-tree, more gazed upon than a towering plane, more
> dazzling than ice, sweeter than the ripe grape, softer than
> swan's feathers and cream-cheese, also, if you would not
> fly me, more delightsome than a well-watered garden, yet
> fiercer, O Galatea, than unbroken bullocks, harder than an
> ancient oak, more deceitful than the waves, tougher than
> both twigs of willow and white vines, more immovable
> than these crags, more violent than a [flooded] river,
> haughtier than a praised peacock, sharper than fire, more
> prickly than briars, more wrathful than a bear in cub,
> deafer than the seas, more implacable than a trodden snake,
> and, what I wish above all I could take from you, quicker
> to flee not only than a stag when the hounds bark after him
> but also than the winds, than the elusive breeze.

The prose renderings give nothing but the sense of the
original, losing the delicate subtleties of the metre and much
of the beauty of the language, as handled by one good and one
first-rate poet and by the cleverest rhetorician that ever dealt
in Latin verse. Coming now to two moderns, Gongora,

---

[1] Vergil, *Eclogue* vii, 37 ff.   [2] Ovid, *Metamorphoses* xiii, 789 ff.

living as he did in the Spanish *siglo de oro*, the Golden Age of their literature, under Charles V and Philip II, was naturally influenced by the Classics, not least the Latin authors, to the extent in fact of sometimes using a Latin word-order contrary to the natural arrangement of Spanish words. The pastoral tradition influenced him, as it did many others of all civilized nations in Europe after the Renaissance, and he continued the praises of Galateia after his own fashion:[1]

> *O bella Galatea, más suave*
> *que los claveles que tronchó la Aurora,*
> *blanca más que las plumas de aquel ave*
> *que dulce muere y en las aguas mora.*

'O fair Galatea, more winsome than the carnations which the Dawn displays, whiter than the feathers of that bird which dies sweetly and dwells in the waters.'

And this was by no means his only Alexandrian reminiscence, for he is one of the many who have been influenced directly or indirectly by Aratos. That poet, describing the dangers of mariners, says that 'a little plank keeps off Death' from them. Gongora combines this with a sailors' jest, as I take it to be, which is as old as Homer and recurs in Plautus,[2] to the effect that sea-water must be poisonous, as those who drink much of it always die (by drowning). In the *Odyssey*, Aias son of Oileus is cast into the sea, 'and so he perished there, having drunk salt water', and in Plautus' *Rudens* a shipwrecked girl, asked what has become of one of her fellow-passengers, replies, 'I think he drank himself to death, for last night Neptune served him with great cupfuls.' Gongora, then, writes of sailors that they are *en tabla redimidos poco fuerte De la bebida muerte*, 'redeemed by a feeble plank from death that is drunk'. But to return to Theokritos, the Spaniard had not the last

---

[1] See G. Brenan, *The Literature of the Spanish People* (London, 1951), pp. 236 ff.
[2] Aratos, *Phaen.* 299; Homer, *Odyssey* iv, 511; Plautus, *Rudens* 361-2.

word, for in the eighteenth century John Gay went to Ovid for the plot of his *Acis and Galatea*, to which Händel wrote the music, and produced the famous song of the Cyclops,

> O ruddier than the cherry,
> O sweeter than the berry,
> O nymph, more bright than moonshine light,
> Like kidlings, blithe and merry.
> Ripe as the melting cluster,
> No lily has such lustre,
> Yet hard to tame as raging flame,
> And fierce as storms that bluster.

One might spend several pages in analysing the resemblances and differences between these four treatments of the same passage, and a long, but by no means dull, treatise might be composed of similar comments on other noteworthy passages in ancient authors, but for such a work as this a few examples briefly handled must suffice.

Aratos also had several imitators, of whom one survives, Nikandros (Nicander) of Kolophon, a contemporary of the last king of Pergamos, Attalos III, 138–133 B.C. He wrote, besides a poem on farming, the *Georgika*, whereof Vergil borrowed the title at least, and another, the *Heteroioumena* (Shape-changings; Ovid took the idea, though not the word itself, for his *Metamorphoses*), a poem in two books, or two poems each of one book, which has or have survived. The work is most extraordinary. The first book, or poem, the *Theriaca* (matters concerning noxious creatures), deals with poisonous serpents, the second, *Alexipharmaca* (antidotes, healing herbs), with the cures for their bites. The contents consist in the one case of natural history, or what then passed for such, in the other of strings of herbal remedies, all set forth in extremely artificial Greek, like none that ever was spoken or even normally written, and crammed with false archaisms, besides genuine rare or obsolete words. The result is both dull and difficult, and certainly not poetical. But he in turn had his admirers, and Aemilius Macer, a contemporary of Ovid, wrote a translation or imitation of it in Latin, of which some few fragments survive. The very obscurity of the work may have acted as a challenge, for it was the great weakness of Alexandrian poetry that it was written by the learned for the learned. Popular writing in both verse and prose, some of it intended for public performance, did then exist, as a few surviving specimens on papyri testify, but it would seem that there was never any connexion between it and the scholars of the Museum or their colleagues in other countries. This meant that the works of those best able to express themselves were cut off from the thoughts and feelings of the people, even of those fellow-subjects (generally forming an upper class) whose language and education were Greek, encouraged not only by its use as the governmental language but by the numerous and apparently very efficient schools which kept up the traditional Greek training in 'music' (*mousike*, the art which the Muses foster; it included not only music in our sense but literature and philology) and gymnastic.[1]

One result of this unhappy divorce was that the Alexandrians were ceaselessly in quest of something, preferably something new, to write about. One solution of their problem was that adopted by both Kallimachos and Theokritos. We have seen that the latter combined the mimes of Sophron with the metre of Epic; the former, when a prominent Alexandrian named Sosibios won the chariot-race at the Isthmian and Nemean Games, did not attempt a Pindaric ode, but wrote a congratulatory poem in elegiacs, using the Pindaric themes (frags. 384, 385 Pfeiffer). Another combiner of the themes of one author with the metre and dialect of another was Herodas, who like Theokritos wrote mimes, but this time in the Ionic dialect and 'limping' metre (the scazon) of Hipponax. A

---

[1] The subject of secondary education in those times has been excellently treated by M. P. Nilsson, *Die hellenistische Schule* (Munich, Beck, 1955).

papyrus has preserved a good deal of his work complete
enough to be made out. The scenes are taken from common
life, some showing clearly the influence of New Comedy. In
the first, a vile old woman tries to induce a young wife whose
husband is away to become the mistress of a rich athlete; in
the second, a brothel-keeper brings suit against a young man
who has kidnapped one of the inmates of his house; in the
third, a schoolmaster, at the request of a mother, thrashes her
unruly son for her; in the fourth, some women visit the temple
of Asklepios, and so on. While not so good as the idylls of
Theokritos, these little pieces have merit, for they are lively
and full of vivid touches, which make one regret that the
author, in accordance with the corrupt taste of the time,
employed a dialect which if not quite obsolete was rapidly
passing out of use, instead of giving literary status to the
actual speech of his day. It is as if someone now, writing little
stories or sketches of life in London or New York, were to
make his characters talk in the style and vocabulary of Queen
Anne's reign; for the dramatic time of the mimes is contemporary.

Another and very curious development was the riddle-
poem. As befitted learned men of that time, the Alexandrian
scholars were very well acquainted with mythology, also with
geography and at least popular and anecdotal history. Hence
to expect them to catch even a far-fetched allusion to some
character of legend, or to some obscure place in the then
known world, was not asking too much. It was a harmless
amusement if they exchanged little poems in which nothing is
called by its proper name, and, as often was done, chose
metrical lines the lengths of which traced out some figure.
Thus, Theokritos composed a *Pan-pipe*, beginning with a
long line (a hexameter) and going on to shorter and shorter
verses, thus tracing the outlines of the instrument with its
row of diminishing reeds. The first line will suffice to give an
idea of the style. Instead of saying simply 'Penelope', which is

what he means, he writes 'Bedfellow of Nobody and mother of Distant-war' (*Makroptolemos*, a paraphase of the name Telemachos, 'fighting far off'). Nobody is (cf. p. 12) what Odysseus told the Cyclops his name was. We have several other specimens of this kind of thing, each a few lines long and each making a figure, axe, altar and so forth. It will be remembered that this harmless fad was revived, without the riddling language, in Elizabethan times. But the *reductio ad absurdum* of all such works was achieved by Lykophron. This man was one of a group called the Pleiad because it consisted of seven writers, hence the name of the French group of poets in the days of Ronsard. Its object was the revival of Tragedy, a laudable aim which, however, did not succeed in producing any noteworthy play. By the most probable account[1] he lived in the third century and saw the embassy from Rome in 273. From him we have one work, which alone survives of all his output, because it was studied and perhaps admired for its extreme obscurity. This is the *Alexandra*, the alternative name of Priam's prophetic daughter Kassandra. In form it is a messenger-speech from an imaginary tragedy, but one of gigantic proportions, for it is 1,474 lines long. A servant of Priam reports that Kassandra has fallen into one of her frenzies, and recounts word for word all that she said. It is a forecast not only of the doom of Troy but of the subsequent adventures of the survivors, Greek and Trojan, of the war, and of their descendants for several generations, down to fully historical times. And throughout, the riddling style is kept up. For instance, the prophetess has occasion to mention Menelaos and his wanderings on the way back from Troy. What she says is this:[2]

And he again – the husband seeking for his fatal bride

[1] In a book of this size, it is often necessary to assume that theory which the author thinks most reasonable, without spending space over debatable matters.

[2] Lykophron 820–4, trans. G. R. Mair in the Loeb edition (New York and London, 1921.)

snatched from him, having heard rumours, and yearning for the winged phantom that fled to the sky – what secret places of the sea shall he not explore? What dry land shall he not come and search?

That is one of the clearest and most straightforward passages in the whole poem. According to a tale started by the early lyric poet Stesichoros and used by Euripides for one of his plays, the *Helena*, Helen never went to Troy at all, and the war was fought for a phantom. After many adventures, Menelaos was wrecked on the coast of Egypt, his phantom wife vanished, and he was reunited to the real Helen, who all this while had lived virtuously at the Egyptian court, under the protection of the king; at least, that is how Euripides tells the story. Such a tax on the reader's literary and mythological knowledge would be well enough if kept up for perhaps a score of verses, but in a poem of nearly 1,500 it becomes intolerable, and conceals what Lykophron here and there displays, a certain amount of poetic or at least rhetorical power.

This concludes the list of Alexandrian poets of whose work anything complete and considerable is now left; a number of other names are known, but their owners are represented by no more than fragments, except for one not unimportant department, epigram. In this age the word takes on more of the complexion it has in our use of it; although many of the little poems are apparently true epigrams, i.e. really meant to be inscribed on a tomb, the base of a statue, or some other monument, many others are simply exhibitions of linguistic and metrical cleverness, and as such often admirable. The subjects vary widely, now literary, now amatory, now abusive, with other expressions of personal emotion. Some again are descriptions of scenery and the like, perhaps loosely connected with the style of inscriptions, as for instance when a dying shepherd asks his fellows to bury him where he can hear the familiar country sounds which he describes. Many others drop all pretence of being inscriptions of any kind, but are addresses, complimentary or satirical, to real or imaginary people, or little stories compressed into the fewest possible words, for example,

> I fell in love, I kissed, I was accepted, I embraced, I am beloved; but who I am and who she is and how it happened, only the goddess [Aphrodite] knows.

The above English version is almost exactly twice as long as the original; our uninflected tongue will not permit of so much compression as Greek. This is epigram 51 of Book V of our collection, known in general as the Greek Anthology, more accurately as the Palatine Anthology, because the manuscript in which it is preserved was once the property of the Elector Palatine at Heidelberg. It has a long history behind it, for four successive collectors have been at work, first Meleagros of Gadara, about 100 B.C., then a certain Philippos, in the time of Caligula (A.D. 37–41), next the Byzantine Agathias, sixth century A.D., and finally Constantine Kephalas, again a Byzantine official, about 900. Later still, in 1301, Maximus Planudes, a learned monk, made a smaller collection, which includes some epigrams not in the Palatine Anthology; these have been picked out and published as a sort of additional book (*Appendix Planudea*) to the main work. Furthermore, there exist a number of real inscriptions in verse, mostly of poor quality, for it looks as though the ancient and medieval editors had skimmed the cream of the available material, which have been and continue to be published and edited. The whole illustrates the continuity of European literature. If Planudes had known English, instead of confining himself to Greek and some not very accurate Latin, he might have included *Somer is icomen in* and *Alisoun* in his gathering. Naturally, the poems of every age were drawn upon by poets contemporary with them, or later, which is why we so often

find a series of little works on the same subject, each trying to
outdo the earlier ones in neat expression and happy thought.
The Anthology preserves to us all we have of a number of
writers, some of them famous in their day, and is a welcome
supplement to the remains of several others; for instance,
epigrams by Simonides, Kallimachos, Theokritos and many
more known authors are included, though here and throughout the collection care must be exercised, since many of the
attributions are doubtful. The Byzantine poems, which are
numerous, are generally in classical metres, a marked indication of the strength of ancient tradition, for the sense of
quantity was by then quite lost and whether a syllable was
long or short had laboriously to be learned out of books.
Some few are in a Byzantine metre; it seems to have been
imagined for some centuries that twelve syllables whereof the
eleventh bore an accent made an iambic trimeter, whatever
the quantities might be. Another interesting fact is that more
than one poet whose works are drawn upon is Roman,
sometimes well known, for they include no less a person than
the emperor Hadrian.

The nationality of these writers may serve to remind us
that Alexandria, although the chief, was not the only intellectual centre of Hellenistic times. Pergamos was an important
home of learning, its scholars devoting much attention, not
so much to the text of Homer, as to the contents. Some set
forth allegorical interpretations of the poet's words; these
included Krates of Mallos in Kilikia, who was also an authority
on grammar, holding anomalist views; in other words, he
respected the apparent irregularities of the language and did
not try, as the opposing school of analogists did, to smooth
them out. Both these activities were imported, it seems, from
Athens, which by this time was fast becoming a sort of
university town, and their chief exponents there were Stoics,
Kleanthes in particular (cf. p. 103) emphatically maintaining
that Homer meant many things allegorically, *allegorikos*, a

word which he was the first known writer to use, and all his school, as already mentioned (p. 104) being much interested in grammatical theory. Demetrios of Skepsis, appropriately, since his native town was in the Troad, wrote at great length on one passage of sixty lines, *Iliad* ii, 816–77, the catalogue of the Trojan forces, native and allied. His average rate was half a book to a line, and there is no reason to suppose him a particularly wordy author; if there had been nothing but verbiage in him, the great geographer Strabo (p. 144), to whom we owe most of our knowledge of him, would have found some better source for his account of the region.

Altogether, this was a golden age for science in all branches. In the exact disciplines, Mathematics took a great stride forward. To the Hellenistic age or shortly before it belong a series of brilliant names. Plato (pp. 94 ff.) regarded Mathematics as a most useful introduction to philosophy; his pupil Eudoxos of Rhodes and Eudoxos' pupil Menaichmos, followed by the third-century mathematician Aristaios, made important discoveries. The third century saw also that great compiler and arranger of mathematical knowledge, Euclid (*Eukleides*) of Alexandria, and, greater still, Archimedes (287–212). Allied to Mathematics is Astronomy, and in the third century flourished the originator of the heliocentric theory of the solar system, Aristarchos of Samos (not to be confused with the Homeric critic), while among those who unfortunately did not accept his theory are counted several excellent observers, from Hipparchos of Nikaia (second century) to the best-known of them all to moderns, Ptolemy (Claudius Ptolemaeus), who died about A.D. 178 and was astronomer, astrologer and geographer in one, becoming a venerated authority in the two sciences and the popular pseudo-science. Geography was very popular, and attracted the attention of several men of ability, besides Demetrios, already mentioned above. Eratosthenes of Alexandria was poet, scholar and scientist, and his nicknames reflect the general opinion that he was good, though not first-rate, at everything.[1] Be that as it may, his was the first reasonably exact calculation of the size of the earth. There survives the greater part of the geographical work of one whom the Middle Ages called simply 'the Geographer', as Homer was known as 'the Poet'. This is Strabo of Amiseia. Born about 63 B.C. and living on till about A.D. 19, he was in a position to consult many excellent works on geography and many respectable historians now lost to us, and although his long history has perished – it was a supplement to Polybios (p. 147) – his geographical compilation is the most important work on the subject we have, and valuable from a number of points of view. In Medicine, the Alexandrian school made discovery upon discovery in the field of anatomy, including the nervous system (which is why *neuron*, in earlier Greek a sinew, has given modern languages the word 'nerve'), and a line of illustrious names closes with that of Galen (*Galenos*), A.D. 129–99, a man of astounding industry whose works, after several important losses, some in his own day, fill many volumes of modern editions. It was no fault of his that an exaggerated reverence for his very real learning and ability made him into an infallible authority in later times, and so hampered the progress of experimental medicine. He would probably have felt great contempt for those who so misused him and welcomed such discoverers as Vesalius, Harvey and their successors who proved him wrong on many points of anatomy, also the many researchers who have in modern times discovered methods of treatment far superior to any that he or his contemporaries ever knew. But these and several other branches of science flourished only in the earlier or Alexandrian part of this period; when Rome became dominant, scientific research withered, not from any positive discouragement of it by the Romans, but from their lack of interest in such matters, for it is a remarkable fact that, although a great, intelligent and practical people, with an

[1] 'Beta' (= No. 2) and 'Pentathlete' (= good all-round man.)

astonishing genius for some kinds of mental activity, particularly law and certain branches of literature, and most unusual diligence in what we should now call applied science, as shown by their engineering, sanitation and other contributions to civilized life, they never in the whole of their history produced one mathematician, physicist, geographer or natural scientist of any original merit. Their most learned men, such as the elder Pliny (p. 250), were industrious compilers of what other nations, generally the Greeks, had found out and recorded, and often grossly uncritical, mingling mere superstitions and popular delusions with facts. We may now leave the Alexandrian, or Hellenistic period proper and consider the progress of Greek literature in the time when Rome, and not any Greek city or foundation, was the centre of the civilized world.

In this period, that is to say from about the fall of Alexandria (30 B.C.) to the collapse of the Roman Empire in the West, Greek continued to be the general means of communication not only in the eastern but to a considerable extent in the western districts. It is noteworthy that the first two surviving communications to the young Church of Rome, the epistles of St Paul and of St Ignatius, are in Greek, and there is no indication that an interpreter was needed for either. Roman children of respectable families learned Greek before they had any formal instruction in their native tongue, and Quintilian (*Inst. orat.* i, 1, 13, see p. 256) warns educators not to keep them too closely and too long at it, lest they should grow up to speak Latin with a foreign accent. It is therefore not astonishing that among the Greek writers of this period are included several native Italians, more than one of whom was able not only to write Greek correctly but to win admiration as a stylist. This, however, becomes less true as we come further down in time, for Latin gradually prevailed throughout the west, ousting not only the other Italian dialects, none of which seems ever to have developed a literature of any importance,

but likewise the native speeches of Gaul, the Iberian penin-
sula, and those parts of Africa which lie west of Egypt and
were under Roman rule. St Augustine, for instance, had
no more than a smattering of Greek and was practically
monoglot.

It is therefore necessary to give a short account of the styles
of prose (for poetry did not flourish much in this period,
except in Latin) which were most in vogue. There were two
principal tendencies, which we know as Asianism and Atticism
respectively. The former we have to form our impressions of
largely from hostile criticism, for it fell decidedly out of
favour later on. It would seem to have abandoned the use of
the period (cf. p. 109) to a considerable extent and made up its
compositions mostly of short sentences, ending with a marked,
almost a versified rhythm. The wording was often very
artificial, and on occasion normal word-order (always much
freer in the inflected languages than in most modern tongues)
was sacrificed and even meaningless words inserted to get the
desired sound-effects. The Gorgian figures (see p. 106) seem
also, from the specimens we have, to have been used to
excess, and poetical ornaments to have abounded. Those who
spoke in this style are accused on occasion of using rather a
singing than a speaking tone. Clearly, all this was highly
artificial, and its chief exponent seems to have been a certain
Hegesias, a native of Magnesia in Asia Minor. It could flourish
only in the numerous schools of rhetoric and among those
who had had a rhetorical training. The other tendency,
Atticism, had this much to be said for it, that it advocated a
return to the great models of Attic prose. If it had clung also
to their fundamental principle of using the current speech
with care and judgement, there would have been little to say
against it. Unfortunately, it insisted on the use of those
admirable writers' dialect, that is of a form of Greek obsolete
for some centuries when the movement grew strong. This
cut it off from the language of the day, thus at once making

the performances of the Atticists artificial and depriving the
current vernacular of much of the improvement which it
might have got if used by men of taste and literary training.
In Latin, where both Asianism and Atticism had their ardent
followers (Hortensius, the most famous pleader of the last
century of the republic until Cicero outshone him, was an
Asianist; Marcus Brutus, the assassin of Julius Caesar, was an
Atticist), there was no archaizing at the early stages, but
artificiality on the one side, dryness on the other, were the
besetting sins of the two schools; for Latin never had the
natural elegance of Greek and needed a certain amount of
ornament to make it a literary language, while this very fact
was a standing temptation to be too ornamental and therefore
highly artificial. There were a number of writers who seem
to have belonged to neither school, and in Greek these
included the scientists and technicians, who were content to
say plainly what they wished to express, and also some of the
historians, of whom the greatest was Polybios. This man, the
last really important Greek historian, was an Achaian who,
after the defeat of the Achaian League, was one of those
taken as hostages in 167 B.C. by the Romans. In Italy he was
treated kindly enough, and won the friendship of some of the
leading Romans, especially of Scipio Aemilianus (see p. 158).
He learned Latin, became interested in Roman history and
the customs of the nation, whose greatness he clearly saw,
and set about writing a work which should explain the rise of
Rome to world empire. His 'pragmatic' history, as he called
it, meaning that it was severely factual, began with the earlier
relations of Roman and Carthage, 266–221 B.C., the account
of which filled two books. The remaining thirty-eight began
in 221 and came down to 120, thus including events which
Polybios had himself witnessed and many more of which he
could learn from men who had taken part in them, to say
nothing of documentary sources of good quality, for he was
allowed access to the Roman archives, and for the older period

L

he had acquaintances who could help him to interpret rather archaic Latin. It is a pity that much of his work is now lost, but we have the first five books and considerable excerpts and fragments of the rest. As a stylist, he is plain to dullness, but his matter is admirable. It is strange that in the preceding age, when much history was written in Greek and the subjects included events so exciting as the conquests of Alexander the Great and the formation of the Hellenistic kingdoms, there arose no one comparable to Thucydides either for style or for impartiality. It was chiefly the lack of style which led to the neglect of most of these writers, with the unfortunate result that we have to construct our histories of those important times from works of far more recent date, some of which will be mentioned later.

It is now time to go back a little and trace the creation of a Latin literature – Latin, not Roman, for of the writers of merit in that tongue but a small minority were actually natives of Rome itself or even its immediate neighbourhood. Paradoxically, the first man of letters of whom we know anything definite was not a native speaker of Latin at all, but a Tarentine Greek named Andronikos. Taken prisoner in the war with Pyrrhos, he was sold as a slave, after the usual fashion, and bought by a member of the *gens Liuia*, who set him to teach his children, for Andronikos was an educated man. Later he was set free, and henceforth he was styled Livius Andronicus, for it was the custom for a freedman to take the *nomen*[1] of his patron, that is to say his former master, to whom he still owed certain duties. He now had his living to earn, and

---

[1] A Roman citizen had at least two names, often three or even more. First came his own name, e.g. Quintus. Of these personal names there were not many, and they were regularly abbreviated, as Q. for Quintus, M. for Marcus, and so forth. This custom was older than the invention of the letter G, C having previously served for the sounds of K and 'hard' G alike; therefore Gaius and Gnaeus were abbreviated C. and Cn., to the confusion of many moderns, who have invented the non-existent names Caius and Cnaeus in consequence. There followed the adjective of his *gens* or clan, always ending in *-ius*; a woman had no name except the feminine of this, for instance Tullia, the daughter of M. Tullius Cicero the great orator, though she might have

did so by setting up a school for Latin-speaking children, for evidently he had mastered the language by that time. Now Greek children learned to read out of Homer, but there was no Latin Homer; consequently Andronicus made one, by translating the *Odyssey* into Latin, using a native accentual metre known as Saturnian. He supplemented his income by meeting a new demand, for dramatic performances at festivals, and composed several tragedies on Greek models. He also was called upon at least once to provide a hymn for a special occasion. His first play came out in 240 B.C., and he was his own producer and 'star', for apparently he had a good singing voice.

The next poet was again no Roman, not even a Roman citizen, and his name was Gnaeus Naevius, from Campania. His great work was an epic, again in Saturnians, dealing with the first Punic War, in which he had fought as an auxiliary, and giving an account of the mythical origins of the enmity between Carthage and Rome. He also wrote both tragedies and comedies, mostly the latter. He died just before the beginning of the second century B.C.

some pet-name in her own family, as Tertia, if she happened to be the third child, or its diminutive, Tertiola. These appellations were called respectively *praenomen* (forename) and *nomen* (name proper), and were often the whole name; for instance, the man we generally call Pompey started life simply as Cn. Pompeius. But often a third name, *cognomen*, was added, in his case Magnus (the Great), always in its origin personal, a compliment or a nick-name, although it regularly passed to his descendants. These were not peculiar to any one *gens*; thus the poets Horace and Persius both had the *cognomen* Flaccus, though they were of wholly different districts and social standing. It seems to have been a mark of familiarity to address a man by his *cognomen* only, less so to use his *praenomen* only; for official purposes his *praenomen* and *nomen* were used, and when it was necessary to describe him in full, as on a roll of citizens, the names of his father and grandfather and that of his tribe were added before the *cognomen*. He might also have more than one *cognomen*, as Q. Fabius Maximus Verrucosus Cunctator, the last being his personal nickname ('Delayer') because of his cautious tactics against Hannibal. All this sorely puzzled the Greeks, whose own nomenclature, as also that of the Semitic-speaking peoples, was much simpler, which is why we do not know the full names of the authors of the second and third Gospels (Marcus and Loukas, i.e. Lucius) or of the Apostle to the Gentiles (Paulus is a *cognomen* of the Aemilii and the Sergii).

Classical Literature

But these names were eclipsed by that of yet another non-Roman, Q. Ennius of Rudiae, a little town between Tarentum and Brundisium. His dates are 239–169 B.C.; he obtained Roman citizenship; he composed plays and wrote another historical epic, embracing the whole of Roman history from the days of Aeneas to his own times, omitting only what Naevius (for whose style and metre he professed contempt) had already treated. One most important feature of his work was that it was entirely Greek in metre and also on Greek models, and what we have left of him, unfortunately including no complete poem, shows that he was struggling to adapt the foreign rhythms, native to a language with little or no stress-accent, to a tongue which had a fairly marked stress, though probably not so pronounced as it is in English or German. The results are not always happy; Ennius was the first to experiment in this direction, at any rate on a large scale. In the dialogue metres his task was much easier, for a happy compromise between Greek principles and the natural rhythm of spoken Latin had been reached by the time of Naevius and was continued in the verse of Plautus (see p. 152). The details, however, are too technical for a book of this kind. Ennius was distinctly a modernist in his literary tastes. For chronicle Epic he had the precedent of his almost contemporary Rhianos (p. 130), also of some earlier writers, such as Choirilos of Samos, about contemporary with Herodotos but somewhat younger, whose subjects included the Persian Wars. When he wrote tragedies, again he sometimes chose a subject from Roman history (*fabula praetexta*, play which wears, i.e. whose chief characters wear, the 'fringed' garment of Roman magistrates), early or recent, but generally he went to Euripides for his originals, adapting, to judge by what is left to us, pretty freely. This he was in a position to do intelligently, for he was trilingual, adding Greek to the Oscan of his native place and being perfectly at home in Latin. Another piece of modern fashion was a didactic poem, apparently mock-serious, on gastronomy; he called it *Hedyphagetica*, literally matters concerning pleasant eating, and his model may have been a certain Archestratos, probably of the fourth century, who dealt with the same subject and apparently in mock-heroic fashion, to judge by his fairly copious fragments. Furthermore, he introduced Latin readers to the latest views on the origin of religion, those of Euhemeros of Messene (late fourth and early third centuries), who held that the conventional gods were simply kings and other prominent persons of early times, given divine honours by admirers or flatterers; for Ennius smattered philosophy. The fact that his *Euhemerus* roused no protests that we know of indicates strongly how divorced Roman religion was from any sort of speculation or what we should call theology. But another activity of this very industrious writer began a long and important series of works, the effects of which still continue. This was a number of compositions in different kinds of verse, on all manner of subjects, but some of them ethical, bearing the general name of *saturae*. *Satura* is the feminine singular of the adjective *satur*, meaning full or replete, and one of its uses was to describe an offering to the gods consisting of a variety of foodstuffs on a large dish. This was called the *lanx satura*, or full dish. Hence it was a not unnatural title for a series of miscellaneous works. The confusion with Greek *satyros* (cf. p. 55, n. 1) led to a late spelling *satyra*, and this in turn to *satira*, which ghost-word has obtruded itself upon modern languages in such forms as English 'satire'.

About contemporary with Ennius (his dates are 250 B.C., or thereabouts, to 184) was Rome's greatest dramatist Titus Maccius Plautus, to give his name its most probable form. He was a poor man, and after various expedients for earning a living, he found something like a competence from the demand for comedies to be performed at festivals or the like, for it was still an unheard-of thing to produce plays simply as an entertainment for any who chose to pay for admission. He was prolific, being the author of not less than twenty-one pieces which survive, whole or in fragments, and quite possibly of about as many more which are lost. Like Naevius before him, but perhaps with even greater skill, he adapted his Greek metres to the natural rhythms of Latin, and like Naevius he may not have been dealing with his mother-tongue, for he was a native of Sarsina in Umbria, and therefore Umbrian, an allied but widely different dialect, was the native language of his people. His plots were taken, with one or two possible exceptions, from New Comedy (cf. pp. 88 ff.), but his technique differed widely from the somewhat monotonous urbanity of Menander and his rivals. Formally, he used a large amount of singing, generally solos or duets. Where he got this idea we do not know, but there is always the possibility that what we may call the music-hall performances of Alexandria (cf. p. 137) and likely enough similar things in the Greek cities of southern Italy (Magna Graecia) gave him the hint. There was also a good deal of what seems to have been recitative. Our evidence is that Italian audiences, then as now, liked a musical performance, approaching opera in its character. Materially, he infused new and rollicking life into the stock plots and well-worn situations, dealing often in the broadest farce, though he was capable of serious scenes as well. He is not a delicate writer, though not often indecent, nor is he very subtle, but his plays are alive and full of zest. I give an outline of a few.

The *Amphitruo*, i.e. *Amphitryon*, is described by the author himself as a tragi-comedy (*tragicocomoedia*). Its subject is the birth of Herakles, Hercules in the Latin deformation of his name. Amphitruo returns from successful war and sends his slave Sosia ahead with the news. Sosia to his horror finds another Sosia at the door of the house and learns that another Amphitruo is within. They are in fact Mercurius and Juppiter (Hermes and Zeus) in disguise, and as they keep their borrowed shapes, confusion and suspicion become rife, although

Alcumena (Alkmene) throughout maintains her dignity. One farcical scene follows another until a sound of thunder is heard and a maid rushes out to say that her mistress has borne twin boys, one of them so prodigiously strong that it was almost impossible to bathe or swaddle him. Amphitruo is about to send for the prophet Teiresias when Juppiter appears in his proper form and explains the whole matter; young Hercules is his son, but Alcumena is perfectly innocent, since she never knew that she was entertaining anyone other than her husband.

The *Aulularia* ('Play about the pot', or more freely, *The Crock of Gold*) has for its central character a miser, Euclio, who has a pious daughter of uncertain name,[1] also a rich and generous neighbour, Megadorus. The daughter having won the favour of the household deity (*Lar familiaris*), he reveals the whereabouts of a buried treasure, which Euclio keeps anxiously concealed, spending none of it to improve his or his family's way of living. Megadorus, knowing nothing of this and persuaded by his sister to marry, asks for the un-dowered hand of Euclio's daughter, who however has been violated by Megadorus' nephew Lyconides; she is with child and Lyconides wants to marry her. Now the plot thickens; Euclio, who has accepted Megadorus' proposal and been driven half mad by the elaborate preparations for the wedding and consequent invasion of his house by a professional cook and his followers, receives a terrible blow, for he discovers that his treasure has been stolen. This so occupies his mind that he can spare little thought for the trifling fact that his daughter has just given birth to Lyconides' baby. Here much of the play is lost, but Megadorus retires in favour of his nephew, the stolen treasure (which has been taken by Lyconides' slave) is restored, and everyone is satisfied.

These two comedies were destined to a distinguished

---

[1] Her name has come down as Phaedria, quite impossibly, for that is a man's name, Phaidrias. Possibly Phaedra.

future. Molière imitated them both and, being what he was, made them even better than the originals, from which he borrowed freely. Naturally, both he and his English imitators (Dryden and Fielding) departed from Latin tradition in sundry details. For instance, Molière's Elise has not to be made an honest woman of in the last act, for being a heroine of Comedy of that period she is necessarily of unblemished, if insipid, character, and her Valère has none but the most honourable intentions. At least she does appear on the stage, whereas Euclio's daughter is nothing but a voice heard behind the scenes as her pains come on her. This is what good imitation means. The later author takes from the older material what he fancies, and adds from his own stores as good or better. A plagiarist, who lacks matter of his own, merely steals from his predecessor and usually tries to disguise his theft.

Plautus claimed for another play, the *Captives*, that it was moral and free from all objectionable language or incidents. What made him so suddenly scrupulous we do not know; generally broad fun and characters far from being exemplars of high morality are freely admitted, though actual indecency of language is not common. Hegio, a wealthy gentleman of Aetolia (which Plautus apparently thought was a city), had two sons. One of these was kidnapped in early youth, the other has been taken prisoner in a war with Elis. He therefore buys several Elean prisoners, in hopes of arranging an exchange for his surviving son. Two of these, Philocrates and his slave Tyndarus, plot to exchange names, so that when the supposed slave is sent to Elis to arrange the bargain, in reality his master will be sent home. Hegio finds this out after Philocrates' departure, and sends Tyndarus to forced labour in a quarry. But Philocrates, having arranged for the liberation of Hegio's son Philopolemus, returns with him, bringing a runaway slave of Hegio's into the bargain, the very slave who had kidnapped his other son. This son turns out to be

Tyndarus, so Hegio's family is reunited. A good deal of fun in the play is provided by a typical character of New Comedy, the parasite Ergasilus. The word *parasitos* means properly a guest at table, and had, to begin with, nothing derogatory about it, but it degenerated into signifying a needy and unscrupulous fellow who attached himself to any well-to-do person who would tolerate him, and in return for invitations to dinner made himself useful or amusing in various ways. Parasites appear as jesters, messengers and so forth in play after play. Middle Comedy called a like character a *kolax*, i.e. flatterer.

The *Captives* has an element of sentimental comedy in it, despite the absence of female characters and love-interest. Another play, the *Menaechmi*, had the honour of suggesting to Shakespere the plot and much of the action of the *Comedy of Errors*. A Syracusan merchant had two sons, identical twins, Menaechmus and Sosicles. The former, accompanying his father on a visit to Tarentum, strayed away and was picked up by a merchant from Epidamnus, who, bringing him home, adopted him, for he was childless. The father died of grief at the loss of his son, and the children's grandfather changed the name of the remaining boy to Menaechmus. This Menaechmus when he grew up set out to look for his lost brother, and arrives in Epidamnus when the play begins. Then ensue much the same confusions as in Shakespere, whose additions to the wild farce are of a nature to give it a somewhat more serious tone in places, although he doubles the misunderstandings by giving the identical twins identical twin servants. It was his idea also to make the parents of the first pair of twins survive, although separated, and to add to the interest by making the father in danger of his life.

One of Plautus' best and funniest plays is the *Miles Gloriosus*, i.e. the *Bragging Soldier*, the name-rôle being the ancestor of a long line of comic characters, including Captain Bobadil and Ancient Pistol. Part of its plot turns on a theme of folktale, the pretence by one person of being two – the reverse, in fact, of the confusion in the *Menaechmi*. Pyrgopolynices is home from the wars with full pockets, and has established himself at Ephesus with his hanger-on Artotrogus ('Loaf-gnawer'), who encourages him in his extravagant lies about his military exploits and his familiarity with a king or two. He has been sent, or so he claims, to recruit mercenaries for his royal employer. Being extremely amorous, he has got himself a mistress, Philocomasium, who is loved by a young Athenian named Pleusicles. With the help of an intriguing slave, Palaestrio, belonging to the soldier but formerly the property of Pleusicles, and of a merry old gentleman, Peri-plectomenus,[1] who lives next door and is Pleusicles' host, the party-wall is pierced and Philocomasium meets her lover. Being seen outside the next-door house, she coolly pretends to be her own sister. Later, the soldier is persuaded that a lady of rank loves him desperately, and for her sake is induced to send Philocomasium away. After an affecting scene of parting, she leaves for Athens, Pleusicles and Palaestrio going with her. Now the soldier, being caught with the 'lady', played by a courtesan hired for the occasion, is so frightened by the old gentleman, who pretends to be the injured husband, that he is grateful for being let off with a thrashing.

The *Rudens* is oddly titled, for the only 'rope' in it is a quite incidental piece of fishing-tackle. Unlike most comedies of this school, it has a flavour of the open air and the sea about it, appropriately, for the scene is on the coast near the city of Cyrene. A rascally slave-dealer, by name Labrax, has sold an attractive girl, Palaestra, to her lover Plesidippus. Thinking better of it, Labrax sails for Sicily, where his wares will fetch a higher price, taking Palaestra and her maid Ampelisca with him. The ship is wrecked, but all concerned manage to swim ashore. They land near a temple of Venus, i.e. Aphrodite, and

---

[1] This is no Greek word and the name is probably corrupt, one of several suspect names in Plautus, cf. p. 153, n. 1.

near the house of a worthy but poor old man, Daemones. Daemones' slave Gripus goes fishing and brings up in his net a wallet containing Labrax' money and the ornaments belonging to Palaestra, who had been exposed in infancy. After sundry complications, Palaestra is proved by these ornaments to be Daemones' daughter. Labrax has his money restored to him on condition of setting Ampelisca free and paying half a talent to Daemones, who in consideration thereof frees Gripus.

An interesting thing about these and the other excellent, if loosely constructed, comedies is that they are what we should call provincial in tone. They freely acknowledge their indebtedness to Greek originals, the characters in them are supposed to be Greeks, or visitors to Greece, which does not prevent them making jokes about or allusions to things purely Roman, and, oddest of all, Plautus calls himself and other Italians barbarians by implication, for *uortit barbare* means 'translated into Latin', *barbaricae urbes* are towns in Italy, and so on. Rome, rapidly becoming supreme in political and military matters, was far from supremacy in things literary, and indeed Roman writers for the most part continued honestly to acknowledge their immense debt to Greece, even when they far excelled contemporary Greek authors.

Plautus was followed by several other comedians whose works are lost to us, unhappily, for it would be interesting especially to know more of some who attempted to adapt Greek dramatic methods to Italian surroundings. Their compositions were known as *comoediae togatae*, toga-wearing comedies, meaning that the characters in them were dressed in Roman fashion, whereas the plays with a supposedly Greek setting were *palliatae*, dressed in cloaks of Greek style. It does not, however, appear from what we know of these authors that they differed much from the Greeks in their plots and characters. For our purposes, a far more important name is that of Terence (Publius Terentius Afer), born about 195

B.C., died 159. As his *cognomen* implies, he was not an Italian at all, but a north African, perhaps what we call a Berber, certainly not a negro, for he was regarded as very handsome by Romans. Enslaved, we do not know how, he became the property of a Roman senator, Terentius Lucanus, who seems to have treated him kindly because of his good looks and his abilities, and set him free. Where and how he achieved such mastery of Latin as made his works models of style and correctness we are not informed; I conjecture that his mother may have been an Italian, even a Roman, woman carried off by some Carthaginian slave-raider, and that her son learned her language from her. At all events, Terence won his way into cultured circles in Rome, being befriended and encouraged by the younger Africanus (Publius Cornelius Scipio Aemilianus Africanus Numantinus, 185/4–129) and his circle, composed of men much interested in literature and philosophy and consequently in Greek authors and their Latin imitators. His talent was for Comedy, and we have the six works he wrote complete. One and all are imitated, much more closely than those of Plautus, from Greek originals, Menander in all cases but one, which is taken from the less known Apollodoros. The metres are mostly those of dialogue, lyrics being rare and recitative not very common. Terence did not translate literally, so far as can be judged when we have none of the originals, and took liberties to the extent of adding to one play scenes and even characters taken from another.[1] Their dates run from 166 to 160. One feature which is apparently original is the use made of the prologue, which in Roman practice was spoken by an actor, usually a junior member of the troupe, and in Plautus nearly always contained an outline of the plot. In Terence the prologues are almost all literary

---

[1] It is commonly asserted that this is technically called *contaminatio*, and certainly Terence uses the verb *contaminare* in mentioning it. But he quotes it as his opponents' word, and Mr W. Beare is strongly of opinion that in their mouths it is a word of abuse, 'mess about', 'spoil', and not a technicality of the day at all.

manifestos, answers to criticisms by unnamed opponents of
the poet, one of whom we know from other sources was himself a writer of comedy, by name Luscius Lanuvinus. The one
exception is a plea for a quiet hearing of the *Hecyra*, which had
been twice interrupted by other and more popular shows.

The earliest play, *Andria*, has a double plot. Pamphilus son
of Simo, an Athenian, has fallen in love with Glycerium, a poor
girl, brought up by a courtesan from the island of Andros
(hence the title of the play), and made her his mistress. His
father wants him to marry the daughter of a friend named
Chremes, but Chremes, disliking the young man's conduct,
breaks off the engagement. Meanwhile Charinus, a friend of
Pamphilus, is in love with Chremes' daughter and naturally
opposed to her marrying anyone else. Simo pretends to his
son that the marriage is to take place at once; Pamphilus,
warned of the facts by his slave Davus, feigns dutiful readiness,
whereat Simo gets Chremes to withdraw his veto and presses
on arrangements for a real wedding. Charinus is indignant at
what he supposes to be the treachery of his friend, and Davus
intervenes by laying a baby which Glycerium has just borne
in front of Simo's house, at sight of which Chremes again
refuses consent. The opportune arrival of a certain Crito clears
up the situation; Glycerium is really Chremes' daughter, lost
years before, and her real name is Pasibula.[1] So Chremes has
two daughters of wealth and position enough to be proper
wives for both young men, and everyone is satisfied.

The *Hecyra* ('The Mother-in-law') has a serious plot.
Another Pamphilus is married to Philumena, whom he loves,
but deserts on finding that she has borne a child an impossibly
short time after the marriage for it to be his. He seeks consolation with a courtesan named Bacchis, and his mother tries
vainly to reconcile the young couple. But Bacchis is able to

---

[1] Glycerium (Glykerion, 'sweetling') is a low-class name, suitable to a
courtesan; Pasibula on the other hand has a respectable flavour and might belong
to any lady of a good family.

prove that the child is after all Pamphilus' own; he had raped Philumena on a chance encounter at night some time before the marriage. So all are reconciled. The play is one of Terence's best, and incidentally throws a curious light on the morality of New Comedy. The rape is passed over as no great matter, nor in any way inconsistent with Pamphilus' generally amiable and gentle character. Certainly the crowd's refusal on two occasions to hear the play out had nothing to do with this incident; they simply went away to see a performance which was more to their taste, on the first occasion an exhibition of rope-walking and a boxing-match, on the second a gladiatorial show.

The *Heauton Timorumenos* ('Self-punisher'; all Terence's titles are Greek) appeared in 163 and is an adaptation of an early play of Menander. Menedemus, a rich Athenian, has been over-strict with his son Clinia (Kleinias, a well-known Athenian name). The young man has left home and gone to take service abroad as a mercenary soldier. His father, deeply remorseful, has moved into the country and there lives a life of self-imposed hardship, sharing in the heaviest farm-work. A sympathetic neighbour, Chremes, has likewise a son, Clitopho, a somewhat rackety youth. Clinia returns from his adventures abroad and is received into Chremes' house. His father is overjoyed and resolved to deny him nothing. Clitopho seizes this opportunity to get his own expensive mistress, another Bacchis, invited; she brings with her Antiphila, Clinia's love, a freeborn girl, who passes as one of her attendants. The whole cortège is soon transferred to the house of Menedemus, but suspicion is aroused when Clitopho, not Clinia, is found to be making love to Bacchis. A rascally slave, Syrus, is, as usual in New Comedy, in the thick of the plots, especially when money is to be wheedled out of one of the fathers. Finally, as might be expected, Antiphila turns out to be Chremes' daughter, and is promptly betrothed to Clinia, while Clitopho also has a wife found for him.

The *Eunuchus* has a double plot, the result partly of borrowing two of the most noteworthy characters from another play of Menander, the *Kolax* (cf. p. 158). These are Thraso and Gnatho, less farcical equivalents of Pyrgopolynices and Artotrogus (p. 156), for Terence does not deal in knockabout farce, but in humour. Thraso has engaged a courtesan, Thais,[1] for his exclusive delectation, but she has a real affection for a much poorer lover, young Phaedria. Phaedria has a brother Chaerea (Chaireas), who is in love with Pamphila, one of Thais' household, given her by Thraso. Phaedria means to give Thais a eunuch; Chaerea disguises himself as one, gets admission to the women's quarters, and makes the most of his opportunities; hence much confusion, especially when the real eunuch appears on the scene, and furious reproaches, complicated by an attempt on the part of Thraso to take back his gift (Pamphila), because Thais has admitted Phaedria to her society. But one Chremes (exceptionally for the nomenclature of New Comedy, a young man; usually it is an old man's name) makes his appearance, helps to repulse Thraso, and proves that Pamphila is no slave-girl but his sister, therefore a freeborn Athenian woman, therefore a quite possible wife for Chaerea, while Thais becomes a client of Phaedria's family and so quite at his disposal.

One reason for an English student to take an interest in this play is that it is the source of *Ralph Roister-Doister.* Udall naturally left out the eunuch and all that goes with him, substituted the perfectly respectable Cunstance for Thais, and added Gavin Goodlucke and Madge Mumblecrust from his own stores. Ralph and Matthew Merrygreeke represent Thraso and Gnatho, the first of a long line of English and other descendants of that humorous pair.

---

[1] Her name has led to a curious confusion. There was a real Thais, an Athenian courtesan, she who appears in *Alexander's Feast* (cf. p. 45). Dante puts her in his Hell, but so confounds her with Terence's fictitious Thais that he puts into her mouth a quotation from the play (*Inferno* xviii, 134–5 = *Eunuchus* 391–2).

Deserting Menander temporarily for Apollodoros, Terence produced a good play turning on a point of Attic law, the *Phormio*. In Athens, as in many if not all Greek states, provision was made for a brotherless female orphan, who being a woman could not herself hold property, by obliging her nearest male relative, not being a half-brother uterine, to marry her, thus keeping the property within the circle of near kin. In the play, Antipho, a young Athenian, is in love with a poor but freeborn girl, and knows that his father would never consent to his marrying her, as she has no dowry and no prospects of one. He therefore gets a parasite, Phormio, to trump up a case against him, alleging that he, Antipho, is the girl's next of kin. Antipho purposely lets himself be cast in the suit; his father returns from abroad and tries to buy Phormio off. Geta, Antipho's slave, pretends that Phormio is willing to marry the girl himself on consideration of a payment of thirty *minae*, about $600 American in bullion value, but many times that amount in purchasing power at that date. The money is really wanted by Phaedria, a cousin of Antipho, to buy a flute-girl whom he fancies. Antipho's father and his friend Chremes between them find the sum, because Chremes has in view a marriage between Antipho and a daughter of his by a second wife, a Lemnian woman whom he had deserted. The flute-girl is bought, the money is ultimately repaid by Chremes' acknowledged Athenian wife Nausistrata, to whose ears the whole plot has come, and of course it turns out that Antipho's sweetheart is the Lemnian daughter. Thus everyone is made happy except the unfortunate Chremes, for evidently Nausistrata will never let him hear the last of it.

Finally, Terence wrote the *Adelphi* (*Adelphoi*, 'brothers'), adapted from Menander with borrowings also from Diphilos. Demea and Micio are the brothers concerned; Demea has two sons, Aeschinus and Ctesipho (Aischines and Ktesiphon; the Demosthenic flavour of the names, cf. p. 113, is accidental).

He is also of puritanical temperament, while Micio is easy-going. Hence when the unmarried Micio adopts Aeschinus, he rears him indulgently and is not offended that the young man sows a fairly large crop of wild oats. But when Aeschinus breaks into the establishment of a slave-dealer and kidnaps one of the inmates, even Micio thinks he has gone rather too far.[1] Then, when it turns out that he has carried off a girl whom Ctesipho, supposedly a model of rigid virtue, had set his heart upon, Demea is furious. Meanwhile Aeschinus has seduced a freeborn but poor girl under promise of marriage, and Micio, strict for once, insists that he keep his promise, as she has borne him a child. Demea finally decides that he has been too exacting; he proceeds to practise affability, and as further evidence of his change of heart proposes that Micio should marry the mother of the girl Aeschinus has seduced. So all ends with a double wedding, and Ctesipho keeps the harp-girl Aeschinus has carried off for him.

Terence, as the failure of the *Hecyra* on its first two presentations indicates, was not a favourite with the generality, for he lacked popular appeal. His patrons off the stage and his admiring hearers on it were men of the upper classes who could appreciate his skill in adapting and translating and the purity of his Latin. This characteristic resulted among other things in his works becoming an approved textbook for schools, a position which they continued to occupy for many centuries, until displaced by Caesar, to the great disadvantage of young students of Latin. More important, perhaps, is the lesson which his works conveyed to those of literary ambitions on how a comedy should be constructed; it is from him far more than from Plautus that modern Europe learned. Incidentally, since Terence drew upon that storehouse of

---

[1] Such establishments, which generally were practically brothels, were tolerated but not approved in antiquity, and their owners looked down upon. Hence, in cities without any regular police force, it seems possible enough that they were raided on occasion by young 'bloods', although the proprietors could and did claim compensation through the law (cf. p. 138).

M

sententious sayings, New Comedy, some of his lines have
passed into proverbs, with the usual accompaniment of mis-
quoting and adaptations. Two of them are

> *Homo sum, humani nil a me alienum puto.*
> (*I'm human; nothing human's foreign to me.*)
>
> – Heaut. 77

and

> *Amantium irae amoris integratiost.*
> (*These lovers' quarrels are but love's renewal.*)
>
> – Andria 555.

If Terence lacked popularity, the authors of Tragedy were
in like case, for that seems never to have been much relished
by holiday crowds. As good evidence as any concerning this is
to be found in Plautus. In the prologue of his *Amphitruo*
(p. 152) Mercurius says

> Next I will tell you the plot of this tragedy. Oh, you
> frowned when I said it was going to be a tragedy? I'm a
> god, so I'll change it. If you like, I will make this same play
> a comedy instead of a tragedy, yet with the same lines. Will
> you have it so, or not? Why, what a fool I am! As if I
> didn't know you want it, being a god. I know what your
> opinion in the matter is; I'll make it a mixture. Let it be
> a tragicomedy, for to make it a comedy from beginning to
> end I don't think proper, with kings and gods coming into
> it.

It probably was not so much the kings and gods the audience
disliked as the solemn tone of the plots and the many long,
sententious speeches which seem to have been a feature of
such plays; seem, for not one specimen has survived and we
must form our opinion of them from quotations and from
what later writers say of their authors. It has already been
said (p. 150) that Ennius wrote tragedies. Next came his
nephew, Marcus Pacuvius or Pacvius, born about 220 B.C.,

died 130. That he was learned and skilled in his art (*doctus* is the word used of him, and implies both), over-fond of extraordinary compounds, against the natural tendency of Latin, which prefers them short and simple, copious, but not a writer of really good Latin, we learn from various writers.[1] The fragments show us that he liked to put philosophical reflections into the mouths of his characters, and that his plots, almost without exception, are taken from the Greek dramatists, though not always from plays which we can identify. Later came Lucius Accius (often miswritten Attius), born in 170 and still alive when Cicero was past his childhood. He alone seems to have found a certain amount of favour, for we hear of productions of his plays at dates after any probable time for his death. Besides being a playwright, he wrote on various subjects, mostly literary, sometimes at least in verse; we have no definite proof that he ever used prose. Again, he was not a Roman, but a *libertinus*, that is to say descended from ex-slaves.[2]

Another non-Roman was Gaius Lucilius, born 180, died 102. He was a Latin who never acquired nor apparently wanted Roman citizenship, although his brother became a Roman citizen and a senator and ultimately the maternal grandfather of Pompey the Great (Cn. Pompeius Magnus). Gaius Lucilius seems to have been in easy circumstances, a member of the Scipionic circle (p. 158), and devoted to literature. He is generally regarded as the father of Roman satire, and what we know of his works (again, only fragments survive) indicates that it was he who directed it into the channels familiar to us, in other words made it satire in our sense and not simply miscellaneous writing. He had strong dislikes, and attacked those of whom he disapproved (some

---

[1] The above opinions are expressed or quoted respectively by Horace (*Epist.* ii, 1, 56), Quintilian (*Instit. orat.* i, 5, 67), Aulus Gellius (vi, 14, 6) and Cicero (*Brutus* 258).

[2] A freed slave was a *libertus*; he and his descendants belonged to the class of *libertini*, who though citizens had certain disabilities.

of them at least prominent citizens) openly and by name. He confessedly wrote for a semi-popular audience; a fragment which survives says that he does not wish to be read by Persius, a good scholar of his day, but by Decimus Laelius, a decent man of some culture; another, to much the same effect, names a certain Junius Congus, presumably again a man of no profound scholarship. His subjects were by no means entirely what we call satirical or libellous, for we have enough left of him to know, for instance, that he discussed the proper spelling of Latin words and wrote epitaphs, or at all events an epitaph, for a member or members of his household. His medium was always verse, of one kind or another, and always very rough, some lines hardly scanning and many being strangely uncouth. But even those who think worst of his style agree that he had vigour in plenty. He was also a ready composer, and his collected works extended to thirty books. That is to say, if we had them entire, a text-edition would be not much less than twice as long as a complete Vergil with brief critical notes, such as is published in the Oxford Classical Texts series, or by Teubner.

Meanwhile prose was developing in Rome, chiefly in the form of oratory, a very necessary weapon in the continual political struggles of those days. Just how early Greek influence came in to instruct users of Latin regarding the best form of a speech it is hard to say, but unless Romans of the third century B.C. and later were strangely unlike Italians of today, there would be no lack of men who could express themselves at least tolerably well on their feet, nor of audiences to appreciate their efforts. Save for a few early pieces preserved for one reason or another, however, the earliest orators of whom Cicero had heard and whom he records in his essay on the history of oratory, the *Brutus*, were little more than names even to him, and we have nothing of theirs; generally there is no reason to suppose that they published their speeches. For us, Latin prose begins with Cato (Marcus Porcius Cato,

234–149 B.C., often called Cato the Elder, or the Censor, to distinguish him from the younger Cato, or Cato of Utica, who committed suicide after the defeat of the Pompeian party in Africa, 46 B.C.). He wrote many speeches, a history (*Origines*, though it dealt with more than the 'beginnings' of things Italian), and several miscellaneous works, one of which, the treatise *On the cultivation of an estate* (*De agri cultura*) has come down to us, evidently with some modernization of its language. It is the most formless thing ever given to the public, a commonplace-book of miscellaneous bits of advice and directions, in which the reader never knows whether the next section will deal with some interesting religious rite or tell him where the best agricultural implements were to be had in Cato's day. His speeches and his history would be less chaotic, for their subjects imposed some kind of form on them; but Cato was a typical rustic, very suspicious of anything scientific, or Greek, though naturally he was not exempt from Greek influence, which was in the very air. The silly tale that he did not learn Greek till he was old needs no refutation; he was a statesman and had dealings with foreigners, therefore he must have known the language of diplomacy and international intercourse; but it is true that he made no serious study of Greek literature till late in life. His good points were that he was courageous, moral within the limits of his narrow, rule-of-thumb ethics, industrious to a degree, and possessed of much native wit and shrewdness, which showed itself for instance in his two excellent maxims for the guidance of an orator, 'Get the matter and the words will follow' and 'An orator is a good man skilled in speaking'. It is a pity that we have nothing but fragments of the 150 speeches and more which Cicero knew, and of the seven books of his *Origines*.

To give a list of other pre-Ciceronian orators would be merely to enumerate the prominent public men of those days; they included, for instance, the well-meaning but unfortunate brothers Tiberius and Gaius Gracchus. Two must be mentioned, because they are the principal speakers in Cicero's best work on rhetoric, the *De oratore*. One is Marcus Antonius, grandfather of the man we usually call Mark Antony, who neither published anything nor let it be known, if he could help it, that his eloquence was the fruit of thorough study and careful preparation. I think it not impossible that his grandson's pose as 'a plain blunt man' and 'no orator', in Shakespere's *Julius Caesar* results from a confusion between the older and the younger bearers of the name. His dates are 143–87 B.C. The other is Lucius Licinius Crassus, whose life was shorter (about 140–91 B.C.). He made no secret of his elaborate and successful study of the art of public speaking, and as he had great natural abilities, including, according to Cicero, refined humour and command of pure but unpedantic language, he stood out among the many good orators of his day. We have just enough quoted from him to know that he paid attention to rhythm, as Cicero (p. 187) was to do later.

History also began to be written in this age. From an early date (how early and how regularly we cannot tell) it had been the custom to prepare every year a whitewashed board on which the head of the State priesthood, the *pontifex maximus*, inscribed the names of the magistrates and any events which he considered noteworthy. Being a priest, he would naturally give relatively much space to sacral matters, but again, as there was no priestly caste or class and nothing prevented him from being a secular magistrate, he would hardly neglect such things as wars, treaties and the like. Someone sometime collected these yearly records (*annales*) into a work, allegedly of eighty book-rolls, called *annales maxumi*, i.e. the Very Great Year-book, or Chronicle. Some use seems to have been made of this by historians, but clearly not very much, and it was in no proper sense a history. The new Greek art, for so it was to the Romans, began to be practised in Greek by Quintus Fabius Pictor, who served in the second Punic War

(217-202 B.C.), and began with the foundation of Rome, coming down to his own times. There were no real traditions of the beginning of the City but, as always when so shocking a state of things existed, a Greek could be found to supply them, and Fabius followed a certain Diokles of Peparethos and apparently added some fictions of his own. Then Lucius Cincius Alimentus tried his hand at the same subject, this time in Latin, and two or three others followed his example. Later, histories of more limited scope were composed. Lucius Coelius Antipater confined himself to the second Punic War; he lived in the second century B.C. Later still, in the age of Sulla[1] and for that reason sometimes called the Sullan annalists, came several writers of varying merit. Quintus Claudius Quadrigarius showed this much critical sense, that he began with the Gaulish invasion (364 B.C.), before which there was a great dearth of documents, aggravated by the devastation of Rome while in Gaulish hands. He seems to have told his story in good plain Latin and not uninterestingly. Valerius of Antium (*Valerius Antias*), his contemporary, had abundant imagination and not many scruples; Gaius Licinius Macer, of about the same date, either was an unappreciated researcher or a notable liar, for he claimed to have got information from certain ancient documents written on linen, whereof no one else seems ever to have heard, except at second hand from him. There were also a few writers, some of them men of considerable prominence, who set down some account of their own times; these included Sulla himself, though the references which we have to his memoirs do not suggest that veracity was their strongest point. They were brought out after his death by a freedman of his, who found them unfinished and edited them for publication.

Thus by the time Cicero was grown to manhood, Rome

---

[1] Lucius Cornelius Sulla Felix, 138-78 B.C., prominent from early in the first century B.C. onwards, all-powerful for the last four or five years of his life. His ultra-conservative constitution survived him only a few years.

had a literature past its beginnings and something at least of a reading public, though hardly large as yet. In passing, a word must be said concerning the manner in which books were brought before the public in antiquity, that is to say in those ages which had anything like a book trade. The material was normally papyrus (see chap. ii, p. 34, n. 1), which was manufactured in various standard sizes, and in rolls of different lengths constructed by gluing together the required number of sheets of the material. On this a trained scribe would write with a reed pen, *calamus* (Greek *kalamos*). Rough notes were made, not in a *liber* or book-roll, but in *codicilli*, notebooks of a form like that of modern volumes, sometimes consisting of wax-coated pieces of wood, *tabulae* or *tabellae*, on which the writing was done with a *stilus*, an instrument not unlike a steel knitting-needle in shape but broad and blunt at one end, sometimes a little volume of parchment sheets, in which case the writing was in an ink which could easily be washed out, thus enabling the sheets to be used again and again, as the wax tablets could be by erasing the letters with the blunt end of the *stilus* (hence 'to turn the *stilus* over' [*stilum uertere*] means 'to erase'). But for publishing purposes, or to make any permanent record, the scribe used one of the standard rolls, and if many copies were called for, the work was dictated to a number of copyists at once. Then, if it was a carefully made edition, their writing was gone over by some competent person (the author, if he was alive and available) and corrected, of course a much slower business than modern proof-correcting, since every copy had to be gone over separately, and different copyists would no doubt make different mistakes. Papyrus also was not cheap, for making it was a skilled occupation, all done by hand; it therefore is no wonder that books were dear and private libraries usually small. The rolls, whether in a public or a private library, were kept in containers not unlike a hat-box in shape, called *capsae*, apparently one *capsa* to each long work, though a huge thing like Livy's *History* (p. 228) must have needed several. A great difference between ancient and modern books was that there was no such sharp line drawn between published and unpublished works as there is now. No copyright existed, therefore there was nothing to prevent anyone who had access to a book from copying it out for himself, or getting it copied, on any piece of papyrus he could find. We have several texts of classical authors written in a less formal hand than that of the regular scribes on the back of papyri containing other matter, such as accounts. The back was the less convenient side to write on, for there the fibres of the reeds ran vertically, whereas on the front they ran horizontally, thus as it were ruling the paper; but it was better than nothing, and these texts are doubtless the work of scholarly people too poor to afford booksellers' prices, or even new blank rolls.

By the middle of the last century B.C. Rome was becoming more and more the intellectual centre of the world, as well as the political. Julius Caesar planned and Augustus completed a great public library; Greeks and Greek-speaking scholars and writers of several nationalities came there of their own accord in hopes of well-paid employment, or were brought there as slaves and afterwards set free to earn their living by their accomplishments. Schools on Greek lines were set up, and teachers of a more advanced type, philosophers and rhetoricians, were to be had, the latter giving instruction, some in Greek and some in Latin. On the whole it may be said that a boy of respectable Roman family had open to him by the first century B.C. courses corresponding to our primary and secondary schools and our universities, although without our complicated apparatus of examinations. A young child of either sex would be taught elementary subjects by a *litterator*, a 'letter-man'; we still speak of teaching children their letters. Later, the boy (girls' education was less regular, though educated women were by no means unheard of) would be passed to a *grammaticus*, which means more than a grammarian, being rather what we should call a philologist. This teacher would give him a thorough grounding in literature, and thus prepare him for the services of a *rhetor*, which meant originally a speaker, but had specialized into the signification of one who taught composition, especially oratory. If so disposed, he might hear a philosopher lecturing on whatever system he favoured, or, if time and money were available, several philosophers of different schools. There was even what might perhaps be called a post-graduate course, generally at Athens, where something like a university was growing up. Such a system was, by the time of Cicero, beginning to supplant the older Roman method, under which the boy, having had his elementary education at home or at a school, would be attached to some more or less prominent man, accompany him to hear him speak in the courts of law or harangue a crowd in the Forum, and generally, under his instructions and by his example, familiarize himself with the duties of a public man who intended to become a candidate for the offices of state.

One result of the new system was that rhetoric was extensively taught and practised. For a speaker of Latin this was a necessary subject for, as already mentioned (p. 147), the language needed some ornamentation if it was to be elegant and forceful; but, as time went on, it became a craze, as it did also in the Greek-speaking world, and was studied for its own sake by men who had no legal or political career in view, and at a time when public speaking had ceased to be an art necessary to anyone's advancement in the service of the State.

To sum up: Rome, in the concluding years of the Republic and at the beginning of the Empire, was on the one hand wide open to Greek influences in everything except politics and military matters; on the other, she was rapidly becoming the intellectual centre of the civilized world and conscious of her own abilities in what had once been exclusively Greek arts, the production of works, both in verse and in prose, which were often of respectable and sometimes of high literary worth. In the following chapter some account will be given of those Latin writers who came forward as rivals to the great classics of Greece, at all events in certain kinds, and of their immense influence on the literatures of later ages.

VI

The Golden Age of Rome

IN THE LAST CHAPTER WE SAW HOW THE WRITERS of Latin learned, fast and intelligently, to improve their language until works composed in it might without absurdity be set up as rivals to the masterpieces of Greece. We now come to a period, something under two centuries in length, during which almost all the really important and brilliant performances in prose or verse were Latin, though there were Greek writers of merit during this time. Afterwards, Latin declines, while Greek continues to put forth works, not indeed of anything like the highest order, but still worth reading and full of interest for anyone who has not let himself be hypnotized by dates and misled by some dogma to the effect that no one after the year *x* B.C., or A.D., could possibly have been a really good writer. The story may begin with a very remarkable man of whose life we know little (indeed, there probably was never much to know), but of his temperament and his genius, a great deal, while his influence is to be found in many later authors in sundry languages. This was Titus Lucretius Carus, born 94 B.C., died 55 B.C., and generally known simply as Lucretius in English, Lucrèce in French. His was one of those sensitive personalities, to be found in all ages and among all peoples, who are intelligent enough to want an explanation of the world about them and of their own inner life, and cannot rest until they find one which they think indefeasibly true, demonstrable by the most cogent arguments, and bringing peace of mind to those who accept it. Probably the majority of such people resort to a religion, if there is one available which satisfies their heart and brain; if there is none at hand, a philosophy of some kind may serve them, and in the time of Lucretius, philosophy was to many thinking people what one of the great faiths is to those of another age. The old State cults had become unreal forms to most educated men, though they generally maintained them as being popular adumbrations of philosophical truths, ethical or physical, or even as being an ingenious device for overawing the naturally unruly mob with the threat of supernatural powers whom it would be most unwise to offend. The various mystery-religions which were making their way from the East had as yet little appeal for sober-minded people, and none of the great ethical religions had got a footing; Christianity, of course, did not even begin till long after Lucretius was dead. Of the philosophies, Epicureanism was the one that appealed to him, for it was simple and also dogmatic, having its orthodoxy from which few or none of its followers dissented. Briefly, it taught that nothing exists except matter, which is composed of indivisible particles, *atomoi*, 'inseparables' (we have adopted the word and paradoxically talk now of 'splitting' that which by definition it ought to be impossible to split), and void, without which there could be no movement. The only channel of knowledge is the senses, which cannot deceive, although we may misinterpret their data. Since no material complex is permanent, for sooner or later its atoms part company, and the soul, being real, is material, man is mortal. His one end is pleasure, and as violent pleasures bring painful reactions, they are to be avoided, bodily desires satisfied in the simplest ways, and attention to be concentrated on the pleasures of the mind, untroubled by silly ambitions after power or wealth. Epicurus himself set the example of a retired life without luxuries and only the most modest comfort, and his most consistent disciples lived much as he had done, avoiding especially the entanglements of a public career. Naturally there were many degrees of fidelity to this regimen, ranging from a general acceptance of Epicurus' doctrines combined with intense political and other activity (Julius Caesar was an Epicurean) to sheer swinish self-indulgence with a slight veneer of philosophy. Religion as such was not opposed, though superstition most decidedly was, but the Epicurean gods, known to exist because we can have visions and dreams of them, and those could not be without a material something to send them, care nothing for mankind, have no duties or activities, create and govern nothing, and spend their blissful and everlasting lives in the *intermundia*, the spaces between the innumerable universes which the system postulates. There, there is not enough matter to damage the divine bodies, which are of very subtle substance, and so they have nothing to fear. Hence there is no reason why they should be hostile to man, who therefore is merely foolish if he fears them, although he may reverence them, since what is excellent is worthy of reverence.

This system Lucretius spent a great part of his life in setting out in the finest didactic poem the world has yet seen. His avowed object was to reveal the truths of Epicureanism to all, and more especially to the addressee of the poem, a certain Gaius Memmius, a politician of no great ability and not very admirable character. Why the poet selected him is not known. In the six books of his great work, he sets forth, firstly, the fundamental principles of the atomic theory, and especially the Epicurean form of it, which introduced a new hypothesis into the system originated by Demokritos (p. 93), namely that all atoms, although generally they fall endlessly downwards through infinite space (a naïve idea which deeper thinkers like Aristotle had completely outgrown, recognizing as they did that our 'up' and 'down' mean simply from and towards the centre of the earth), yet are subject to a capricious and unpredictable swerve, which prevents anything from being absolutely determined beforehand, however complete a knowledge of their movements one might postulate. It is a quaint attempt to get rid of Demokritos' determinism. These expositions occupy the first two books; the third discusses the soul, brings forward elaborate proofs of its mortality, and insists with grave eloquence on the lack of anything to be feared in death, which is simply non-existence, and therefore 'more carefree than any sleep' (iii, 977). Book iv sets forth the Epicurean theory of perception; it is due to the continual casting off of very thin shells or skins from all material objects, which impinging on our eyes and other organs of sense produce the impressions that we have. A long discussion of sexual passion closes the book, with the usual insistence on its purely material and physical nature, nothing being caused by any supernatural agent. Book v sketches the history of the universe and of living creatures, and includes a crude theory of evolution, a fairly common doctrine among Greek philosophers, made the easier for them because their traditional religious ideas, never definite enough to form a creed, did not include a creation-myth. Book vi is of miscellaneous content, giving rational explanations of a kind (for neither Epicurus nor Lucretius was a scientist) of various phenomena ending with a description, taken from Thucydides, of the great plague at Athens near the beginning of the Peloponnesian War. The title is *De Rerum Natura*, *Concerning the Nature of Existents*.

That the poem is incomplete is obvious to anyone who reads through it attentively. Perhaps the most outstanding sign of this is the repetition of several passages, which apparently the poet had composed but not found a final place for. It is said that it was edited after its author's death by Cicero, meaning no doubt the orator; if so, he did not take his duties very seriously, for there is no trace of another hand filling gaps or otherwise rearranging the material. The style is admirable throughout, copious, eloquent, most ingenious in what Lucretius regarded as a great difficulty, the expressing of Greek philosophical ideas in Latin, of whose 'poverty' he complains (i, 136 ff.). It is also diversified with many episodes of pure and exalted poetry, such as the moving address to

Venus with which the whole begins and the several laudations of Epicurus as the greatest benefactor of mankind in all history. Lucretius had a vivid and pictorial imagination, and his enthusiasm for his subject prevented him from ever becoming dull, even in the most technical parts of his exposition.

Vergil (pp. 202 ff.) was his earliest great admirer and must have known his work nearly by heart, to judge from his frequent imitations of and allusions to it. Since then his popularity has fluctuated. Epicureanism was anathema to most orthodox Christians, few of whom took the trouble to find out what it really taught, and after the classical age interest in and study of the poet began with the Revival of Letters, when Poggio Bracciolini (1418) the great humanist discovered a manuscript of him, which was extensively copied, and the copies formed the basis of the earlier texts. Modern editors since Lachmann (1850) use as their leading authority two manuscripts preserved in Leiden, which go back to a copy made in the fourth or fifth century. On the whole, then, we have a fairly good text, probably not differing very widely from those copies which resulted from Cicero's editing of the original and presumably were produced by the copyists employed by Atticus (p. 194).

Lucretius' tastes were somewhat old-fashioned, and he clearly shows, in grammar and even to some extent in metre, the influence of Ennius (pp. 150 f.), of whom he speaks warmly. In this he was out of tune with a strong tendency of his time, close imitation of the Alexandrians and adoption of their methods. There grew up a school of what we may call Alexandrianizing poets, centring around a noteworthy personality, a *grammaticus* (p. 171) named Valerius Cato; we do not know his *praenomen*. He seems to have been a most amiable man, poor and frugal all his life, but an inspiring teacher; someone, we do not know who, wrote a little epigram on him, Alexandrian in metre and substance alike, which styled him 'Cato the *grammaticus*, the Siren of Latium, the only reader and maker of poets'. The verse is the hendecasyllable, Tennyson's 'metre of Catullus', in which he wrote that amusing trifle 'O you chorus of indolent reviewers'. The mention of the Siren is typically obscure, for usually a Siren is the embodiment of sensual temptation which leads men astray. The unknown author would have his readers remember what it was that the Sirens on the *Odyssey* sang to its hero,

> For never yet has any man sailed by in his dark ship until he had heard the honied strain from our lips, but ere he goes his way he has been delighted, and has more knowledge. – *Od.* xii, 186–7.

Cato, then, is the giver of knowledge (and pleasure as well) to the Latins, and his sweet utterance is the cause of both. We know at least the names of a few of his pupils, if we may call them so, and we have nearly the whole output of the most famous of them all. Gaius Licinius Calvus Macer was both orator and poet, and was apparently at his best when accusing a disreputable follower of Julius Caesar, by name Vatinius; later writers couple him with Catullus in a way which suggests that they thought one about as good as the other, and we know the subjects of some of his poems, all quite consistent with Alexandrianism. His short life (82–about 47 B.C.) was plainly an active one. Furius Bibaculus was celebrated for his lampoons, but that he could write in quite a different fashion when he chose is plain from another of the surviving tributes to Valerius Cato, which is from his pen. C. Helvius Cinna (the 'Cinna the poet' of *Julius Caesar*) has left us practically nothing, though Catullus was of opinion that one of his learnedly obscure poems, the *Smyrna*,[1] would endure. So we come to the survivor of the group, who was also, so far as we can judge, the best poet of them all, Gaius Valerius Catullus. Born at Verona in 87 B.C., he would seem to have been a man of moderate fortune who lived beyond his means. His life was

[1] Not the city, but the mythical heroine, better known as Myrrha, for whom see Rose, *Handbook of Greek Mythology*, pp. 124 f.

N

short, lasting until about 55 B.C., or not much later, and his whole career centres around one event, his removal from Verona to Rome or its immediate neighbourhood. There two things befell him; he joined the circle of Valerius Cato and he fell in love with a woman whom he calls Lesbia, her real name being almost certainly Clodia, the sister of Publius Clodius, a ruffianly partisan of Caesar and one of Cicero's worst enemies, whom he spent much eloquence in abusing. Clodia was a beautiful and fascinating woman with no morals at all, and Catullus, passionately in love with her for some time (the dates are vague), later hated her with equal fervour, and recorded his love and hatred in some of the most poignant poems ever written in any language on such topics. No one since Sappho had expressed private and intense feelings so effectively, and no one in the Roman world was to do so again. However, this was not Catullus' only theme. He wrote some vehement attacks on Caesar and his partisans, and translated a part of Kallimachos' *Aitia* (p. 128), the section known as the *Lock of Berenike*, which records how the queen's severed hairs, made a votive offering for her husband's safe return from his wars, became a minor constellation and were recognized by Konon the astronomer; a bit of courtly compliment which gave Pope the ending of *The Rape of the Lock*. He also wrote two charming epithalamia or marriage songs, one for a real wedding, that of two of his acquaintance, and one for an imaginary one, with a Greek setting. He produced a marvellous *tour de force*, in a difficult and erratic metre known as the galliambic, on the legend of Attis, the beloved of the Great Mother Kybele and the prototype of her self-emasculated priests. He composed an epyllion, quite in the best Alexandrian manner, having for its framework the wedding of Peleus and Thetis, but spending much of its moderate space over the tale of Ariadne and her desertion by Theseus.[1] This is in hexameters,

[1] For the relevant legends, see my *Handbook of Greek Mythology*, pp. 25 f., 106, 265.

not yet quite as good as those of Vergil in technique, but a vast improvement on earlier attempts; his elegiacs, including the translation from Kallimachos, are not so successful, the metre needing further adaptation to the natural rhythms of Latin. In that metre and in several others, including his beloved hendecasyllables, he composed a number of short poems on a variety of topics, mostly personal. Influenced though he was by the Alexandrians, he was a better poet than any of them when he wrote on matters which deeply concerned himself, and they were never his exclusive models, for one short translation and several reminiscences show that he had studied Sappho to some purpose.

A greater literary influence, though a much worse poet, was the supreme prose writer of that day, Marcus Tullius Cicero, whom we usually call Cicero simply, though our ancestors frequently named him Tully (so for instance Ascham in *The Scholemaster*). Though he lacked all the more important qualities of a poet, he had technical skill, and made his contribution to the development of the Latin hexameter, besides producing spirited renderings of some passages of Tragedy in the metres of the original Greek. We know him and his life intimately, thanks not only to his more formal works but also to his bulky correspondence, much of which survives. He has been overpraised and overblamed by many writers, but the fact is that he was a patriot, not lacking in courage, of amiable principles in politics, but too skilled in advocacy not to see that a good case could be made out for or against almost any movement of the day, whether conservative or radical, and therefore prone to waver when confronted with a situation in which neither side was manifestly wrong or right. His most annoying fault was his boundless vanity, which made him exaggerate his own really considerable services to the State more than he ever did his incomparable abilities as a speaker and writer. Twice in his life, once in 63 B.C., when he was consul, and once late in 44 and early in 43, when the

Republicans made their last stand against the powers of what proved to be a disguised, if moderate despotism, he saw the situation clearly and took what was, for him, the only possible stand. On the former occasion, he was successful; on the latter he was fighting vainly but bravely against the inevitable course of events, and paid for his courageous stand with his life. In times when the issues were less clear-cut, he advocated a policy of union between all men of good will of the two principal orders in the State, the senators, who were all either magistrates or ex-magistrates and had collectively a great and often ill-used amount of power in their hands, and the *equites*, among whom were the principal men of business and financiers of the day. He also hoped to see emerging a citizen of such outstanding worth and wisdom that the rest would willingly follow his advice in public matters, and for a time he hoped he had found such a leader in Pompeius Magnus. It was an attractive ideal, but when the leader did in fact appear in the person of Octavian, the future Emperor Augustus, his sane policy had the backing of military force, and his early career was marred by bloodshed, though once in power, he was meticulously careful to preserve the outward forms of constitutional government. It was a weakness of Cicero that, being himself accessible to reasonable argument, he underestimated the overwhelming importance of brute force in the troubled conditions then prevailing. Lucan, wise after the event, saw more clearly when he put into the mouth of the younger Cato the words

> True liberty [i.e. the continuance of the Republic] went when we let in Sulla and Marius; now that Pompey is gone from our affairs, even the phantom of it is lost; no one henceforth will be ashamed to be a despot. – *Phars.* ix, 204–6.

Cicero's political and literary careers are so closely bound together that it is impracticable to describe one without saying something of the other. He was a 'newcomer' (*nouos homo*) in

politics, that is to say a member of a family none of whom
had ever held one of the important magistracies. Not being
rich, he had but one access to public life, his own abilities, and
the obvious method of getting known and winning influence
was by succeeding as a pleader. Roman juries, like those of
Greece, were large and had great power in their hands. A
majority vote determined the issue, and naturally the force
with which the cases for prosecution and defence were put had
a great deal to do with obtaining such a majority. Barristers
like ours did not formally exist, but it had long been the duty
of prominent men to defend their retainers (*clientes*, literally
hearers; we still speak of the 'clients' of a pleader) when they
had business before any court. This was extended so far as to
allow anyone to state the case of any litigant, whether in what
we should call a civil or a criminal trial. Obviously, to take
part in some suit which had excited wide interest was an
excellent advertisement for an ambitious man, the more so if
he won his case. There were no fees, but the litigant, who
might owe his civic rights to the eloquence of his defender,
would naturally feel obligated to do something for him in
turn, such as supporting his candidature for a magistracy, and
everyone who might need good speaking to maintain his cause
before a court or sway the electorate in his favour would
remember and note the name of the orator in question. Cicero,
in almost the first case of his which is known to us, showed
that he had tact, eloquence and courage at his command.
While Sulla was in power, a certain Sextus Roscius had been
so imprudent as to fall heir to a considerable estate, which
however had been confiscated and bought for a nominal
price by Chrysogonus, a hanger-on of Sulla. Roscius set out
to recover his property by showing that the former owner,
his father, had been illegally put to death and the confiscation
of the estate was void. Chrysogonus then employed a certain
Erucius to accuse him of having murdered his father. Cicero
defended Roscius, proved his innocence, and managed not to

offend the all-powerful dictator. Having succeeded, he yet
found it advisable to leave Rome for a while, and spent his
retirement in further studies of oratory under Greek masters.
Some few years after Sulla's death and his own return, he
came forward to lead the prosecution in a test case. Roman
magistrates, after their year of office, were regularly given a
department (*prouincia*) to manage, and this was often a
province in our sense, a dependency of Rome. Gaius Verres, a
particularly objectionable specimen of the worst politicians of
the day, had thus become governor of Sicily, and used his
powers, unlimited and unchecked so long as the governor-
ship continued, to rob the unfortunate inhabitants of the island
on what seems to have been an unprecedented scale. Returning to Rome, he was accused of extortion, the only legal
means of getting any sort of redress. He had on his side the
interests of his whole class, the senatorial order, many of
whose members were only too ready to let a villain escape his
deserts in order to have opportunities of filling their own
pockets by similar means. Hence every possible kind of
chicanery was used to secure an acquittal for Verres. Cicero
outmanœuvred his opponents, and Verres went into volun-
tary exile when the proceedings were half over.[1] Cicero
published the speeches he would have made had the trial continued to its normal end, and they formed a powerful indictment of the existing system, and had no doubt their share of
influence in reforming it. He was now a rising man, little as his
appearance was welcomed by those who wished to continue

---

[1] Exile, *exsilium*, was not formally a punishment in Roman law, though
outlawry (*aqua atque igne interdictio*) and, under the Empire, *relegatio* (confine-
ment to a named district) were. An accused person, at all events one of any
social standing, was under no restraint, and so, until the last vote was cast, he
was at liberty to walk out of the court and depart from Rome to some place
technically independent, such as Massilia (Marseille). This could be regularized
by passing a decree to the effect that he had 'changed his domicile with the
intention of remaining permanently abroad' (*solum uertisse exsili causa*). It
does not appear that there was normally anything corresponding to our extra-
dition. Verres retained at least a great part of his plunder, and ironically he was
in the end murdered to get some valuable objects which were included in it.

passing offices of state and consequent opportunities for profit
and power from hand to hand among a comparatively small
group. He was elected praetor, and later, in 64 B.C., six years
after the trial of Verres, consul for the next year, along with a
worthless but fortunately inactive member of the family of
the Antonii. As consul, he had and seized his opportunity.
Catiline (Lucius Sergius Catilina), a desperate and bankrupt
rake with a kind of wild ability, had gathered around him a
number of persons like himself to whom any disturbance in
the State would be an advantage, because it might involve a
wholesale cancelling of debts – if necessary, by murdering the
creditors. Cicero had behind him the Senate, many members
of which no doubt were genuinely anxious to prevent disturbances, while others would be glad to shift responsibility
for vigorous measures on to the shoulders of the energetic
consul; which was done by passing the 'final resolution of
Senate', as it was called (*ultimum senatus consultum*),[1] about
equivalent to declaring martial law in a modern State. Cicero
had taken measures to stop breaches of the peace in Rome and
kept himself informed of the progress of the conspiracy. He
then, in full Senate, delivered one of his most famous speeches,
telling Catiline plainly that all his plans were known and bid-
ding him depart, which he at once did. Nothing then remained
for him save open armed rebellion, which was crushed in a
single sharp engagement by such forces as were available to
the government, most of the military power of the Republic
being then in the East under Pompey. Meanwhile a number
of the leading conspirators had been arrested and put to death
by Cicero in virtue of his emergency powers. The chief
literary record of all this is the series of speeches, all short and
all brilliant, in which Cicero set forth and explained his action;
they are collectively known as the Catilinarian Orations.

---

[1] This was a formal resolution 'that all office-holders (mentioned in detail,
from the highest to the lowest) should see to it that no harm befalls the State'.
How they were to 'see to it' (*dare operam*) was left to their discretion.

Unfortunately, his laudable conduct so inflamed his vanity that he never was done praising it and seeking to have it praised by others. He seems also to have thought himself more powerful than he really was, and five years after his consulship he was outlawed on an obscure legal issue connected with his execution of the Catilinarians. The motive force behind this was the new political coalition, generally called the First Triumvirate and consisting of Pompey, the most prominent public man of the day, Julius Caesar, the ablest statesman then alive, and Marcus Licinius Crassus Dives, an immensely rich man with political ambitions in excess of his abilities, but useful to provide funds (Pompey was not rich and Caesar chronically in debt). The agent of the triumvirate was Clodius. By 57 B.C. Cicero was back again and made his peace with the real power of the day, in support of whom he delivered a number of speeches of one kind or another, some against his real convictions. It is hard to see what else he could have done, short of remaining permanently away from Rome and Italy. On one occasion he failed conspicuously. Clodius had an opponent as ruffianly as himself, a certain Titus Annius Milo. The two, with their attendant gangs, clashed and Clodius was killed. Naturally, Milo was impeached, and Cicero, who spoke on his behalf, lost his nerve in a court surrounded by an armed guard to preserve the peace. He later published the speech he ought to have made, in which Milo appears as a high-minded patriot; Milo himself drily remarked that if it had been delivered at the actual trial, he would never have known how good the mullets were at Massilia. This was in 52; not long afterwards came the Civil War. Cicero came forward as a not very vigorous supporter of Pompey, but after his leader's defeat and death found himself treated with clemency and courtesy by Caesar, before whom, in 46, he delivered some two or three speeches on behalf of other Pompeians. Now followed the assassination of Caesar (March 15, 44 B.C.), and what might be called the constitutional party, with Cicero at its head, made a stand against Mark Antony, who clearly aimed at supreme power and was in armed rebellion against the Senate. Cicero delivered a long series of orations against him, the most famous of which, the Second Philippic (for he gave them a general title borrowed from Demosthenes, cf. p. 112) was not actually spoken but published as a political pamphlet. The event was decided by the action of a youth not yet twenty years old, Octavian, the adopted son of Caesar, who had behind him Caesar's memory and the loyalty of his veterans, to which was added his own genius and his cold, single-minded ambition. He supported Cicero and the Senate for a while, then allied himself to Antony, and the Senatorial government collapsed. Cicero was one of the many who were got out of the way in the resulting 'purge', and was murdered by Antony's emissaries on December 7, 43 B.C.

In all his speeches, Cicero steered a middle course, stylistically, between the excesses of the Asianists and the too unemotional, over-plain manner of the Atticists. From the latter he took their wholesome regard for a normal vocabulary, without poetical flourishes or use of uncommon words or empty, sounding phrases. From the former he borrowed their attention to effective rhythm, especially at the ends of sentences and other natural pauses, such as we mark by commas and semi-colons. The details of his methods here are highly technical, but this much must be said, for it is of importance for the later history of prose. He regularly gave each closing rhythm (*clausula*) a base, which normally consisted of a cretic (a long syllable followed by a short one and then another long), and after it a short run of alternating long and short syllables, two, three or four in number. For the cretic, a molossus (three long syllables) might be freely substituted, and there were other modifications, giving rise to allowable, though less common cadences. The commonest forms were $- \cup - - \bar{\cup}$, as (*pati*)*entiā nostra*, $- \cup - - \cup \bar{\cup}$, as (*iac*)*tabit audacia*, and $- \cup - - \cup - \cup$, as *filii comprobauit*. Now these three rhythms found their way, through many later authors, into medieval Latin prose of the more formal sort, where naturally accented syllables took the place of long ones. Hence the three 'runs' (cursus) as they were called, the cursus planus, or plain run, as nostris infúnde, the tardus (slow, as (incarnati)ónem cognoúimus, and the uelox (swift), as gloriam pèrducámur. From medieval Latin they were picked up to some extent by the vernacular literatures, and echoes of them are often to be heard in the more stately kinds of English prose, from Tudor times onwards. The A. V. and the Book of Common Prayer, for instance, furnish examples, conscious or unconscious, thus: omnipotent reigneth (planus); (for)give us our trespasses (tardus); gracious Queen now assembled (uelox). If ever a really searching and thorough study of our prose rhythms is made (no small task), it should start with this inheritance, through the Middle Ages, from the usage of Cicero and the many writers who followed him more or less closely. In his other works, use is made of these clausulae, but they have not as yet been so minutely analysed as the speeches.[1]

Cicero was of course interested in rhetoric all his life, and never ceased to practise it. His first work, little more than a schoolboy effort, which got abroad without his knowledge or consent, is known to us as the De inuentione, i.e. on the choice (and arrangement) of subject-matter. It is in two books, and sums up the precepts of the time. Years later, in 55 B.C., one of his periods of comparative retirement from political life, he wrote a far more important treatise, the De oratore, i.e. 'Concerning the (ideal) orator'. It is in form an Aristotelian[2] dialogue, the speakers Antonius and Crassus (p. 168). It might be said that it gives a good and interesting account

[1] The speeches were analysed by the great Polish Latinist Th. Zielinski, in two works, Das Clauselgestz in Ciceros Reden (Leipzig, 1904) and Der constructive Rhythmus in Ciceros Reden (Leipzig, 1914).
[2] That is, a work in which successive speakers set forth their views in orations or essays of considerable length, not brief questions and answers.

of how Cicero himself became a persuasive and eloquent speaker, but such fundamental things as the psychology of persuasion and the differences between close logical reasoning and the sort of argument which will sway a popular audience are left to Aristotle (p. 101) and the other Greeks. Besides a little handbook in the form of a catechism, the *Partitiones oratoriae*, i.e *The Orator's Classifications*, for the benefit of his rather stupid son Marcus and his nephew Quintus, he composed the *Brutus* (cf. p. 166), in which, besides his sketch of the earlier orators, he gave an account of his own career. To this he added the *Orator*, in which he set out to persuade Brutus that true Atticism was not so narrow as those of his school imagined, but included a variety of styles; and by way of illustration, he translated two of the most famous Attic speeches, Aischines' indictment of Ktesiphon (p. 113) and Demosthenes' immortal reply. There survives only the preface to this work. A final contribution to the subject was due to a piece of good nature on Cicero's part. His friend Gaius Trebatius the jurist was puzzled by the crabbed Greek of Aristotle's classification of arguments, the *Topica*; Cicero wrote a Latin *Topica* for him, shorter, clearer and with illustrations from Roman law.

Cicero, like most intelligent Romans of that day, was interested in philosophy, but it was with a Roman's interest. Neither he nor any of his fellow-countrymen had much talent for or interest in metaphysics or logic, still less perhaps in physics, then recognized as a branch of philosophy, not a separate discipline. What many besides Lucretius (p. 174) were looking for was a guide to life, and therefore ethics was the part of the subject which attracted them. And politics (in the proper sense of the word, ethics as applied to the community, not the individual), being a further part of the same subject, was naturally included. So it is not remarkable that Cicero, after some early efforts in the direction of ethics, which included translations from Xenophon and Plato, wrote

a work of his own *On the State* (*De re publica*), begun in 54
B.C., finished about three years later. His ideal state, for he had
Plato's masterpiece in mind, was a highly idealized Rome,
and its equivalent of the Greek's philosopher-king was the
younger Africanus. As Plato had ended with the famous myth
of Er the Armenian, who was granted a vision of the next
world, so must Cicero, and his myth took the form of a dream
in which Scipio was shown what rewards awaited him and
other righteous men, after bodily death. Although the rest of
the work was lost for centuries and even now is but partly
known from a defective palimpsest,[1] this dream survived, was
lengthily commented upon by Macrobius (p. 269), and is
known to us from several manuscripts; the views it sets forth
may be described as Platonizing Stoicism. Like Plato again,
Cicero followed up his *Republic* by a work in some five books,
On Laws (*De legibus*), whereof three books have come down
to us, though not quite complete. They are enough to show
that his idealized Rome was to be given an idealized Roman
constitution. Both these works are in the form of Aristotelian
dialogues (see p. 188, n. 2).

A rhetorician as well as a practical orator, Cicero did not
like a too drily scholastic fashion of setting forth any doctrines,
which accounts for the manner of his odd little work,
addressed to Brutus and not much later than the book which
bears his name (p. 189), the *Paradoxes*. Stoicism, to which
school Brutus belonged, was fond of startling statements, as
'that only the (Stoic) sage is rich', which they supported by
ingenious dialectic. Cicero treats them as themes for declamations, characteristically adding a personal touch; thus the
discussion of the maxim 'that every unwise man is mad' turns
rapidly into an attack on Clodius. He was himself an Academic,

[1] Literally a manuscript which has been 'scraped again', i.e. from which the
original writing has been more or less thoroughly erased to use the parchment
for some other text. The underlying writing can generally be made out to
some extent at least, formerly by the use of chemical reagents, more recently
by infra-red rays.

that is a member of the school which, taking its rise from
Platonism, had developed a theory that real knowledge is
unattainable and the best we can do is to follow whatever
approximation to the truth seems to us most reasonable. This
left an Academic free to do as Cicero did and adopt pro-
visionally a system of ethics from one of the other schools, in
his case Stoicism. In 45 he wrote a work, known to us as the
Prior Academics, which explained the tenets of his school; he
then re-wrote it, because he heard that Varro (p. 198) wished
to be one of the speakers in some work of his. We have one
book left of each of the two editions. Far more important is
the *De finibus bonorum et malorum* (*On the Extremes of Good and
Evil*), five books of dialogue which expound Epicurean, Stoic
and finally Academic ideas on the subject, with criticisms of
the first two schools. The author and several of his acquaintance are the speakers. This was still in 45, and it took some
three months to write. Cicero obviously worked very fast,
without, however, descending to slovenly style. It must have
become second nature with him to write not only correct but
highly eloquent and forceful Latin. The matter, by his own
modest admission, is never original; as he tells Atticus (*Ad
Atticum* xii, 52, 3), the works are 'copies, and so cost less pains,
for I supply only words, of which I have plenty'. Within a
year of finishing the *De finibus*, he had completed the *Tusculan
Disputations*, five books in which he instructs a young man
that death is not to be dreaded, pain can be endured, grief overcome, other 'disturbances of the mind' (*perturbationes animi*)
alleviated, and that virtue is sufficient for happiness. Between
the two works he himself underwent a severe affliction. His
daughter Tullia, his favourite child, died and he was for a
time nearly mad with grief, to the extent of half-seriously
entertaining a project of deifying her.[1] Becoming somewhat

[1] It was nothing unusual in the Hellenistic monarchies for a king, occasionally some other prominent person, to be given divine honours, normally in
recognition of eminent services to those who thus honoured him. But this was
a public and official procedure as a rule, though exceptions occurred; for

calmer, he was helped by his own vanity. It occurred to him that although composing consolatory addresses to the afflicted was a stock practice, the great model of such things being one by the Platonic philosopher Krantor, no one yet had addressed himself on that subject; and he set about doing so. The work is lost to us, though for a while a forgery, probably by the humanist Carlo Sigonio, passed for genuine with some. Another lost work, the *Hortensius*, deserves mention. It was named after Hortensius the orator, who appeared in it as an opponent of philosophy, confuted by the other speakers. It was therefore an exhortation to philosophic pursuits, a protreptic work, to use the Greek technicality for such things. It was admired for its style, therefore students of rhetoric and literature read it as part of their regular course, and thus it was read by St Augustine in his early days, and was the first influence to turn his mind to serious things.

About this time, during which Cicero seems to have spent almost every waking hour writing or dictating, he hastily composed his three books *On the Nature of the Gods*, most of which has survived. Again in dialogue form, it expounds first the Epicurean and secondly the Stoic theology, both being then criticized by an Academic; the last book went on to set forth Academic doubts concerning theism generally. Still in this period of political retirement and literary activity comes the little work which Cicero called *Cato Maior*, we generally *De senectute* (*On Old Age*). The elder Cato (p. 167) sets forth to Scipio and his friend Laelius his reasons for not being displeased at growing old. A motive for it was that Atticus and Cicero himself were beginning to feel their years.

Divination was a subject much discussed in and before the days of Cicero, therefore it is not surprising that he wrote on

---

instance, Epicureans had a kind of cult of their founder. The model was followed for posthumous honours to Julius Caesar, Augustus and most of his successors, but for a private individual to attempt it in Cicero's time was eccentric to a degree.

it. In the two books *De diuinatione* his brother Quintus is represented as using the stock Stoic arguments to prove that the future can be discerned, whether by inspiration or by science, and Marcus argues against them. Its date was 44 B.C., and a kind of continuation of it is the treatise *Concerning Fate* (*De fato*), in which Cicero expounds to Hirtius, one of the consuls for the following year, arguments for and against the proposition that all actions are predetermined. Two more works, of nearly the same time, survive, the essay *On Friendship*, or *Laelius* (because Laelius, discussing friendship, uses his dead friend Scipio as an example) and the three books *On Duties* (*De officiis*), addressed to his son, which abandons the dialogue form. Two or three other works on philosophic subjects are known to have been written by him, but have not survived.

Unoriginal though they are, these writings have a considerable importance. To the specialist, they are a valuable source for the reconstruction of numerous Greek works known to Cicero but lost to us. To the non-specialist they have a different but not a lesser interest, for they long held a place as manuals especially of ethics, which perhaps they have not yet quite lost; at least, the author knew a delightful old man who re-read 'Tully's Offices' every year. That they, especially the *De officiis*, were almost proverbial in such a connexion may be seen, for instance, from the poem *Morality* by that very minor poet Thomas Little (late eighteenth century). Speaking of the 'plain good man', he says,

> *Nor could he act a purer part*
> *Though he had Tully all by heart.*

In other words, however much he had studied ethical theory. To anyone interested in human history, they must retain their place, as setting forth in an attractive manner the problems and attempted solutions which occupied thinking men in one of the most important periods known to us.

Finally, mention must be made of Cicero's immense correspondence, through which we know him perhaps better than any other ancient. A very large part consists of his letters to his intimate friend Titus Pomponius Atticus (later Quintus Caecilius Pomponianus Atticus, for he was adopted by the will of his uncle Q. Caecilius in 58 B.C.). This was a very remarkable man, a consistent Epicurean who was also possessed of considerable abilities and a genius for friendship. His dates are 109–32 B.C.; heir to a fortune, and recipient afterwards of sundry legacies, he augmented his wealth by his talent for business. He always avoided politics, and his relations with men of all parties and none were characterized by great generosity in financial matters, for many whom he knew (Cicero was one of them) were chronically short of money, owing to the many expenses which a public career involved. Perhaps the best testimony to his tact is that he was on good terms not only with Cicero and the younger Cato, but also with Antony and Octavian. A prudential withdrawal to Athens in the troublous days of the early first century B.C. resulted in such improvement of his knowledge of Greek that he spoke it like a native Athenian, and this sojourn abroad got him his *cognomen*. His abiding interest was for literature, and all his household consisted of literate persons. He published, among other things, the works of Cicero, and it would seem that he also put forth good copies of Greek authors; at all events, we hear now and then of editions called *Attikiana*, and we know of no other name which would explain their existence. On his own account he wrote a work on Roman chronology, the *Liber annalis*, or *Book of the Years*, and other pieces dealing with topics from Roman history. One was in Greek and treated of Cicero's consulship. To him, Cicero, from shortly before his election as consul, wrote often and frankly, sometimes oftener than once a day. We have his letters, though not Atticus' replies to them, and these hurried notes, as they mostly are, tell us more of their author's character and real feelings than his formal works, besides casting a welcome light on affairs of that day, on Latin as informally used by educated persons, and every now and then on the spoken Greek of the time, for Greek words abound in them. In addition, we have a large number of letters to various friends and acquaintances, varying in tone from jocular or excited scribbles to formal communications obviously intended to be shown to others than the addressees. Furthermore, the answers from a number of correspondents are preserved. It would seem that none of these letters, which contain matter throwing perhaps too much light on contemporaries, was published until about the time of the Emperor Claudius (A.D. 41–54), but published they ultimately were, including a considerable number that have not come down to us. Among other things, they served as a model to future letter-writers, including the younger Pliny (p. 259); for letter-writing was an acknowledged branch of rhetoric, and model letters (see p. 236) were a common exercise. It is not long since *Complete Letter-writers* ceased to be composed in English, to say nothing of other modern languages, but in our own times, the very ease with which news may be communicated to friends in any part of the civilized world has caused the art to be neglected. Much of what an ancient, or a modern of, say, the seventeenth century, would have put into a letter is now omitted because the correspondent will have read of it in his newspaper or heard it over the wireless, and not a little which might have been written down is simply telephoned.

After Cicero, all Latin prose of literary importance was written either in more or less close imitation of his style, or in deliberate departures from it. Naturally, in his own day he had his critics, and also there were writers who used other principles of style, notably the Atticists. To this school, if to any, Julius Caesar may be said to have belonged, witness the very un-Ciceronian Latin of his surviving works,[1] the *Commentarii*

---

[1] Besides the *Commentaries*, and some juvenile works of no importance, he

o

de bello Gallico and *de bello ciuili*, i.e. *Notes for a history of the Gallic and Civil Wars*. In Cicero's opinion they are like athletes stripped for action or, as he phrases it, they are 'naked, straight and handsome' (*Brutus* 262), and apparently no later historian tried to put elaborate dress upon them. But they are as different from anything Cicero himself would have written as any Latin work well could be. In the words of a modern journalist of good taste, Caesar's style is 'drily vivid',[1] yet it has the air throughout of simply stating the facts, in the one case concerning his campaigns in what are now France, Belgium, Western Germany and England, in the other in Marseille, Spain and Greece. How true his accounts really are was and is a disputed point; it is to be remembered that he was not writing for the benefit of posterity, but for his own defence against vigorous and often unscrupulous opponents, and for propaganda among the undecided. Some of what he says is second-hand, and his sources not always trustworthy, notably in his accounts of the fauna of the German forests and of the religion of the Germans. Some of his first-hand statements are obviously coloured; for instance, he glosses over the failure of his first campaign in Britain. But of actual misstatements of facts known directly to him it is hard to find any plausible example.

Another historian, and this time an original and excellent stylist, is Sallust (Gaius Sallustius Crispus), a Caesarian who, after a somewhat disreputable political career and a term of office as governor of the Roman province of Africa, which he plundered freely, settled down to write very able political

---

wrote a treatise on grammar, *De analogia*, dedicated to Cicero and composed on his way to Gaul, perhaps in 54 B.C.; a rather bulky work, *Anticato*, in reply to a laudation of Cato by Cicero, a number of speeches, well thought of by good judges in antiquity, and some verse, including a famous critique of Terence, known to us through Suetonius (p. 261), which calls him a half-Menander.

[1] Anonymous critique of a 'novel in the London *Times* of April 3, 1958. I have no means of discovering the reviewer's name.

pamphlets under the disguise of history with a high moral tone. His dates are 86-35 B.C., and his known writings three in number, of which we have two. He composed a history of the years 78-66, lost except for some fragments, a work *On the conspiracy of Catiline*, evidently his earliest attempt, and another on the campaigns against Jugurtha king of Mauretania. The former has Caesar for its hero, the supporter of strong but constitutional action, humane, patriotic and free from all self-seeking. Cicero plays a diminished part, and Cato is shown as the unpractical, if well-meaning and honest, foil to the clear-sighted Caesar. The *War with Jugurtha* is really a laudation of Marius, who was by this time a kind of patron saint of the 'popular' party to which Caesar belonged. The foil this time is Metellus, praised for his many virtues but shown as a typical noble with the typical noble vice of haughtiness; and after him Sulla, again shown in a favourable light, with just enough emphasis on the fact that his most notable service during the war was simply to carry out Marius' orders. No doubt the *History* took a similar line. But the greatest merit of Sallust's works is his style, that 'superhuman rapidity' which Quintilian (*Instit.* x, 1, 101-2, cf. p. 256) would not hesitate to set up as a rival to Thucydides (p. 120) himself. Archaisms help out the general tone of old-fashioned uprightness which colours the whole; the sentences are generally short or, if long, merely strung together from shorter units, rather than forming periods. The descriptions are always vigorous, and at their best when they convey the effect of hurried, confused action, as in the battle-scenes of the *Jugurtha*. The speeches are pointed and effective; and everywhere the author seems to cram into as few words as possible a maximum of meaning. In places, Sallust freely acknowledges his indebtedness to some of the greatest Greeks by almost literal translations from them. He provided history with a fitting style, from which Tacitus (p. 257) learned much; but he was himself no historian, but a pamphleteer.

There are, however, three pamphlets attributed to him which in my opinion he certainly did not write. They are an invective against Cicero, and two addresses, one a speech and the other a letter in form, to Caesar.

Several minor historians flourished at about the time when Sallust was writing. One was Aulus Hirtius (cf. p. 193), who wrote a continuation to Caesar's *Gallic War* (Book viii of the existing text) and perhaps an account of the operations at Alexandria and Caesar's return to Italy, which survives under the title *Bellum Alexandrinum*. Someone also has given us an account of the campaign in Africa in 46 B.C., and another and very bad writer, who however had first-hand knowledge of the facts, of that in Spain in 45. Another minor writer was Cornelius Nepos, who produced biographies, many of which survive, of men noteworthy in various capacities (generals, kings, Roman and perhaps Greek historians), also a compendium of history in three books. Those biographies which survive are mostly jejune and rather dry, and the style is poor; the Lives of Atticus and the elder Cato are more interesting.

A much more important author was Marcus Terentius Varro, usually called Varro simply. Born in 116 B.C. and surviving till 27, he became the most erudite man Rome ever produced, although he also took an active and not undistinguished part in public affairs and was in danger of his life in the proscriptions of 43. His productions ran into hundreds of book-rolls, mostly on learned subjects. It seems to have been his habit to write one major work on some topic, such as Roman antiquities or language, and add to it several shorter ones on particular points. But he also produced works of a purely literary type, notably his *Menippean satires* (or *miscellanies*), for the model of which compare p. 104. His greatest performance was his *Roman Antiquities*. Of all this there remains to us one work practically complete, the three books *Concerning Agriculture* (*De re rustica*), written in his eightieth year, and six books of the work *On the Latin Tongue* (*De lingua Latina*). Although the *Antiquities* are lost, they were so extensively drawn upon by later writers that we know a great deal about their contents. They were entitled in full *Antiquitates rerum humanarum et diuinarum*, that is to say the ancient history of the civil constitution of Rome and of her religious usages. The latter especially were treated at great length, for Varro was a Stoic, and as such saw in every cult some popular adumbration of what he conceived to be the fundamental truths of theology, and therefore an object worthy of sympathetic attention, and of course of interpretation in the light of his philosophy. He was not a distinguished stylist, but the fragments of his more popular works show lively humour and a vividness of description which must have redeemed them from dullness. His learning is so copious that it overflows everywhere, and we can gather scraps of useful information from the most unlikely contexts.

Second to Varro in erudition was Publius Nigidius, surnamed Figulus ('the Potter') on account, it was said, of the following incident. He was an astrologer, and on it being objected to him that people born at the same moment or very near it might have different fortunes, he set a potter's wheel in motion, flicked it twice with a paintbrush, and then showed the two marks some way apart. The heavens, he said, revolved much faster than the wheel, and so a very small difference in the time of birth was enough to account for varying destinies. Besides his astrology, a pseudo-science then gaining ground rapidly in the West, he was a neo-Pythagorean. Pythagoras' followers had ceased to be of any account, politically or philosophically, by about the time of Plato's death, although they survived long enough to influence him in some ways. Nigidius was one of those who foreshadowed the mystical and non-rational tendencies of the following centuries, and therefore took an interest in those parts of Pythagoreanism which could be interpreted as favouring their views. One result was the composition of a mass of spurious

'Pythagorean' works, attributed to early members of the school, and full of shameless borrowings from later philosophers, who were traduced as having themselves stolen from the Pythagoreans. Nigidius may have dabbled in magic also; at least, that was his reputation in later times. But he was also a serious scholar, and wrote extensively on a variety of topics, not all of them theological or mystic, though some were. The loss of his works is to be regretted from the historical point of view at least, though probably their purely literary value was but moderate.

When at last the establishment of Octavian (Augustus) in supreme power and the overthrow of his great rival Antony brought long-lasting peace to the world and a vast improvement in the machinery of government both at home and in the provinces, a marked difference was soon apparent in public life. It was no longer possible for any but one man to gain supreme power, and those who were politically ambitious must ultimately depend for their advancement on the favour of that one man, not of the corrupt urban multitude who in practice had been the electors of magistrates and the approvers of new laws, at least on all ordinary occasions. Hence oratory was at a discount, though still of importance, especially in the courts (to which was now added the Senate for certain political cases); but rhetoric remained as popular as ever, in fact became a craze and was sometimes the life-long study of men who put it to no use which Cicero or Caesar would have regarded as practical. Both in Greek and in Latin, it was taught, after the elementary stages were passed, by setting the pupils to compose speeches on imaginary themes, known as *controuersiae* and *suasoriae*. In the former, the 'controversy' regularly turned on some imaginary point of law; two statutes would be supposed to exist, and a case invented in which they might seem to contradict one another. For instance: in a certain city, great honours are decreed to those who distinguish themselves in war; in the same city, the penalty for robbing a holy place is death. A valiant citizen breaks his weapons in fighting the enemy, who are attacking the place. He takes dedicated arms from a temple and with them routs the enemy. Is he to be rewarded or executed? In a *suasoria*, the speaker was to imagine himself called upon to 'persuade' some real or mythical person to do or refrain from something; for instance, to advise the younger Cato for or against killing himself. Clearly, this made for artificiality, since none of these speeches was meant really to convince anyone, and the specimens we have in such writers as the elder Seneca ('rhetor') prove this. They consist regularly of short sentences, each containing or trying to contain some clever turn of phrase, what the Romans called a *sententia*, at any cost of remoteness from the language of genuine debate or pleading. This taint spreads to much of the subsequent literature, which all too commonly was divorced from any sort of natural human speech. On the other hand, great writers, such as Vergil or Livy, made rhetoric their servant, and, keeping the ability to write plainly, knew how to ornament their diction when the subject called for it and to invent new and telling phraseology.

The Imperial government was on the whole favourable to literature, and Augustus in particular, who was a master of propaganda, saw the importance of getting educated opinion on his side, and so did all he could, especially through his very able helper Maecenas (p. 202), to enlist men of talent to influence the growing numbers of those interested in literature. Scarcely an Emperor for the first two centuries of the Empire was without some pretensions to ability as a writer or speaker, and even the most tyrannical, such as Domitian, were well content that literature should flourish, provided always that it referred to them and their government, if at all, in tones of courtly and ingenious flattery.

Hence during the Augustan period, the government was able to attract and encourage several writers of outstanding merit. First in date and importance comes Vergil[1] (Publius Vergilius Maro), a member of a family neither wealthy nor distinguished, his father being a small landholder near Mantua (Mantova). Born on October 15, 70 B.C., he was given a good education, literary, rhetorical and philosophical, the last being under an Epicurean teacher, Siron by name. Shy and awkward, he failed utterly as a pleader, and henceforth devoted himself to literature, beginning to write at an early age,[2] but his career was interrupted by the civil wars, one consequence of which was that land was confiscated wholesale to form allotments for discharged soldiers. The seizures included the property of the elder Vergilius, but the son's genius came to the rescue. About 39 B.C. he published the ten *Eclogae* (*Selections*) or *Bucolica* ([*Poems*] *of the Countryside*) and thus attracted the attention of Maecenas, who may be described as the untitled Minister of Propaganda of the new government. Vergil's work consisted of extremely good and poetical adaptations of Theokritos (p. 132), full of allusions to contemporary events, which without unmanly flattery of Octavian extolled him and yet protested against the injustices done to the poet and his fellow-citizens of Mantua, while one magnificent poem, the fourth, predicted the coming of a golden age, heralded by the birth of a child. The child has never been satisfactorily identified, but the probabilities are that Vergil hoped for a son to be born to Octavian who should finish the work begun by his father of restoring peace and order to the distracted world. Henceforth the poet's personal prosperity was assured. He was compensated, it would appear, by the gift of an estate near Naples, and encouraged, even urged, to write more.

[1] The current misspelling Virgil (Virgile, Virgilio) has nothing but medieval and modern usage to recommend it.

[2] Besides the spurious poems (see p. 209), we have a little collection called *Catalepton* (Greek *kata lepton*, 'in small portions') of short pieces in various metres attributed to Vergil. It is probable that several of them are genuine early works of his, and the mastery of language and metre shown in the *Eclogues* presupposes long and diligent practice. He would never publish anything he thought imperfect.

The immediate result was the *Georgics*, begun about 36 B.C. and composed during the following seven years, for Vergil was a slow writer and his own most fastidious critic. Octavian was anxious to repopulate the countryside, which, owing among other things to the competition of cheap imported corn, was no longer occupied by hardy peasant farmers and small stockbreeders, as it once had been, but more and more by great estates (*latifundia*), which raised cattle on a large scale rather than cultivated the soil, and were managed for the most part by bailiffs with gangs of slave-labourers under them. Vergil's work, the next-best didactic poem after that of Lucretius (p. 176), was the production of a country-bred man, who did not idealize rustic life out of all recognition, for he insists on the hard work involved and does not minimize the dangers from unfavourable weather, cattle-plagues and other handicaps. Yet he draws a balance decidedly in favour of the small proprietor, such as his father had been. His advice is 'praise large estates, but cultivate a small one' (*Georg.* ii, 412–13). The poetical value of the poem lies not only in the magnificent digressions, on the glories of Italy, on the delights of country life, and, in varying tones as the situation changed, on the state of public affairs, but in the choice language in which he sets forth precepts which, by the testimony of later writers on the subject, were practically sound as well. They cover all the country activities, tilling the fields, arboriculture, the choice and breeding of large and small cattle and of horses, the preparation of vineyards and the care of the vines, and finally the keeping of bees, with a long concluding passage which gives the mythical origin of an alleged method for producing a new stock if the existing one died out.

Rome lacked a Homer, although some critics tried to persuade themselves that Ennius (p. 150) supplied the want. Vergil, prompted by Augustus, spent the rest of his life in composing his great epic, the *Aeneid* (*Aeneis*, poem concerning Aeneas), which he never completed to his satisfaction and

even wished to destroy when his last illness came on him, in
19 B.C. Fortunately for posterity, Augustus would not allow
this, and we have the poem as it left its author's hand, with
inconsistencies in the plot left standing and several verses not
finished, but with most of the work done, as no one else
could have done it. The problem was twofold, to give the
Latin-speaking world a new and modernized *Iliad* and
Odyssey and to embody the ideals of the Augustan régime.
Vergil hit on the idea of taking for his hero Aeneas (Aineias),
a prince of the junior branch of the Trojan royal family, who,
according to a tradition as old as Homer himself (*Iliad* xx,
316–17), survived the war and ruled over the remaining
Trojans. Later authors gradually elaborated a story[1] that he
emigrated to the West and founded, among other things, the
sanctuary of his mother Aphrodite at Eryx in Sicily. In time
the belief became established that either he or some descendant
of his had founded Rome. Vergil adopted the latter alternative. Aeneas is fated to settle in Italy, and the first six books of
the poem are concerned mainly with his adventurous journey-
ings towards his object, thus making a kind of *Odyssey*. Driven
on to the coast of Africa by a storm which Juno raises,[2] he
makes his way to Carthage, just founded by Dido, a Tyrian
princess. Juno, wanting to ruin his prospects of gaining Italy
by delaying him permanently in Africa, plots with Venus
(Aphrodite) to make Dido fall in love with him; the plot
succeeds, but before long Aeneas, reminded of his duty by a
peremptory message from Juppiter, leaves Carthage reluctantly; Dido, after pronouncing a formal curse on him and all

[1] There may be a grain of fact underlying this. The clan named after the
doubtfully historical Aineias, the Aineadai, seem to have actually moved west
and perhaps introduced the cult, at Eryx, of their local mother-goddess.

[2] Juno had long been identified with Hera, who in Homer is the implacable
enemy of Troy. She was also identified with the chief goddess of Carthage,
Tanit, and so has all the more reason for opposing the founder of that city's
greatest enemy and final destroyer. How the rather insignificant Venus rose
to be identified with so important a deity as Aphrodite is a question which has
never been satisfactorily answered.

his descendants, kills herself. Aeneas sails to Sicily, and there celebrates funeral games on the anniversary of the death of his father Anchises. He then, after leaving the weakest of his followers behind, goes on to Cumae, where he consults the Sibyl and, guided by her, enters the underworld, meets the ghosts of Dido, of many of his dead comrades, and finally of his father, who foretells his future and reveals something of the glories of the future Rome. This ends Aeneas' Odyssey, for the earlier part of his adventures since the fall of Troy form the subject of a long narrative to Dido at a banquet in Carthage. Now begins his Iliad. Latinus, king of the Latins, has a daughter Lavinia, who is destined to marry a foreigner. Aeneas is an obvious candidate for her hand, but has a rival favoured by Latinus' queen Amata, in the person of Turnus king of the Rutulians, who is not of pure Italian descent. A chance quarrel leads to an outbreak of war; Aeneas gets allies by visiting Euander, an Arkadian who has settled with a small following on the future site of Rome. Instructed by him, Aeneas gets command of a large body of Etruscans, in rebellion against their cruel king Mezentius, who have been told by a diviner that no native of Italy must lead them. Thus reinforced, he returns to his camp near the mouth of the Tiber, defeats Turnus and his followers in a series of battles, and finally, by agreement, fights a duel with Turnus and kills him.

The narrative is diversified by episodes rather suggested by than imitated from Homer; extraordinary adventures, with divine interventions now and again, during Aeneas' wanderings, with occasional allusions to episodes in the *Odyssey*; a much more elaborate visit to the world of the dead, containing the results of post-Homeric eschatological speculations, in which Vergil obviously was interested, for he appears to have abandoned Epicureanism by this time; a magnificent musterroll of the Italian peoples as they flock to the standard of Turnus; armour made for Aeneas by Vulcan (Hephaistos), as it is made for Achilles in the *Iliad*, but this time the decoration of the shield is a series of pictures from the future history of Rome, culminating in the defeat of Antony at Actium; there is even a truce between Aeneas and the Italians, which is treacherously broken, as that between the Achaians and Trojans is in Homer (p. 8). Of smaller imitations and reminiscences there are far too many to list. The great difficulty is the character of Aeneas himself, who has to be at once an Epic hero, an embodiment of the ideals and destinies of Rome, and at least a suggestion of Augustus and his policy. It is only fair to say that Vergil handled this complex figure better than anyone else could have done, but here and there the poem suffers from such multiplicity of aims. Another weakness is the patent dislike of the poet for slaughter and warfare generally, which makes the battle-scenes far less lively than in Homer; but this is to a great extent compensated by the deep pathos with which the deaths of several outstanding characters (Pallas, son of Euander, Camilla, an Amazonian ally of Turnus, Mezentius and his son Lausus, Turnus himself) are invested. The episode of Dido, again, is narrated with such sympathy for her that the verdict of most readers is against Aeneas, despite the obvious intention of the poet to show his sense of duty to his destiny rising superior to even strong and genuine passion.

The style of the whole poem and the manner in which many episodes are handled show the influence of much post-Homeric literature; for instance, Dido would not be so moving a figure were it not for the reminiscences of Medeia in Euripides and in Apollonios (pp. 73, 130), and there are many passages which imitate or otherwise borrow from noteworthy models in Greek poetry of all ages and also the older Latin writers, not least Ennius, whose very rhythms are now and then introduced with impressive and archaic effect.

The influence of the Aeneid can be traced in all later Epic, both classical and post-classical. Direct imitations of it are patent in such writers as Valerius Flaccus and Statius (pp. 253,

252); in Silius Italicus (p. 251) the slavish following of Vergil is one of the features which make him insufferable. The moderns, besides indulging in much futile controversy as to whether Homer or Vergil was the more admirable poet, learned chiefly from the latter how to construct and diversify a long poem. It is an unfortunate fact that many of the attempts to revive or continue Epic tradition, whether Homeric or Vergilian, have had but poor results, and the present outlook is very unfavourable for that sort of composition, though some of our longer novels, or sequences of novels, have now and then something of an Epic flavour. However, literature owes much to a tradition which, besides the great Italian writers, has given us *Paradise Lost* in serious and *The Rape of the Lock* in burlesque poetry. One standing difficulty for a modern is that the so-called Epic machinery, the frequent interventions of gods, must be entirely unreal to him, mere stage-properties, and well worn at that. He must therefore either omit them altogether or (as Milton does) alter them to suit a wholly different theological outlook. In antiquity, this difficulty did not exist, for to early Epic such incidents were of a kind which had occurred now and then, in popular belief and probably in that of the poets themselves, and so might occur again, while to such writers as Vergil, the traditional gods were still objects of public and private cult, and stood for realities of some sort, at least for some kind of direction of human history by a superhuman power.

As to the posthumous effects of Vergil's other works, Pastoral poetry is now out of fashion, and deservedly so, for after Vergil it became artificial and empty to a degree. Theokritos had had imitators who, to judge from what is left of them, were sometimes pretty but seldom anything better. We know the names of two, Bion and Moschos. The latter may have lived about 150 B.C., the former somewhat later; we do not know his date. Better work than theirs was done by two nameless writers, one the author of the eighth Theokritean idyll, a charming though quite artificial description of a singing-contest between two shepherd-boys, and the other the composer of a lament for the death of Bion, which rises in places to real poetry and has the distinction of suggesting to Milton much of the framework at least of *Lycidas*, though that owes quite as much to the first idyll of Theokritos himself and the tenth Eclogue of Vergil. In Latin the *Eclogues* found imitators, but of no great poetical powers. One, T. Calpurnius Siculus, lived under Nero, whom he flatters outrageously, another, Nemesianus (in full, M. Aurelius Olympius Nemesianus), of Carthage, was of the third century, and besides his bucolic attempts wrote a didactic poem on hunting. That Pastoral had a great revival in and after the Renaissance is well known; it was attempted, often not badly, in Latin by a whole series of writers, from Ioannes Baptista Mantuanus to Milton and beyond, and in the vernacular by a host of others, including, in our own tongue, Spenser and Pope. But its best and truest followers were those who, like Burns and others, wrote of the country people of their day as they saw them and in the dialect they used, without attempting to be either Theokritean or Vergilian, and thus caught the spirit and something of the tone of those masters by going for material where they went. If Theokritos could be brought to life and made acquainted with Ayrshire Scots, he would accept Burns' Hallowe'en as a companion piece to his own description of a harvest festival in the seventh idyll, rather than any of the performances of the sedulous imitators of him and his Latin follower.

Didactic poetry has on the whole come to little. It was attempted by a number of Latin writers, mostly minor, but without rising to the heights of either Lucretius or Vergil. A certain Grattius, of whom we know nothing except that he came from the town of Faliscae, whence he is sometimes surnamed Faliscus, wrote a poem on hunting (*Cynegetica*), whereof a part survives. An unknown writer, possibly that

Lucilius who was a friend of the younger Seneca (p. 244), took Mount Etna for his subject, and the resulting poem, *Aetna*, was absurdly attributed to Vergil by some later readers. It is not without interest as an exposition of ancient theory concerning volcanoes, and it now and then has poetical merit, though not of the highest order. Ovid (p. 224) gave the *genre* a humorous turn in his *Arts*, and there were others, the most noteworthy being Manilius, who wrote, under Augustus and Tiberius, five books concerning astrology, in which he evidently believed, though he was no great expert on the subject. He was highly ingenious in getting dull technical matter into correct hexameters, and occasionally, when the subject allows it, he shows a certain eloquence which is sometimes even poetical. But none of the greatest post-classical work has been of this kind. Even Pope is not at his best in the *Essay on Man*, and while John Philips' *Cyder* is pleasant reading, no one would call it a great poem. Today, if a writer wants to be interesting and discursive on some topic which might be the subject of a technical handbook, garden-ing, for instance, on which Columella (p. 267) composed a book of not contemptible verse, he uses prose.

The greatness of Vergil and the immense esteem in which he was justly held resulted in sundry masterless works being passed off as his. The most notorious of these is also the poorest, the *Culex* (Spenser's *Virgiles Gnat*). A shepherd is bitten by a gnat as he lies asleep, kills it, and finds that its bite has roused him in time to avoid the attack of a poisonous snake. Haunted in sleep by the ghost of the gnat, he makes it an elaborate miniature tomb. This rather silly little story is embellished with a good deal of mythological and other information, supposed to be imparted by a speaker who clearly is Vergil to a 'holy child', Octavius, obviously the future Octavian (Augustus). The metre is of a kind posterior to Ovid, and the whole the patent forgery of some foolish pedant. The *Ciris*, dealing with the story of Skylla, who betrayed her father Nisos king of Megara, for love of his enemy Minos king of Crete, is much better, and that it is somehow related to Vergil is proved by several phrases which they have in common. It is probably the production of some tolerable minor poet who knew Vergil's works well. Of the *Aetna* I have already spoken (p. 209). The *Copa* (*Hostess at the Inn*) is a charming sketch in elegiacs of the invitation a woman gives to travellers to stop and refresh themselves at what we might perhaps call her road-house; Servius the commentator on Vergil says it is his, but it is not at all like his style. The *Moretum* has no external authority earlier than the Middle Ages for attaching it to Vergil; it is in a somewhat later kind of hexameters than he wrote, and is a sympathetic sketch of the early morning occupations of a peasant, who sets forth on his day's work provided with a bannock and a *moretum*, a preparation of herbs and cheese pounded together. Whoever composed it was a very tolerable poet, with a kindly interest in the poor and a knack of gentle mock-heroic. He lived under the early Empire.

Vergil had a friend who resembled him in little save that he was amiable, unambitious and an excellent poet. This was Horace (Q. Horatius Flaccus), 65–8 B.C. Son of a *libertinus* (see chap. v, p. 165, n. 2), he was given a good education by his father, caught up in the civil wars which followed the assassination of Caesar, served under Brutus, escaped with his life to find his estate confiscated, got a small governmental post, and by his own account (*Epp*. ii, 2, 51) sheer poverty emboldened him to try his hand at verse-writing. Here he found his true occupation, for he had such skill as no Roman had hitherto possessed at certain kinds of metre, and withal something to say. He was not a profound thinker, nor a fanatical enthusiast for any doctrine, nor had he very strong emotions to express; but he had shrewd common-sense, a genuine feeling for sane, right living, sympathy with various moods and much interest in mankind and its curious and often ridiculous ways. His first attempts were adaptations of the metres and something of the manner of Archilochos (p. 30), which he collected and published in a book of moderate size entitled simply *Epodes*, from one of its characteristic metres, a longer line followed by a shorter one. Sometime during the composition of these little pieces he was introduced to Maecenas, who evidently was favourably impressed, encouraged him to publish and attended to his material wants by giving him a small estate in the Sabine territory (it has been recognized from his description of the neighbourhood and is one of the local 'sights'), on which he lived in modest comfort, besides having a residence of some kind in Rome. He easily made his peace with the government, of which he had never been a very formidable opponent, and thenceforth was a loyal supporter of Augustus, though, like Vergil, he never descended to low flattery, which indeed would not have been acceptable to the Emperor. About 35 B.C. he brought out a book of 'familiar talks' (*sermones*) as he called them, satires as most people have styled them since, containing among other things gently humorous rebukes, not so much of gross vice as of follies of various kinds. He followed this up with a second book, about five years later, containing still better work. A new departure was three books, brought out in 23, of lyric poems, the *Odes* as they are generally called, his own name for them being simply 'poems', *carmina*. The metres are those of the Greek solo lyricists (pp. 33 ff.), among whom, again by his own testimony, he especially admired Alkaios (*Odes* ii, 13, 26 ff.; Alkaios in the shades has a 'golden' lyre, and his music is 'fuller' than Sappho's; the other ghosts listen to both with attention, but prefer him). It therefore is not wonderful that his most serious poems are generally in the metre named after that poet. To write in this or any other metre of solo lyric needed many delicate modifications before it would fit the rhythms of Latin, and Horace made them, no doubt after long practice, and with some few small

P

improvements added as he wrote more odes, as we can see if we examine them carefully. The subjects vary, and Horace has arranged the poems in such order as to bring out the variety. Thus in Book i, No. 27 is a banqueting scene; the speaker, presumably Horace himself, quells an outbreak of rowdy drunkenness and extorts from another guest a confession of an unfortunate love-affair. No. 28 is a monologue by the ghost of a drowned traveller, cast ashore near the tomb of Archytas the great mathematician, to whom he addresses reflections on the brevity and uncertainty of our life, followed by an appeal to a passing sailor to give his body at least formal burial. No. 29 is a humorous reproach to a friend who is thinking of giving up his philosophical studies to go campaigning in the East, No. 30 an eight-line hymn to Venus, who is asked to enter the house of a certain Glycera, and No. 31 a prayer to Apollo, with a passing reference to his new and splendid temple just erected on the Palatine by Augustus. All these poems, and the rest of the collection, are in exquisitely subtle language, artificial indeed, but somehow sounding natural as Horace uses it, and written with full mastery of the difficult metres. Translation of them has been attempted times without number, but adequate rendering into a modern language is still to seek, owing not only to the general felicity of diction which Horace shows but specifically to the amazing skill of his word-order, which exploits the possibilities of a highly inflected idiom to the full. He is equally successful with the lightest and the most serious themes; of the latter, the most famous are the six 'Roman' odes which begin Book iii, and advocate the traditional virtues of the nation, moderation, hardihood and so forth, with sufficient complimentary references or allusions to Augustus to remind the reader that these were the very principles which his government endeavoured to revive. Great events of the time have their adequate commemoration, notably the triumph over Antony and Kleopatra and all that they stood for, at Actium (*Odes* i,

37). Horace was justifiably proud of his achievement, and proclaims in the last poem of the collection that he has erected an imperishable monument to himself.

Thus he had given his nation a modernized Lucilius, adapted to the tastes both literary and social of the age, and brought into Latin the full range of Greek technique in the composition of all but the most elaborate choral lyric poetry. His successes did not turn his head, for he continues to refer to himself in the most modest way, never concealing but rather gently emphasizing his lowly origin and in particular speaking with tender gratitude of his father; his mother he never mentions, though there is a passing reference to his nurse (iii, 4, 9; her name was Pullia), therefore it is probable that she died while he was a small child. His affectionate loyalty to Maecenas shows itself in poem after poem, and we know that he was also on almost familiar terms with Augustus himself, who thought highly of him and wrote to him in a friendly, jocular manner on occasion.

There was another form of composition which Lucilius had used and Horace now took up, the letter in verse. As already mentioned (p. 195), the epistle was a recognized form of literature, and the rhetoricians could and did give directions for its composition and models of how to write it. It must not be quite formless, yet not too formal, something between casual conversation and elaborate oratory or history. It therefore was a fit matter for verse which should not be too pretentious, while preserving a tone somewhat above everyday language. The subject of such a work might be anything the writer pleased, provided that it could be adequately handled at moderate length; for there is no topic on which one might not conceivably write to an acquaintance. For a man like Horace, who could chat agreeably in verse on all manner of subjects, it was an ideal form of expression, and the collection of twenty *Letters* (*Epistulae*) which he brought out about 20 B.C. contains some of his best work. It varies from a charming letter of introduction (No. 9), which I think may very well have been actually sent to Tiberius, the future Emperor, to recommend an acquaintance who wished to join his staff, and some directions (No. 13) to a messenger on the right manner of delivering a presentation copy of the *Odes* to Augustus, through gently philosophical disquisitions to a comparatively long address (108 lines) to Maecenas, containing a broad hint that he wishes to write no more verse but devote himself to the right ordering of his remaining years.[1]

But whatever Horace's intentions were, he was not left to philosophize for the rest of his life. Augustus wanted a poem addressed to himself, indeed sent the poet a jocular letter in which he asked if he was afraid that it would harm his reputation with posterity to have it known that they were on friendly terms. Horace produced what was asked for, in the form of a long letter in verse, dealing with the state of literature and also with what had already begun, the controversy between the Ancients and the Moderns. It was published (no doubt Augustus had been sent a separate copy beforehand) with another, addressed to Julius Florus, an officer on Tiberius' staff in the East, as a second book of *Epistles*. Sometime in the concluding years of his life he wrote a third letter on literary topics, published separately (it is 476 lines long), and generally called the *Art of Poetry* (*Ars poetica*), sometimes the *Letter to*

[1] Incidentally, I think it is a misunderstood passage in the *Epistles* which presented the Middle Ages with a new writer on the Troy-saga. Chaucer (*Hous of Fame*, 1468) mentions a certain Lollius among those who 'were besy for to bere up Troye'; now Horace begins the second Epistle thus: *Troiani belli scriptorem, Maxime Lolli, dum tu declamas Romae, Praeneste relegi*, i.e. 'while you, Lollius, were practising rhetoric at Rome, I have been at Praeneste, re-reading Homer.' But to an unskilled Latinist, such as I was when I first read the *Epistles*, it might seem that *declamas* governs *scriptorem* and that to 'declaim Homer' was to compose something elaborately eloquent on his subjects. The real Lollius was a young man of good family, in whose prospects Horace evidently took a friendly interest, for he addresses him again in No. 18, with some worldly-wise advice. A modern editor or two have actually misconstrued the passage as above, but without making young Lollius a composer of Epic on the Homeric model. It would, I think, be found on examination that a few more ghostly writers could be exorcised by discovering the literary errors which set them haunting.

the Pisos, from its addressees, a father and his sons, probably
Lucius Calpurnius Piso (49 B.C.–A.D. 32) and his family. It is
founded on a handbook by a certain Neoptolemos of Parion,
the outlines of which, for part of it is preserved, can be made
out under the informal treatment of poetry generally and
drama in particular (perhaps Piso tried to write plays) of
which the poem consists. Being by Horace, it contains much
common-sense and good advice on composition, and is the
ancestor of an honourable line of similar pieces, including
Vida's Latin poem *De arte poetica* (about 1525), Boileau's *Art
poétique*, and Pope's *Essay on Criticism* (1709). It hardly need
be said that it has been misunderstood, like other products of
ancient criticism. No one ever became a great poet by studying it, but not many writers do not need to be warned by it
of various absurdities into which they might easily fall.

Horace's lyric vein was not allowed to run dry, for Augustus
wanted a hymn for his Secular Games of 17 B.C., and the poet
obliged with as fine a poem as such an occasion is likely ever
to produce. It never was included in a book of odes, but
survives separately and is usually called the *Carmen saeculare*.
There were also exploits of various members of the Imperial
house to commemorate, and if there can be said to have been
a court poet it was Horace, now that Vergil was dead. Odes
on these events, together with some shorter pieces, made up a
fourth book, which is not his best, but much better than anyone else could then have written. Its date is somewhere about
13 B.C.

These two great poets were never forgotten by posterity,
least of all by writers of every age and every degree of merit.
Vergil came to be regarded as a repository of all learning, at
least (as in Dante) all secular learning and wisdom. For late
antiquity, we may refer to the *Saturnalia* of Ambrosius
Theodosius Macrobius, an official of high rank under the late
Empire (he flourished about A.D. 400). This, his longest work,
was of the same kind as that of Athenaios (p. 237), and in it

there is a long discussion of Vergil, extending to several books, in which his 'deep learning' (*profunda scientia*, iii, 2, 7) and other admirable qualities are set forth. Another side-light on the reverence felt for him is thrown by that curious and muddle-headed pretender to scholarship, Fabius Planciades Fulgentius, about a century later than Macrobius. In his *Exposition of the contents of Vergil according to the moral Philosophers* (*Vergiliana continentia* for short), he professes to have been instructed by the poet himself that the *Aeneid* is an edifying allegory of human life. With this start, it is not wonderful that to the Middle Ages Vergil was a powerful sorcerer, to whom many tales of wonder attached.[1] But, apart from his personal renown, Vergil was an important contributor to the lasting popularity of the Troy-saga, especially to its pro-Trojan colouring. It was not only medieval Europe which held that

> *Omere made lyes,*
> *Feyninge in his poetryes,*
> *And was to Grekes favorable.*
>
> – Chaucer, *Hous of Fame*, 1475–7.

Later antiquity even produced an ingenious rhetorician, Dion of Prusa, surnamed Chrysostomos (Golden-mouth), who proved to the citizens of New Ilion that their city had never been taken by the Greeks at all.[2] But more important are two alleged contemporaries of the siege, known to later times as Dares and Dictys. A papyrus found at Tebtunis in Egypt contains a fragment of the work of the latter, in Greek of perhaps the second century A.D.; it had already been suspected that a

[1] See for particulars D. Comparetti, *Virgil in the Middle Ages*, trans. from the Italian by E. F. M. Benecke, London, 1895, and later ed.; J. W. Spargo, *Virgil the Necromancer*, Cambridge, Mass., 1934. Spargo notes that the magical tradition is relatively late (twelfth century) and supposes it to be of German, not Italian origin. Certainly many of the tales were not originally told of Vergil.

[2] Dion Chrysostom, *Orat.* xi (10). He lived in the first and early second centuries, cf. p. 277.

Greek original of his work existed. This impudent forger gave out that he had been a follower of Idomeneus the Cretan chieftain during the war, and favoured the world with his memoirs. Another fictionist may have written in Greek, but we have him in a sixth-century Latin text; his alleged name was Dares the Phrygian, and so he could tell the tale from the Phrygian, that is Trojan side.[1] Dictys found a translator in a certain Lucius Septimius, who probably wrote in the fourth century of our era, and the Middle Ages took both writers at their face value. Their real worth, save as a link in the long history of the saga, is *nil*. It need hardly be said that with the coming of romances of chivalry the classical heroes became medieval knights, which indeed, save for outward details, is not very far wrong, since both alike are members of an aristocratic, land-holding class, but the details are prominent; Homer's Trojans, for instance, would not have elaborately romantic love-affairs, still less write pathetic letters to their mistresses, as Chaucer's Troilus does. One great addition to the narrative was made when Troilus, who appears in classical tradition as a young son of Priam, slain by Achilles, is made to fall in love with the faithless Cressida (her name is variously spelled and is in any case a corruption of Chryseis), thus furnishing Chaucer with the plot of one of his finest poems and Shakespere with material for that strange and bitter comedy which bears the names of the lovers. The popularity of the themes connected with Troy did not end with the Middle Ages nor with the times of the first Elizabeth and her successor, for scarcely a month, certainly hardly a year, passes without some work, long or short, appearing which handles some part of the story, seriously or by way of parody or burlesque, in prose or in verse, in one European language or another. Naturally the specifically Roman sympathies have now evaporated. For a while, Trojan origins were claimed

[1] Post-Homeric authors continually regard the Trojans as a kind of Phrygians, which in Homer they certainly are not.

by modern European countries; in Britain, the story of Brut
and his conquest of the island was not only a theme for
imaginative writing, from Layamon onwards, but was
actually accepted as sober history for so long that there was
need of the stinging criticism of it by Buchanan in Book ii of
his *Historia Scotorum*. This whole fiction was but a continuation of the tendency which we saw in the story of Aeneas. All
respectable nations had fabulous origins, for choice either
Greek or Trojan; therefore the British nation and all its
component parts must have such an origin, regardless of such
trifling difficulties as the Latin name of a Trojan hero (whose
native language, according to a writer cited by Buchanan,
was Welsh), and etymologies marvellous even for their date.
Perhaps we ought not to quarrel with an artificial legend
which has given us such good verses as those of Kipling,

> Oak of the clay lived many a day
> Or ever Aeneas began;
> Ash of the loam was a lady at home
> When Brut was an outlaw man;
> Thorn of the down saw New Troy Town,[1]
> Whereof was London born;
> Witness these three the ancientry
> Of Oak and Ash and Thorn.

As to Horace, it has already been said (p. 212) that attempts
to translate him have met with but poor success. Imitation has
proved more profitable. It would be an endless task to give
anything like a list of the odes, poetical addresses and so
forth which have taken their inspiration from him. I mention
a single instance, interesting because geographically it could

---

[1] Troynovant, the alleged original name of London. It is pretty certainly
made up from the tribal name Trinobantes, found in Caesar and Tacitus. The
Middle Ages made but little difference between *b* and *v* in writing and in some
Romance languages, notably Spanish, the two sounds were confused in pronunciation, while such trifles as the different vocalization of *Troia* and *Tri-*
would trouble etymologists of that time not at all.

hardly be further from Rome to be in Europe at all. In *The New Shetlander*, No. 44 (Autumn, 1956), p. 11, appeared a pretty little poem, 'Da wal gaet', in the local dialect. It is confessedly an imitation of Horace, *Odes* iii, 13, the address to the fountain of Bandusia, near his farm, and takes for its subject a well ('wal') which the author remembers from his earlier days, when it was the water-supply for the near-by houses. It is amusing to speculate what Horace would have thought if it could have been foretold him that he would be read with affectionate interest and imitated in a tongue as yet unborn, in a land which to him was the very ends of the earth. Adaptations of passages in the *Odes* with modern names and allusions in place of the classical ones are also common enough; some will be found in Thomas Moore, for example. Perhaps the most fruitful sources of suggestions to moderns have been the Satires and Epistles. I have already (p. 214) spoken of the *Ars poetica* and its long line of successors; the most obvious, and the best, adaptations to modern language, metre and background of the moralizing and critical poems are without doubt those of Pope, who loved Horace, as Matthew Prior had done before him, witness his picture of himself driving through The Hague with 'on my left hand my Horace, a nymph on my right' (*The Secretary*, 1696). That Prior read his Horace assiduously is plain from nearly every poem he ever wrote; but it was Pope who imitated him with such ability as to be often as good as the original, sometimes better, or at least more vivid, for he was less restrained than the Latin poet in his personal allusions. Thus, both alike complain of the false taste of the day for empty shows on the stage; what they would have thought of the modern cinema, with its expensively photographed settings and 'stars' who as often as not cannot act, is an interesting speculation. Horace's stricture may be roughly translated thus:

> On steps the player, decked in foreign gauds,
> And clapping hand on hand at once applauds.

> *But why the noise? He has said nothing yet.*
> *He wears Tarentine wool dyed violet.*
>
> – *Epp.* ii, 1, 204-7.

Pope, taking his hint from the older writer, livens the picture by bringing in the greatest actor and most famous tragedy of the time:

> *Booth enters – hark! the Universal peal!*
> *'But has he spoken?' Not a syllable.*
> *What shook the stage, and made the People stare?*
> *Cato's long Wig, flow'r'd gown, and lacquer'd chair.*
>
> – *Imitations of Horace*, Epistle i, 334-6.

And one might easily cite a hundred passages in which English wit and sarcasm contend with Latin.

One important branch of poetry neither Vergil nor Horace attempted, at least on any large scale; the former is supposed to have written a few short pieces in elegiacs. Alexandria had set the fashion for telling love-stories in this metre (cf. p. 130), but, so far as we know, no one of that age had tried to do what Mimnermos in his time (p. 27) and Antimachos in the fourth century B.C. had attempted, to tell of his own amours, real or imaginary, in a series of poems. This certainly the Latins now did. The first of the series was C. Cornelius Gallus, a native of Forum Iulii (Fréjus), who rose high in the service of Augustus, fell suddenly through his own folly, and committed suicide, while still quite young. He was a thorough Alexandrian in taste, imitating especially the obscure style of the minor poet Euphorion, for some reason very popular with the writers of his time (he was born in 69 B.C.). His works were excluded from the public libraries after his disgrace and death, though not destroyed, for Quintilian knew them (p. 256); we have lost them. They included a number of poems addressed to a woman whom he called Lycoris, her real name, or at least what may be termed her stage name, for she was an actress,[1] being Cytheris. She was a beauty, and notorious, having been the mistress of several men, including Mark Antony, and it seems that she left Gallus for some more profitable admirer. We can judge of the value of these pieces only by Vergil's obvious admiration for them and equally obvious friendship for their author; the tenth *Eclogue* is addressed to Gallus. The next name is that of Albius Tibullus, an acquaintance of Horace, who addresses one of the *Epistles* to him (*Epp.* i, 4). He was attached, not to Maecenas but to a contemporary patron of literature, Marcus Valerius Messalla Corvinus, himself a writer and speaker of some merit. He was in comfortable circumstances when Horace wrote to him, though he had, like Vergil and Horace himself, suffered losses through the confiscation of property to provide allotments for soldiers. His works, besides several pieces not on amatory subjects, consist of addresses, in his first book, to a woman he calls Delia (her real name was Plania), and in the second, to a courtesan named Nemesis,[2] of whom he was much enamoured, without deceiving himself as to her character. Of the other poems, one in particular (ii, 1) is a charming description of a country rite, the annual lustration of the fields, i.e. the tracing of a kind of magic circle about them to keep good in and evil out. There are two other books (some would run them together into one) of what is commonly called the Tibullan corpus. They contain, besides one poem which may be a stray composition of Tibullus himself, specimens of the work of other members of Messalla's

[1] She was a *mima*, appearing in a kind of farce called *mimus*, which differed from most plays in that the female parts were played by women. Neither the plays themselves nor the women who took part in them were of high repute for morality or decency. As to the name, it was the convention, at least when mentioning a woman of any position or shred of reputation in amatory poetry, to use a name which was not hers but scanned like it, as Lesbia for Clodia, Delia for Plania, and so forth.

[2] Probably her real name, for there is no tradition that she had any other and there was no need to be reticent about a woman of her class and profession.

literary circle. They are of very unequal value, but six are the pretty love-poems of someone who calls himself Lygdamus and six more the clearly real addresses of a Roman lady, by name Sulpicia, to her lover. A more important poet is Sextus Propertius, a native of Asisium (Assisi), most of whose life centres around his affair, lasting some six years, with a freed-woman named Hostia, but in his verse Cynthia. Three books, of dates ranging from a little before 31 B.C. to about the end of 23,[1] are concerned more with Cynthia than with any other topic, even the recurrent one of excuses for not writing what might be called official poetry, as Maecenas tried to induce him to do. A fourth, not earlier than 16 B.C., still has two poems concerning her, one a macabre account of how her ghost visited him, but the rest is on other themes, especially anti-quarian, with a very fine elegy, as we might call it, on the death of a lady of noble family, into whose mouth he puts a really moving address to her surviving husband. Propertius has throughout more power and intenser passion than Tibullus, also more display, perhaps too much, of his mythological learning, which, after the Alexandrian fashion, is considerable. Whether he or Tibullus is preferred is now, as it was in the time of Quintilian (*Inst. orat.* x, 1, 93), a matter of taste. Last of the series, and on the border between Golden and Silver Latin, comes Ovid (Publius Ovidius Naso), of Sulmo (Sulmona), who was sent to Rome for his education and there distinguished himself in the rhetorical schools. He was in-tended for a public career, but abandoned it after holding one minor magistracy, to devote himself to poetry, for which he had a great natural aptitude, so far, that is, as versification went, for he lacked the deep feelings of a true and great poet. On the other hand, there never was a cleverer rhetorician in verse, nor anyone who could tell a story in verse better, unless

[1] The dates are approximately certain, the arrangement less so; some would divide the traditional second book into two. The text-tradition of Propertius is unfortunately bad, apparently going back to one copy which was both defective and confused by the misplacing of pages, hence many uncertainties.

it be Chaucer, who like many poets of the Middle Ages and Renaissance, knew his work intimately. One of his earliest publications was the 'Loves' (*Amores*), in five books, which he revised and shortened to the three which we have, presumably by omitting those poems which he thought poorest and perhaps re-writing some of the rest. Being obviously of independent though modest means, he never attached himself to either Maecenas or Messalla, and though his poems breathe decorous loyalty to Augustus and his government, he wrote nothing of the nature of even the most indirect propaganda. Another early production was a series of typical rhetorical exercises. To write a letter supposed to be from some well-known person on an occasion famous in myth or history was a variety of the *suasoria* (p. 201), when it was not simply narrative; Ovid produced fourteen letters in eleg,acs, addresses from heroines (hence the general title, *Heroides*) to their husbands or lovers; Penelope to Odysseus, Briseis to Achilles, Laodameia to Protesilaos, and so forth. Much later, he enlarged and revised the book, adding a letter from Sappho to Phaon (cf. p. 37) and pairs of letters supposedly exchanged between Paris and Helen, Leandros and Hero, Akontios and Kydippe. Sometimes a doubt has been expressed, but I think unnecessarily, about the genuineness of these additional letters. If they are spurious, they are early and very good imitations of his style, and that he had imitators is certain. One, called Sabinus[1] (we do not know the rest of his name), wrote an answer or answers to some of the original fourteen *Heroides*, and someone, whose name is completely unknown, composed an amusing little poem, the *Nut-tree* (*Nux*), which deceived many into taking it for genuine Ovid. It is the complaint of a nut-tree growing by the roadside and so exposed to the pilfering of every passer-by.

---

[1] This we know from Ovid himself, *Ex Ponto* iv, 16, 13–14, where he specified only a reply by Odysseus to Penelope's letter, but there may of course have been others. He adds that Sabinus died young leaving a poem, apparently epic, unfinished. We know no more about him.

Ovid's masterpieces are a kind of mock-serious didactic, the *Art of Love* (*Ars Amoris*, or *Amatoria*) and the *Cure of Love* (*Remedium Amoris*). He began by writing a poem about cosmetics, the *De medicamine faciei*, to give it its probably medieval title, of which a hundred lines survive, but the *Arts* themselves are much longer, more elaborate and infinitely more readable. The *Art of Love* deals with the relations between the courtesans of Rome and their admirers, Books i and ii from the men's standpoint, Book iii from the women's. As it was proper that a man should sooner or later give up such affairs and settle down to decorous married life, the *Cure* discusses the best ways of falling out of love again. Between them, they give us a brilliant picture of the amoral, but not unrefined or even unintellectual, life of the Roman *demi-monde*, and they are interspersed with all manner of interesting episodes, including mythological excursuses, which Ovid handles lightly and well, at least as well as any surviving Alexandrian.

All these works are in elegiacs. Ovid was a past master of that metre, and gave it its final form, as Pope did to the couplet which he made his own. Departures from his norm of euphony and rhythm are in future either the result of imperfect skill or belong to Epigram, which goes its own way. He now tried his hand at hexameters, and here again he showed both his skill and his limitations. His verses lack the variety of rhythm and pauses which are so characteristic of Vergil, and tend to be too much like one another, too regular and smooth, and thus have something of a machine-made effect, though each one taken by itself is a good line. His model seems to have been Kallimachos, with hints taken from Nikandros (pp. 127, 136). Like the former, he wrote a long poem which consists of a number of episodes of moderate length ingeniously joined together in a framework of narrative and, like the latter, he took for his subject tales of shape-changing, his title being *Metamorphoses*. The fifteen books into which it is divided begin with the greatest metamorphosis of all, from chaos to the ordered universe, and end with the latest event of the kind, the change of the man Julius Caesar into the officially recognized god Diuus Iulius. He had not quite finished revising this, his longest work, when his career at Rome was brought to a sudden end, by a sentence of relegation to Tomis (probably Constanza, on the Black Sea). The reason is unknown. The official excuse was the alleged immorality and consequent ill-effects upon public ethics of the *Arts*, a feeble figment which no one can have seriously believed. He himself repeatedly says that he was guilty of no great crime, but had been imprudent, seen what he ought not to see, and been betrayed. The old story that he was one of the lovers of the notorious Julia, granddaughter of the Emperor, is merely silly; he was about fifty years old, distinguished only for his literature, and she could make her choice among the richest and handsomest young men of the Empire. But that he was somehow privy to some intrigue of hers is likely enough. He was good-natured, and of too shallow character to understand how profoundly Augustus was hurt by her flagrant ignoring of his own honest attempts to raise the level of morality among his people. Consequently he could probably have been beguiled or flattered into acting as her go-between or in some such capacity. At all events, he was relegated (cf. p. 184, n. 1), and never recalled. He still, however, had his poetry to console him. After a burst of despair on the eve of leaving Rome, during which he burned much that he had written, including the *Metamorphoses* (fortunately preserved to posterity in copies belonging, one must suppose, to his acquaintance), he began composing again while still on his way to Tomis. The total result was the five books of *Tristia* (understand something like *carmina*, i.e. sad poems or compositions) and the four *Ex Ponto* (messages from the Black Sea), which contain endless variations on the sadness of his lot, the horrors of the climate and the savage peoples of the country, and his desire for recall or at least removal to a more tolerable place of exile. They also tell us much about himself, including an autobiography (*Trist.* iv, 10). Besides these he relieved his feelings against those former friends who had turned against him in his misfortune by writing his *Ibis*. The original poem of this title had been Kallimachos' polemic against Apollonios (cf. p. 130); Ovid addresses no real person, but a lay figure, whom he curses at length, invoking on him all the horrible dooms he can think of, mythological or historical, always in allusions which sometimes are puzzlingly obscure. He also worked at an ambitious project, no less than the versifying of the Roman calendar, the history of which he had probably studied in Verrius Flaccus (cf. p. 264). He says he had written twelve books, i.e. one for each month, before his banishment (*Trist.* ii, 549), but we have only the first six, in a partly revised edition dating from after the death of Augustus (A.D. 14). Perhaps he had no more than drafted the rest. At all events, it is an ingenious poem, full of interesting, though second-hand, information and typical prettinesses to boot. Its title is simply *Fasti* (*The Calendar*), and it has received elaborate treatment in the large edition in five volumes (London, 1929) by the late Sir J. G. Frazer, besides many others, whole or partial, large or small, several being of great merit.

Ovid survived Augustus by about three years. Tiberius, always meticulously careful to follow the precedents of his great predecessor, made no move to recall him, and he died at Tomis, where, despite his incessant plaints, he seems to have settled fairly comfortably, even to the extent, if we will believe his own testimony,[1] of learning the local speech and composing a poem in it. He was at all events not in want, for relegation did not involve confiscation of property, at least in the form inflicted upon him. Nor were his works in any effective way suppressed, though some of them (including a

---

[1] *Ex Ponto* iv, 13, 19 ff. It was a panegyric on Augustus and his household. The Getae, he assures us, thought it very fine.

tragedy, *Medea*, which was well thought of in antiquity) are lost to us. They were indeed excluded from the public libraries, but there was nothing to prevent private individuals possessing and reading copies, witness for instance the persistency with which the younger Seneca imitates him in his prose. The Middle Ages read him, though with a somewhat uneasy conscience, as not being an edifying author, and even this was remedied by commentaries which set out to prove that his many narratives concealed sound moral teaching couched in allegories. From the Revival of Letters to the coming of the nineteenth-century Romantic movement he was assiduously studied; as he definitely is not a Romantic, his popularity with the critics then waned, but the latest opinion seems once more to be somewhat in his favour. Such ups and downs are common enough in the case of every author who has any decided and well-marked manner; he will be more or less liked according as the fashions in literature change. Ovid's absolute worth is naturally unaffected by these fluctuations. A poet of the calibre of Vergil, Lucretius or even Propertius he assuredly is not, for as already said he lacks deep feeling; but within his limits he is a consummate artist in words, witness especially the fact that his extremely artificial language sounds perfectly natural when the reader has gone through a few pages of him. He can feign any emotion well enough for his purposes, and thus lead up to its rhetorical expression, sometimes at excessive length. Read as he is meant to be, a moderate amount at a time, he is never dull. He has been called the poet of love. If this means the deeper sexual emotions, he does not deserve the title, but for the delicate handling of light *affaires* he has no rival, unless it be a few of the best French artists in that kind. His Corinna, to or about whom the *Amores* are generally written, is a lay-figure, but a very dainty one, worthy to take her place, as she does, among Herrick's 'mistresses'. I do not attempt to give anything like a list of the works, or even the classes of works, which show

Q

Ovidian influence, but mention merely as a specimen the poetical letter. Probably that English poem which most resembles one of the *Heroides* is Pope's *Eloisa to Abelard*; but it seems a tenable theory that if Ovid had not shown the way, Browning would have had to find some other form of expression for two of his best works, the *Epistle of Karshish* and *Cleon*, although Ovid himself would have been the last man to fill any such poems with serious reflections, religious and philosophical.

The Augustan age was one in which prose composition flourished, although the supreme importance of oratory was gone. The great name in this kind is that of Livy (Titus Livius) of Patavium (Padua). He was born about 59 B.C., and died in or about A.D. 17, was on good terms with more than one member of the Imperial family, and devoted most of his life to the composition of his immense history of Rome, in a hundred and forty-two books, whereof thirty-five (i-x, xxi-xlv) have come down to us fairly complete, thus enabling modern readers to judge of the value of the whole. It must be said that it is far from a critical and scientific history, as we now understand it. Practically no original research seems to have been made, at all events for the periods covered by what we have (753-167 B.C.). Livy contents himself with getting his facts from the earlier writers, Latin and Greek, criticizing here and there, at least to the extent of preferring one of two or more divergent accounts, or of expressing doubt on some details. How he handled more nearly contemporary events, down to the death of the elder Drusus in 9 B.C., we cannot tell, but certainly there were abundant sources, literary and other, at his disposal if he could use them. But his great contribution was the impressive picture he draws of the events as he understood them, set forth in one of the best styles achieved by any Latin writer, varying from extreme simplicity when he has nothing to relate except the minor incidents of the year (he uses the annalistic method throughout, like, for instance,

Thucydides, cf. p. 121) to high eloquence when he describes or comments on a great event or, again in the manner of Thucydides, uses the convention of speeches from the leading figures of the story to evaluate the situation. To this must be added his high moral tone, clearly genuine and not, as with Sallust (p. 197), a pose. His own statement of the value of historical study has already been quoted (p. 120), and whatever his scientific defects it cannot be thought an unworthy attitude. Of some minor writings of his practically nothing has survived, and the history itself, which he seems to have called no more than *Ab urbe condita*, 'From the foundation of the City', was much too large for the lazy readers of later antiquity, wherefore they contented themselves with jejune epitomes, of which one and parts of another still survive,[1] or with writers of short popular historical works who went to Livy for their material and adorned their extracts from him with rhetorical flourishes of their own; for instance, the sketch of Roman military history by Annius Florus (we do not know his *praenomen*), probably the same as the minor poet Florus who lived under Hadrian.

Livy, good though his style is, shows at least in one respect a departure from the prose standards of Cicero. Here and there his language has a poetical colour, oftenest a specifically Vergilian flavour, whereas the rule had been, ever since Isokrates (p. 109), to give prose a vocabulary all its own and avoid poetical locutions, except of course for actual quotations in verse. He cannot, however, be reckoned among the anti-Ciceronian stylists, who are rather of the next generations.

I have already (pp. 120, 229) pointed out that Livy is of the school of 'Isokratean' historians. This lasted far beyond antiquity, indeed flourished until the modern conception of history as an exact science came to the fore, with the unfortunate result in some cases that its practitioners forget that

---

[1] One such at least was current about the end of the first century, as we know from Martial (see p. 254), xiv, 190. It was a little parchment book.

history should also be literature. The well-worn phrase 'the lessons of history' is a remnant of such a view of the study of the past, and so perhaps is the foolish proverb about history 'repeating itself'. As regards the style of Livy, its influence on moderns is not absent, though perhaps the historians of our own day show little trace of it. Anyone who, ignorant of Latin, reads a few chapters of Gibbon's *Decline and Fall* will form some notion of the combination of stateliness and clarity which marks the Roman historian at his best.

Though the greatest, he was not the only noteworthy writer of prose or of history at that time. An older man (76 B.C.–A.D. 5), prominent in public life, was the addressee of Vergil's fourth Eclogue, Gaius Asinius Pollio, consul in 40 B.C., whose talents as a soldier and statesman were respectable and his abilities as a writer, so far as can now be judged, not contemptible. His history of the Civil Wars has not survived; as a man of letters, his chief fault was perhaps his too great opinion of his own importance, which led him to carp at other authors, Cicero included, his best-known comment being on Livy, who, he implied, used not *Latinitas* (Latinity, pure Latin, such as educated Romans spoke and wrote) but *Patauinitas*, 'Paduanity', the dialect of his native region. Probably he referred to small details of pronunciation and hence of spelling, long since normalized away from the copies from which our manuscripts descend.

Another historian of the time whom we know almost entirely through an epitome was Pompeius Trogus, a Gaul, as his *cognomen* shows, whose grandfather was given Roman citizenship by Pompey the Great, hence his *nomen*. His work, which extended to forty-four books, was perhaps meant as a kind of supplement to Livy, for it was an account of the rest of the known world, under the rather misleading title *Historiae Philippicae*. It did indeed have much to say of Philip II of Macedon, father of Alexander the Great, and his successors, but it began with the foundation of Nineveh by the mythical

Ninos and ended with the absorption of the Hellenistic realms into the Roman Empire. Trogus followed Greek authors throughout, arranged his material well, disliked the practice of introducing speeches in what purported to be the very words used, and wrote very respectable Latin. Someone named M. Iunianus Iustinus, whom we usually shorten to Justin, cut his work down to an amount occupying 240 pages in Ruehl's Teubner edition; if we had the whole, it might extend to some 3,000. But even the shortened form is worth reading.

Meanwhile Greek literary activity was by no means at a standstill, although no author of the first rank appeared among writers in that tongue. But several of a certain importance who lived and wrote in or near the Golden Age of Latin literature have been already mentioned, and two outstanding critics whose works survive are now to be briefly recorded. The first of these is Dionysios of Halikarnassos, who, coming to Rome about 30 B.C., spent over twenty years there, during which time he learned a certain amount of Latin and became much interested in Roman antiquities, on which he wrote a large work that still survives in part. As history it does not rank very high, but it preserves a good deal that is interesting from earlier writers. The style is what might be expected from a rather wordy and rhetorical author who was an uncompromising Atticist (cf. p. 146). We have twenty books, whole or fragmentary, which bring us down to the year 271 B.C. More important are the same author's works on literary history and criticism, for his taste was very good and he judged of other men's writings better than he himself wrote. There have come down to us four sections of a long work *On the Ancient Orators* – those which deal with Lysias, Isokrates, Isaios and Demosthenes, the last being, as we might expect, far the longest and most elaborate. A sort of appendix to this treatise discusses the minor orator Deinarchos, and we have some fragments of further studies of the orators and the works attributed to them. There are also preserved two essays on Thucydides, one on Plato and the historians, one on a point of literary chronology (someone had naïvely suggested that Demosthenes had learned his eloquence from Aristotle, and Dionysios shows that he had delivered some of his most famous speeches before the philosopher had written his works on rhetoric). All these are addressed, as a sort of open letters, to sundry Roman acquaintances. More important is the long and able treatise *On Composition* or, to render the Greek title literally, *On the arrangement of Words*. These writings, despite certain limitations, entitle their author to a very respectable place in the history of criticism, and his right to such a place has been generally acknowledged. Several of them are easily accessible to an English reader in the editions of the late Professor W. Rhys Roberts, which contain excellent English translations.[1]

A minor critic of about this time, whose work is a kind of compromise between a rhetorical handbook and a treatise on literary criticism generally, is alleged to have been called Demetrios, and his title is simply *On Style*. We know nothing of him, save that he cannot possibly be Demetrios of Phaleron, a statesman and writer of Athens, whose dates are approximately 350–283 B.C., and who is known, among other things, as the first person to publish a collection (now lost) of the fables ascribed to Aesop. This Demetrios is seen by his style and the general manner of handling his subject to be of good Graeco-Roman date, about the last century of the Republic or the first of the Empire.

Far more important than Demetrios (if that was his name) or even than Dionysios is an anonymous writer whom we have known for centuries as Longinus, a name which there is practically no reason for giving him. At the top of the one

[1] W. Rhys Roberts, *Dionysius of Halicarnassus, The Three Literary Letters* (1901); *Dionysius of Halicarnassus, On Literary Composition* (1910). See also his editions of *Demetrius, On Style* (1902); *Longinus, On the Sublime* (1907).

authoritative manuscript of his work some unknown Byzantine has written 'Of Dionysios or Longinus', and in inferior copies the 'or' has disappeared, giving rise to the imaginary name Dionysius Longinus. The worthy Byzantine was simply suggesting the names of the first two rhetoricians he could think of, Dionysios of Halikarnassos and Cassius Longinus, a statesman and writer on rhetoric of the third century A.D. But the treatise *On the Sublime* (as it is generally called; the Greek word is *hypsos*, literally height or elevation) is too good for Dionysios, far too good for Longinus, besides making it clear from certain internal evidence that it is not later than the first century of our era. Its immediate occasion was a treatise, now lost, by another critic, Caecilius of Kale Akte in Sicily, whom 'Longinus' finds superficial. Not content with examining passages from various writers which satisfy his canons of elevation, and exposing the hollowness of merely pretentious and bombastic expression, the author seeks to discover what mental qualities are necessary for sublimity, and points to a number, natural and acquired, but sums all up in an excellent aphorism of his own, 'Sublimity is the echo of a great mind'. It is unfortunate that this admirable work is disfigured by a number of gaps; evidently our manuscript tradition goes back to a copy which had lost several leaves.

All these writers knew in various degrees what true excellence of style is; the story of the corruptions which followed will be told in the next chapter.

VII

The Silver Age and After

AFTER AUGUSTUS, LITERATURE UNDERWENT SOME strange vicissitudes, due in part to the characters of successive Emperors, partly to a general, though not universal, depravity of taste, both Greek and Latin. Under Tiberius (A.D. 14–37), a soured, suspicious, unoriginal man, freedom of speech was curtailed far more than under his great predecessor, and his principate saw no great writers. Caligula, or to give him his proper name, Gaius (37–41), always unstable and after the first few months of his reign a dangerous, sadistic maniac, was hardly one to encourage intellectual activity of any kind. Claudius (41–54) had literary tastes and ambitions, and his numerous faults did not include wanton cruelty. Nero (54–68) was a clever amateur in poetry and music, besides sundry other arts. He did something to encourage literature, but his childish vanity and childish rages when frightened or jealous rendered his patronage of it unreliable. Of the next dynasty, Domitian (81–96) again posed as a patron of literature, but his jealous despotism left no room for free speech whatever. This state of things came to an end under the 'good Emperors', Nerva to Marcus Aurelius Antoninus inclusive (96–180), and under them also, especially the earlier ones, we meet the last Latin writers of paganism who had any claim to greatness. Meanwhile Greek literature was moving towards and passing through what is quaintly known as the Second, or New, Sophistic period. By this time 'sophist' meant 'rhetorician', and extraordinary enthusiasm was aroused by men who, while endlessly clever in the handling of words, seem to have had nothing to say that was worth saying and wasted much ingenuity in setting forth unreal themes such as have already been described (p. 200). Under them, the worst features of Asianism seem to have revived (cf. p. 146), but also literature took two new and not un-interesting directions.

One is of merely historical interest; prose invaded the precincts of verse and we have specimens of speeches which are really hymns or other expressions of emotion. One of the most famous producers of this kind of thing was also one of the latest writers of this period, Aelius Aristeides (about 117 or 129–189),[1] a hypochondriac who spent most of his life besieg-ing Asklepios with requests for miraculous cures and making extraordinary experiments in the belief that they had been supernaturally communicated to him. His wretched perform-ances have come down to us to the number of fifty-five, for he was much admired in later times as well as while he lived. Their only merits are that they are unusually good imitation Attic and that they throw some light on certain strange facets of contemporary life.

The other novelty is of more lasting interest. This age saw the birth of the prose romance; it can hardly be called the novel yet, though some specimens are not unlike the Italian *novella*, long short stories, to use the paradoxical modern term. The earliest, fragmentary, specimen we have is perhaps of the first century B.C., the latest is Byzantine. Most of them follow one and the same general pattern. Two young people meet and fall in love. They marry, or intend shortly to marry, and then are separated by some cause such as the departure of the man for military service, the kidnapping of one or both, the supposed death of one, or whatever the author thinks most exciting and plausible. While separated, their constancy is continually tested, but they emerge triumphant from all

---

[1] The odd divergency of possible dates for his birth arises from his mention-ing the positions of certain stars, but not the year, when he was born. The data he gives will fit 117 and 129 equally well.

ordeals, and at last are reunited and, we are to understand, live happy ever after. One composition of this kind, though not the only one that is readable, stands out from among the rest. It is the famous *Daphnis and Chloe* of Longus, to whom we can neither attach a date nor restore the rest of his obviously Roman name. In it, the main characters, two foundlings brought up by kindly country folk, are something more than lay figures, for the awakening of their love for each other and their gradual realization of what it is are drawn with a psychological insight rare in these novels generally. But the *genre* did not pass away with the end of classical literature, but has its descendants in the many stories, especially amorous, in every literature of Europe, sometimes independent, as in Boccaccio or Marie de France, sometimes forming episodes in longer works, as the narratives inserted in (for instance) *Don Quixote* and sundry of the earlier English novels, as far down as Dickens' *Pickwick Papers*.

Two more developments of Greek literature of this age deserve mention. It has already been said (p. 195) that letter-writing was a recognized branch of literature. One consequence of this was that many of the 'sophists' wrote and published whole series of letters, sometimes to and from frankly imaginary persons, characters from New Comedy and from pastoral poetry, sometimes allegedly written by well-known historical figures. Specimens of the former are easily accessible in the Loeb series;[1] the latter incidentally produced one of the most celebrated controversies in all English literature. An unknown rhetorician of not very early date and little knowledge of history composed some letters under the name of the notorious Phalaris, tyrant of Akragas in Sicily. Sir William Temple, taking part in the peculiarly silly debate of the Ancients and the Moderns, spoke of them as genuine pieces and belauded

---

[1] *Alciphron, Aelian, Philostratus, The Letters*, ed. and trans. by A. R. Benner and F. H. Fobes. Philostratos, Nos. 2, 32, 33, 46, gave Ben Jonson the materials or *Drink to me only*.

them; Wotton replied, and in the second edition of his work on *Ancient and Modern Learning* got the assistance of his friend, the great Richard Bentley, who contributed a brief treatise showing that the letters were spurious.[1] Meantime the Hon. Charles Boyle, a member of a great and justly respected family, but personally an impudent and foolish young man, who was then an undergraduate of Christ Church, had put out, or at least let his name appear on the title-page of, an edition of 'Phalaris', in the preface of which he was rude to Bentley. This was followed by an answer to the treatise on the letters, again nominally by Boyle, but actually by the combined forces of Christ Church, who were further supported by various London wits, and above all by Swift, in his famous *Battle of the Books*. Bentley, not a little annoyed at the utter lack of courtesy shown by his opponents, enlarged his work and produced, in 1699, the immortal *Dissertation upon the Epistles of Phalaris*, which is not only crammed with miscellaneous learning but contains some of the most telling sarcasm in our language, for Bentley, in this as in everything else, was superior to all his opponents put together. Except for Swift's contribution, all that they wrote is either forgotten entirely or remembered only as illustrating Bentley.

Another offshoot of the Second Sophistic is a quantity of miscellaneous writings, their contents loosely connected by some common subject, as natural history or the like. The best of these, so far as erudition goes at least, is a certain Athenaios, who produced, some time in the second century A.D.

[1] It throws a somewhat lurid light on the condition of classical philology in England at that time that not only beginners like Boyle and non-specialists like Swift and Temple, but professional scholars of some repute seem to have been honestly unable to see, by a mere glance at the letters, that they could not possibly have been written by Phalaris or anyone else who lived in the sixth century B.C. These were the ancestors of the many readers who, a century or so later, needed to have it proved to them that Chatterton's Rowley poems were forgeries, were deceived by Ireland's Shakesperian discoveries, and could not at once recognize that 'Hardyknut' and sundry other sham ballads were contemporary productions, and very poor ones at that. Bentley's scholarship was in most respects about two hundred years ahead of his time.

(incidentally perhaps the date of the *Epistles of Phalaris*), fifteen books under the general title *Deipnosophistai*, i.e. 'The Dinner Specialists'. He supposes a number of scholars of his day, notably the grammarian Ulpian (not to be confused with the great jurist of that name) to meet at a dinner, where they fall to discussing, and illustrating with long quotations, for they all have prodigious memories, everything which can by any ingenuity be connected with what they have before them, foodstuffs of sundry kinds, dinner-guests, luxurious habits and so forth. The result for us is that there is preserved a very large number of fragments from authors both in verse and in prose whose works are lost, and for that reason Athenaios is valuable; as literature, his performance is dull and his characters mere mouthpieces. Another author of somewhat similar kind is Aelian (Claudius Aelianus), a native of Praeneste, but writing in Greek, the fashionable would-be Attic, which he managed fairly well. Two long works of his survive, besides some letters (see p. 236, n. 1) and fragments. One is called, literally, the *Various Enquiry*, the other *Concerning Peculiarities of Animals*, and both are readable, though often inaccurate, credulous and silly. Aelian probably, Athenaios certainly, has been handed down partly in epitome. The former, when he deals with literary matters, sometimes is faintly reminiscent of the entertaining miscellanies of the elder Disraeli.

To return now to Roman literature, the reign of Tiberius saw no great authors and not many small ones. History is thinly represented by the epitome of Velleius Paterculus (his *praenomen* is uncertain). This was an old soldier who had seen Tiberius at his best, as commander of Roman armies on important campaigns. Admiring him in this capacity, he evidently could find nothing but good in him and the rest of the Imperial family, and so, after getting everything down to about 150 B.C. into a single book and everything down to the beginning of Julius Caesar's career into about a third of another, he devotes the rest of his work to a laudatory account of the

Caesars and their exploits. For this, he has been called a flatterer, unjustly; it is rather the case that he was a simple, honest fellow, who knew nothing of politics or court intrigues, or if he heard of them would believe no evil of his old commander. His style is tolerable, considering that he was more familiar with the camp than the study. Another more or less historical work of this date is the *Memorable Doings and Sayings* of Valerius Maximus, a collection of anecdotes illustrating traits of character, good or bad, arranged under proper headings, as 'chastity', 'cruelty' and so forth, and each of the nine books divided into a Roman and a foreign section. No doubt it was intended for the use of orators and rhetoricians, who liked to adorn their speeches with such illustrations. The style is pretentiously bad, but the work was much read, in the original and in epitomes, and several well-known stories got abroad from it. Tiberius is flattered, and some fragments of good sources, such as the missing parts of Livy, are preserved.

Another minor writer was Phaedrus (or perhaps Phaeder, a known Latin form of the Greek name Phaidros; it happens that no one mentions him in the nominative case). Son of a schoolmaster living in Thrace, Phaedrus had a slender talent which he exploited by composing the earliest surviving collection of Aesopic fables. They are in iambic trimeters, neatly enough expressed, and we have them from two sources, the surviving manuscripts of them, which manifestly give but a selection (some of the five books extend to less than 200 lines each; an average 'book', *libellus*, of verse would be perhaps 600–800), and some additional fables extracted in the fifteenth century by Niccolò Perotti from a fuller copy which has not survived. Others can be and have been more or less convincingly restored from prose paraphrases found in sundry medieval manuscripts, including the collection of someone named Romulus, of whose life and date nothing is known. Phaedrus is described in his manuscripts as a freedman of the

Emperor (*Augusti libertus*); the persons whom he addresses in his fables, when anything is known of them, seem to have been freedmen of some wealth and position; he had a grievance against Seianus, the all-powerful favourite for some time of Tiberius; a part at least of his work was written when he was old. We know no more of him. He passed unnoticed, except perhaps for a mention in Martial (see p. 254)[1] until the time of Avianus (see p. 241), but later ages liked fables, and he was then read, excerpted and paraphrased. For a time he was a popular text for young students of Latin, but seems now to have gone out of fashion.

The fable in its proper sense, that is a moral or gently satirical apologue in which the characters are all or mostly the lower animals, credited with the power of speech, is as old as Hesiod in European literature and may very well have come in from the east, ultimately from India.[2] However that may be, Greek tradition credited the bulk of such tales to Aesop (Aisopos), said to have been a Phrygian and to have lived some time in the sixth century B.C. If there ever was such a person, we know nothing about him, for the Life of Aesop which has come down in three forms[3] is a chapbook perhaps of about the first century A.D., originating in Egypt, and taking a good deal of material from the *Words of Ahikar*, a popular Oriental romance. As already mentioned, the earliest known written collection in any European language was that by Demetrios of Phaleron (p. 232), which is lost; the next after Phaedrus is in Greek scazons (cf. p. 32), the author being an otherwise unknown Babrius, which is an Italian name; but as already mentioned (cf. p. 238) there were native Italians who chose

[1] Martial, iii, 20, 5, asks if Canius Rufus, a literary acquaintance, is imitating *improbi iocos Phaedri*, 'Phaedrus' naughty stories'; now *iocus* might translate Gk. *geloion*, one of the words for an Aesopic fable. Very little in our Phaedrus could be called improper, but something of the kind may have been cut out by shocked educationists of the past.

[2] Brief account in (Sir) W. R. Halliday, *Greek and Roman Folklore* (New York, 1927), pp. 101 ff.

[3] Full account in B. E. Perry, *Aesopica* i (Urbana, Ill., U.S.A., 1952), pp. 1ff.

Greek rather than Latin for literary puposes. Babrius' date was some time in the second century, if not earlier,[1] and an interesting feature of his work is that his metre is influenced by that of Latin. Since every Latin disyllable, or longer word having its penultimate syllable long, is accented on that syllable, it follows that Latin scazons always have an accent on the first syllable of the last foot, unless, as very rarely happens, that ends in a monosyllable. Babrius so arranges his words that the penultimate syllable of every verse bears an accent. His style is simple and neat. Next, of surviving authors, comes Avianus, a man so obscure that we do not know the rest of his name, or even if it is not really Avienus. He dedicates his work, Latin elegiac paraphrases of Babrius, to someone called Theodosius, who can hardly be either of the Emperors of that name, but might well be Macrobius Ambrosius Theodosius (cf. p. 268), in which case his date is probably fairly late in the fourth century. Besides these nameable writers, we have a multitude of Aesopic fables in both Greek and Latin, the former including several in verse and several more clearly paraphrased from verse, whether that of Babrius (whose work has not come down complete) or of someone else. The Greek ones alone number some four hundred, the Latin ones about three hundred more,[2] and both extend well into the Middle Ages. No one manuscript in either tongue containing anything like all of these (to say nothing of the many extant in non-European idioms), the earlier editions of 'Aesop' contained merely selections from this mass of material. The amusing thing is that as late as Bentley's time (cf. p. 237) these productions were imagined to be the genuine work of the Phrygian, and he thought it worth while to point out

---

[1] Oxyrhynchus Papyrus No. 1249 (in vol. x of that collection) is a scrap of a copy of Babrius, and the handwriting cannot be later than A.D. 200. This puts out of court all earlier suggestions as to his date.

[2] I do not try to give exact figures, for the number varies from one modern edition to another, some including and some excluding fables found incidentally in various authors such as Horace.

that they are quite late Greek. The reason, or at least a reason, for their number and continued popularity was their use in elementary education. Quintilian (*Inst. orat.* i, 1, 2) recommends that, as a first lesson in composition, children should be set to tell fables, first orally, in plain but correct language, then in writing. It seems likely that what we have in the prose of various ages, from late classical to medieval, is largely fair-copies from the teachers, or approved compositions of the brighter pupils, and as many have come down in several slightly different forms, again some at least may result from elementary exercises in paraphrasing, a branch of composition on which much stress was laid.

The popularity of this simple branch of literature was great and lasting. Phaedrus, Avianus and 'Romulus', Babrius and the authors of the prose fables, were succeeded in modern times by much better writers, La Fontaine being the chief, while many others in various tongues, for instance Gay in English, showed no small ingenuity in their re-tellings of the ancient tales and inventions of new ones in imitation of them. Parodies on the traditional style are to be found, particularly among American writers, and not a few of them, notably those of Mr Thurber, are full of ironical wit. It goes without saying that translations into all manner of languages abound also.

The most famous literary family under the early Empire, renowned also as generous patrons of literature, was the Annaei, whose best-known members bore the *cognomen* Seneca. The elder bearer of this name has already been mentioned (p. 201); his son, often called Seneca philosophus to distinguish him from his father, was one of the most popular writers of his day. Perhaps the kindest view of his character is that he was a neurotic; certain it is that the high moral precepts that he sets forth, taken from Stoicism with excursions into the writings of other schools, including the Epicurean, to show that despite their errors they saw something of the truth, agree but poorly with his conduct. To do him justice, he never pretended to have reached anything like perfection, but only to be striving after it; but a multi-millionaire cuts an odd figure when he preaches the simple life, a moralist ought not to descend to low flattery, followed by witty abuse of the man he had flattered, and an eloquent advocate of stern uprightness should not, under any pressure, consent to write the defence of a matricide. Seneca the younger was born about the beginning of our era, at Corduba (Cordova) in Spain, was relegated by Claudius to Corsica on a trumped-up charge of being the lover of Caligula's sister, Julia Livilla, recalled in 49 and made tutor to Nero, wielded great influence, along with Burrus, the commander of the Praetorians (the household troops), till Burrus died in 62, and three years later was implicated in a conspiracy to assassinate Nero and forced to commit suicide.

He wrote both prose and verse. In the former medium, his style is lucid, clever, rhythmical, of Asianic tendency, and therefore un-Ciceronian, and popular in his own day and afterwards, although the best critical taste justly found fault with it. Besides a number of philosophical essays, several being oddly described in our manuscripts as dialogues, which they are not, he composed the deplorable *Consolation to Polybius*, a freedman of Claudius and an able and influential official, for the necessary work of what we should call the Civil Service was then largely done by members of the Emperor's personal household. Polybius had lost his brother, and to write a 'consolation' to the bereaved was a usual thing (cf. p. 192); but Seneca descends to unmanly laments over his banishment, mingled with the basest flattery of Claudius and his entourage.

I am ashamed, I am ashamed [says Lipsius, Seneca's first critical editor]. Whoever published this was an enemie to Seneca and his glorie.

R

Messalina, Seneca's enemy, after bringing about Polybius' death, came to a violent end herself, and Agrippina, the next Empress, mother of the young Nero, recalled Seneca. Not long after, Claudius died, by poison as was suspected, and Nero succeeded. Seneca would naturally be expected to write something in congratulation of his pupil; but he need not have produced his wittiest work, the *Apocolocyntosis* (a title of rather doubtful meaning), which not only contains a prophecy, put into the mouth of one of the Fates, of Nero's glorious reign, but describes in broadest farce the old Emperor's undignified death and unhappy experiences in the other world. It is something to be able to set against these performances his 'Consolation' to his mother, written from Corsica and containing the usual stock arguments against grieving over exile. He was a good son.

He had a friend, Gaius Lucilius (often called Junior, to distinguish him from the satirist, cf. p. 165), who was interested in poetry (it is possible, but a long way from being proved, that he wrote the *Aetna*, p. 209), and, seeking moral perfection through philosophy, seems to have taken him as his spiritual adviser. To him Seneca addressed his *Natural Questions*, which we have in a rather battered state, divided into an uncertain number of books. It preserves a good deal of ancient physical speculation, and, still more informative, a fair amount of Etruscan lore concerning thunder and lightning, on which much of their elaborate divination was based. It need hardly be said that Seneca draws moral lessons from it all.

This Lucilius is not to be confused with Lucillius (Loukillios), as he seems to have spelled his name, a contemporary writer of epigrams, many of which are preserved in the Anthology (p. 141). He composed what we call epigrams, brief, witty utterances in elegiacs, generally dealing with someone's weaknesses of character or oddity of person, and commonly having their point in the last verse, or even word; I translate one of the shortest:

> You *dye your hair, my dear? Perish the thought!*
> *'Tis coal-black still, as 'twas when it was bought.*
> – *Anth.* xi, 68.

But to return to Seneca, his most pleasing work in prose is the long series of 'Moral Letters' addressed to Lucilius, which, besides their moralizings, contain many really good and vivid sketches of contemporary life and events. We have 124, and there is evidence that our set is not complete, one of several gaps in our tradition of the prose works.

As a poet, Seneca, besides a number of short pieces which we have, and some passages in verse scattered through his prose writings, composed several tragedies. It had long been usual (cf. p. 78) to use this form for poems which were never seriously meant to be performed on the stage, though some at least of them may have been publicly recited. Seneca's were plainly not intended for real actors, but are exhibitions of his great cleverness in sententious rhetoric and at the same time expressions of his philosophic views. Certainly by him are the *Mad Hercules, Trojan Women, Medea, Phaedra* (all on Euripidean themes; the *Phaedra* is hardly from the *Hippolytus* which we have, but perhaps from the other lost play on the same subject, in which the character of Phaidra was differently handled), *Phoenissae* (*Women of Phoenicia*; the title is Euripidean, the work consists merely of three disjointed scenes dealing with the attack on Thebes by the Seven), *Oedipus* (the outlines of the plot are from Sophokles, cf. p. 64), *Agamemnon* (very unlike Aeschylus' masterpiece, p. 59, though necessarily following the same general plot), and *Thyestes*.[1] Attributed to him are the long *Hercules on Oeta*, of about the same plot as the *Trachinae* of Sophokles (p. 66), which is probably spurious, and the *Octavia*, the only surviving Latin play on a historical subject, the murder by Nero of

[1] The subject is the 'Thyestean banquet', see my *Handbook of Greek Mythology*, p. 247.

his first wife, daughter of Claudius and Messalina. In this not uninteresting piece, one of the characters is Seneca himself! It may have been written in the time of Vespasian (69–79). Both these works clearly show Senecan influence in their style.

The posthumous reputation of Seneca was very great. The Christians correctly perceived a resemblance between his ethics and their own, the reason being that he and they alike drew on contemporary moral philosophy. Hence he was often felt to be something very like a Christian himself, and someone forged a correspondence between him and St Paul. But his subjects, also the general manner of his writing, gave models to practically everyone who wrote philosophical and especially ethical essays in modern languages from the Revival of Letters on, to say nothing of the great use made of him in the Middle Ages. As to his plays, it is not too much to say that for the earlier period of modern European drama, till well on in the seventeenth century, it was he rather than the great Athenians who was the model. Seneca did not use the 'god from the machine' beloved especially of Euripides (cf. p. 71), but he likes a ghost; the *Thyestes* begins with a scene between the phantom of Tantalos and a Fury, the *Agamemnon* with a long speech from that of Thyestes, and in the *Oedipus* there is a reported scene of necromancy, carried out by Teiresias, as a result of which the bloodstained spectre of Laios utters an elaborate but obscure warning of the horrors to come. It need hardly be said that ghosts are very familiar creatures on the Elizabethan and Jacobean stage, headed by that of the elder Hamlet. Seneca loves gore, witness the detailed descriptions of the murders of Hercules' children by their insane father and of those of Thyestes by their uncle, to say nothing of various other killings up and down the tragedies; certainly here we have at least one of the ancestors of Tragedy of Blood. His Medea spends a long scene, part reported by her terrified duenna, part supposed to be enacted before the audience, in elaborate magical rites. Whatever Greek models he may have had are lost to us, and so here we look for dramatic forerunners of the various witches from *Macbeth* onwards. Perhaps most noteworthy of all, his sententious heroes and heroines find their echo in very many characters, most notably those of Chapman on the English and Corneille on the French stage, who explain their troubles and set forth their resolves in language certainly no less eloquent than that of their Latin predecessor. Even the choruses of Seneca's plays, whose part is mostly to utter lyric reflections between the acts, return in later times, for example in Ben Jonson's *Catiline*, a play which contains many strongly Senecan features throughout.

Still dealing with the family of the Annaei, we come to Seneca's nephew, Marcus Annaeus Lucanus, usually called Lucan in English. He was a precocious youth, who early showed great fluency in composing verse. He seems to have thought of himself as a rival to Vergil, for a scrap of one of his early poems ran 'And how much do I lack | Now to a *Gnat?*', that silly composition (p. 209) evidently passing with readers of his day as genuine Vergil. His life was short. Born in 39, when his education was finished he was summoned to Nero's court and shown favour for a while, but he was obviously a better poet than Nero and not very tactful in concealing it, hence he found himself slighted, was implicated in the same conspiracy which brought his uncle to his death, and died in the same way, by opening his veins. It is said that with his last breath he recited some lines from his epic poem about a soldier dying from loss of blood.[1]

His chief work, the *Pharsalia* ('matters concerning the Battle of Pharsalos', at which Caesar defeated Pompey in 48 B.C.), is an extraordinary performance for a man who died at 26. It is unfinished, and its ten books, the last incomplete, are marred by falsified history, bombast, a tendency to dwell upon bloodshed and agony, gratuitous display of not very profound

[1] Probably *Phars.* ix, 808–14.

learning, and blunders of various kinds, to say nothing of Lucan's far from infallible taste in many things. Yet its merits are great, and were soon recognized.

> There are some [says Martial, putting words into the mouth of Lucan himself or his poem], who say I am no poet, but the bookseller who sells me thinks I am. – Mart. xiv, 194.

Quintilian (*Inst. orat.* x, 1, 90), would have rather sided against the bookseller, for after praising some features of Lucan's style, he adds that he thinks him a better model for orators than for poets. But, poetical or not, Lucan at his best can rouse the reader with genuine eloquence, not mere clever rhetoric. Examples are the admirable speech of Cato on hearing of the death of Pompey (*Phars.* ix, 190–214), the entrance of Pompey's glorified spirit into the realms of the good (*Phars.* ix, 1 ff.), and, perhaps finest of all, the dream in which Pompey, on the eve of his decisive defeat, sees himself once more in Rome, a young man again, the idol of an applauding crowd (*Phars.* vii, 7 ff.). Like his uncle, Lucan had a taste for the macabre, and quite outdid him in that respect by his horribly impressive witch-scene in Book vi, 507 ff., where Sextus Pompeius consults Erichtho, an expert in all kinds of black magic, to learn the outcome of the civil war. Lucan's popularity did not end with the downfall of ancient civilization, witness the frequency with which he has been edited and commented upon, well or ill,[1] by scholars of most European nations, the attempt by Thomas May (1595–1650) to supply the parts of the work which Lucan did not live to write (May's hexameters are far from contemptible, and catch much of the tone of Lucan's own), and the translations made both by May and by the much greater Marlowe (Book i, in 1600).

Contemporary with these Spaniards was a young Etruscan, Aulus Persius Flaccus, whose short life (December 4, 34–

---

[1] See the amusing preface to Housman's edition.

November 24, 62) was long enough for him to develop an amiable and virtuous character and to produce one little book which has never ceased to find appreciative readers, despite its extraordinarily contorted style. He came early under the influence of Lucius Annaeus Cornutus, a Stoic who has left us a curious little work in Greek[1] on the interpretation, according to the tenets of his school, of mythology. With a zeal for Stoicism which he caught from his teacher, Persius combined an enthusiasm for the Republican writers, especially Lucilius, and for Horace, and so a contempt for the over-refined style of the minor poets of his own day, among whom, though of course Persius does not mention him, was the Emperor himself. These views he set forth in six satires, one on the degeneracy of modern taste – not only Midas in the legend, but everyone in Rome, has asses' ears – the rest on ethical themes. The whole work comprises but 664 lines. A modern reader can have access to at least the matter, if not the peculiar manner, of the satires from the neat rendering in verse of the late Professor J. Tate (Oxford, 1930) or the revision of Gifford's old translation in the Everyman series, No. 997 (London, 1954).

Nero had a courtier, Gaius Petronius, who according to Tacitus was the *elegantiae arbiter*, the man to whom all questions of taste were referred. A voluptuary, he lacked neither energy nor courage on occasion, and when at last a false charge of treason brought him to an end he bled himself leisurely to death, destroying before he died his signet-ring, which might have been used to forge evidence against others, and sending Nero a full and detailed account of his most secret perversions. This man is almost certainly the author of the *Saturae* (Medley) of which we possess considerable extracts. It is the first surviving picaresque romance, an

[1] It is entitled *Sketch of the traditions of Hellenike theologia*. If this is his own, Cornutus means by the last two words 'Greek account of the gods'; if on the other hand it was added by some Christian copyist, they mean 'heathen theology'.

obvious parody on Greek novels (see p. 235), with a wandering rascal, Encolpius, and an impudent boy, Giton, for the virtuous hero and heroine, south Italy for the foreign lands in which the adventures take place, and a quick succession of incidents, sometimes highly indecent but always lively, the chief being the account of the dinner to which Encolpius and a friend are invited at the house of Trimalchio, the local millionaire of some provincial town (in Rome, by the standards of that day, he would have been thought but moderately well-to-do, and his elaborate entertainment is apparently a stale imitation of fashionable frolics in the capital). This part has been translated many times into English and other modern languages; most of the rest is generally left in the original. But of imitations Petronius has had his full share, the most famous being the adventures of Gil Blas.

The principate of Vespasian may be the time when Quintus Curtius Rufus flourished; the date we assign to him depends on the interpretation of one rather obscure passage. His subject was the life and death of Alexander the Great, and his ten books, of which the first two are lost, give an entertaining account, in good Latin, of what he had learned from some earlier writers on that topic. Obviously, his chief aim was to provide pleasant reading, and in this he succeeded. He is confessedly uncritical, and may be ranked rather among the authors of half-historical, half-fictional works such as are rather popular now than among serious historians. 'I copy down', he says (ix, 1, 34), 'more than I believe', and again (x, 10, 12), 'I report what is rather handed down by tradition than believed'.

The short reign of Vespasian's son Titus saw the end of the most assiduous reader and writer of that age, Pliny (Gaius Plinius Secundus) the Elder. He filled several public offices and wrote voluminously, but of his works only the famous *Natural History* (*Naturalis Historia*, perhaps more nearly meaning 'inquiry into the visible world') survives. This extends to thirty-seven books. The first is introductory, the next five treat of the structure of the universe and of geography, after which comes a long series which is biological (zoology, Books viii–xi, botany, xii–xix, use of plants in medicine, xx–xxvii, medicinal use of animal matter, xxviii–xxxii), and the rest deals with minerals, and so with art, which makes use of mineral products. The whole is a most interesting and curious mixture of information, true and false, for Pliny was not a first-hand observer, but a diligent collector of information from earlier writers, Greek and Latin, the former now and then misunderstood. It is fortunate that his masterwork has come down to us entire, for it was diligently excerpted, stolen from without acknowledgement, and generally made use of by many lesser writers, and it is seldom that such extracts and epitomes have not displaced the longer original. Pliny, who was born in 23 or 24, at last fell a victim to his scientific curiosity combined with unselfish humanity. During the eruption of Vesuvius which buried Herculaneum and Pompeii in 79, he, being then in command of the fleet at Misenum, set out on a rescue expedition to the scene of the disaster, and took the opportunity of observing the eruption from as close as possible. He was overcome by the bad air and died of asphyxiation.

The time of Domitian was not unfavourable to some kinds of literature, despite the total absence of free speech. The Emperor had literary pretensions himself, and instituted a competition, the Agon Capitolinus, at which compositions in verse and prose were submitted. Poems, good and bad, large and small, were composed by a number of writers, some of whom deserve mention. The bulkiest and dullest was the *Punica* (i.e. epic on the Second Punic War) of Silius Italicus (the rest of his name was Tiberius Catius Asconius; such long names were coming into fashion). Silius, an ex-consul of Neronian times who survived all his colleagues, set forth his version of the war in seventeen books of appalling dreariness, for he had enough metrical skill to write quite good hexameters, but neither taste nor common-sense, witness for example his battle-scenes, in which he tries to make his heroes fight in Homeric fashion. This is much as if one were to represent the battle of El Alamein as decided by a sword-duel between Montgomery and Rommel. He also introduces all the stock Epic ornaments, divine interventions, sports, a visit to the underworld. His excuse was presumably that all these things are found in Vergil, for whom he had an almost idolatrous reverence; but even the younger Pliny (p. 259), who was indulgent to all pretenders to literature, could find nothing better to say of him than that he 'wrote poetry with more industry than genius' (*Epp.* iii, 7, 5). Martial indeed (*Epigr.* vii, 63, 1) says his works will live for ever, but Martial was writing a complimentary poem and Silius was rich, therefore a possible source of profit. He does not seem to have found modern imitators, unless indeed Sir Richard Blackmore can be accounted his successor.

Much more tolerable, though far from faultless, was the most popular poet of the time of Domitian, Publius Papinius Statius of Naples.[1] From him we have five books of occasional poems, the *Siluae* (one of many ancient names for a miscellany; hence for instance Ben Jonson's title 'Underwoods'). They are mostly in hexameters, though he now and then experiments with lyric metres, and are consistently clever, once or twice poetical, though for the most part they are simply versified addresses of compliment to prominent people of the day (including, of course, the Emperor) with whom he was in one way or another acquainted. These, and some lost pieces, are his minor works; his chief performance was the *Thebais*, or epic on the attack upon Thebes by the Seven. This is the work, not of a great poet, but of an ex-

---

[1] Not of Toulouse, as Chaucer (*Hous of Fame*, 1460, Skeat) imagines. This was a common medieval blunder, occasioned by confusing the poet with Statius Ursulus Tolosensis, a rhetorician who flourished about the middle of the first century A.D.

tremely clever man, versed in every device of rhetoric, having
the leaning towards grisly horrors which we noted in Seneca
and Lucan (pp. 246, 248), but also a tenderness towards
young people and for the unfortunate, a taste which now and
then is good, and occasionally a passage worthy of a greater
genius. Being very artificial, the poem has been disparaged
beyond its deserts for a century or so, after having been over-
valued in many earlier ages; Chaucer for example ranks its
author with Vergil, Ovid and Homer (*Troilus and Criseyde*
v, 1792),[1] and Pope thought highly enough of him to translate the first book of the *Thebais* in his youth and revise it later
in life. There are signs that modern criticism is dealing more
justly with it. Statius also began, but never lived to finish, an
epic on Achilles (the *Achilleis*), of which we have what he
completed, one book and part of another.

There is something of the romantic about Statius, and this
is more clearly marked in a contemporary who died with his
work unfinished, Gaius Valerius Flaccus Sentinus Balbus (the
second and third of this list of names are those by which he is
generally known). He began under Vespasian and partly
completed under Domitian an elaborate epic on the Argonauts, largely but not entirely imitated from Apollonios of
Rhodes (p. 129). Exactly how he meant to handle the end
of the action must be a matter of conjecture, for as we have it
he gets no farther than the meeting of the Argonauts with
Apsyrtos and an ensuing debate as to whether Medea should
be surrendered to him. But Jason is rather less of a lay-figure
than in some tellings of the story, since he and his comrades
help Aietes in a war and he fights valiantly, thus giving Medea
some reason to love and admire him, and other episodes are
handled with considerable freedom. His language is generally clear and pleasant to read, rhetorical of course, but not

---

[1] The stanza of which this line forms part is a fine imitation of Statius' own
farewell to his poem, *Theb.* xii, 810-end. The Latin writer, however, bids his
work reverence Vergil, and says nothing of other poets.

overladen with rhetoric. His metre is correct and workman-
like, his character-drawing not contemptible. Altogether
Quintilian may be right in saying that his early death (as it
seems to have been) was a great loss to literature (*Inst. orat.* x,
1, 90). What he might have accomplished had his life been
longer is a futile question; as it is, he is at least an agreeable
'idle singer of an empty day'.

One of the most interesting writers of the time was Martial
(Valerius Martialis), a native of Bilbilis in Spain, who came to
Rome, no doubt counting on the patronage of the Senecas,
a year or so before their downfall. This threw him on his own
resources, without a wealthy supporter. There was a fairly
wide public for light literature, but no such means of satisfy-
ing them as is furnished by our modern periodicals, daily and
other, and therefore no salaried post for one who had all the
qualities of a good gossip-writer or 'columnist'. Even so well-
liked a poet as Statius, who plainly had some moderate means
of his own, supplemented his income by writing libretti for
the extremely popular *pantomimi* of the day, a kind of ballet-
dancers whose performance was accompanied with vocal and
instrumental music on comic or serious themes. Martial was
good at one thing only, epigrams like, but better than, those
produced by Lucillius (p. 244), and though no doubt the
collections of them which he put forth year after year sold
well, there was nothing like our copyright or the royalties
paid to an author by his publisher. Hence his work is full of
appeals to any who could give him anything to give, or to give
more. Apart from this there was abundant material in the
gossip and scandal of Rome, no doubt augmented by him
with invented tales about imaginary or insignificant persons,
and in addition there was the inexhaustible topic of flattery,
especially of Domitian, who was regularly referred to as
'lord and god', was intolerant of the least hint of adverse
criticism, and apparently had an unlimited appetite for the
most exaggerated laudation. Martial had no scruples, no

shame and no self-respect, and so would furnish as much of this as even Domitian wanted, while on the other hand he was ready to pander to the foulest tastes of a corrupt 'smart set' by writing epigrams which were sheer filth. But subtracting these, we have left a mass of clever and amusing productions, never lengthy, sometimes no more than a single line, varying in tone from neat praises of people for whom he felt some genuine admiration, through biting wit, to occasional tenderness, for he seems to have been personally an amiable man and a lover of children. Certainly the death of a little slave-girl, Erotion, of whom he made a pet, and who died just six days before her sixth birthday, was a real grief to him, and he made her the subject of more than one really beautiful little poem. The assassination of Domitian and the accession first of Nerva and soon afterwards of Trajan gave the capital an entirely different tone, and seem to have spoiled Martial's market. The younger Pliny paid his expenses to return to Spain, and there he lived the rest of his days on an estate given him by a wealthy countrywoman. From Spain he sent one more volume of epigrams, some of which rejoice in the quiet life he now leads, while others are full of regret for the excitements and diversions of Rome.

As to his influence on posterity, it can be summed up in one sentence. No one since his time who writes verse epigrams in any European language uses any other style than that of Martial, as near as he can imitate it.

Enjoying Domitian's favour, yet flattering him but moderately and falling into none of the vices of his court, was the most celebrated rhetorician, or rather educationist, of the day, Quintilian (Marcus Fabius Quintilianus). This was another Spaniard, educated in Rome, brought back there by Galba when he seized power in 68; surviving Galba and the other short-lived Emperors of those troubled months, he appeared occasionally as a pleader in the courts, but mostly occupied himself with teaching. In this he was brilliantly successful, but his private life was unfortunate, for his wife and children predeceased him. He was a reformer, rejecting the artificial flourishes of the common rhetorical schools[1] and advocating a return to the more realistic teaching and manlier style of Cicero's day. We have from him one work which is at once important and certainly his own, the *Institutio Oratoria* (Training of an orator), one of the most admirable treatises on education ever written, for Quintilian was wholly of the elder Cato's opinion (p. 167) that an orator must be not simply an able speaker but a good man. The one serious defect in his system is that it is too bookish, with a typically Roman neglect of scientific knowledge and first-hand observation. Of its twelve books, the first and the tenth are of especial interest to a modern reader, the former giving his views on early training, the latter containing a long list of what we should perhaps call recommended reading in authors both Greek and Latin. The rest of the work treats of more technical matters. His dates are about 30–96.

After Domitian's death, four writers who had remained almost if not completely silent under his despotism began to speak out, enjoying to the full the 'rare happiness of the times, when one may think what he will and say what he thinks' (Tacitus, *Hist.* i, 1). Of these, three attracted notice and approbation; the fourth was neglected till long afterwards.

Undoubtedly the greatest of the three was Cornelius Tacitus (his *praenomen* is uncertain). His exact dates are unknown, but he held office of one kind or another under all the Flavians, was consul in 97 under Nerva, governor of Asia about 112, and lived at all events until near the end of Trajan's principate (97–117), perhaps later. What is probably his earliest work, though direct evidence that he wrote it is weak,

---

[1] Hence it is doubtful if he really composed the two sets of declamations (one containing nineteen themes treated at length, the other 145, originally 388, handled more briefly) which are attributed to him, for they show the very faults which he deprecates. But they are possibly early works, composed before he formed the views of his maturity.

is the *Dialogue on Orators*, in which he professes to record a conversation heard in his youth between several eminent men of the day, the chief subject under discussion being the reasons why oratory no longer flourishes. For a while, but without sufficient reason, the work was identified with one known to have been written by Quintilian, *On the reasons for the decay of eloquence*. The style is unlike that of Tacitus' universally acknowledged works, but the difference of subject-matter is reason enough for this; the model for such an essay would naturally be Cicero, and hence some flavour of Cicero's sentence-structure and rhythm was called for. In his other writings, Tacitus, so far as he had a model, followed Sallust (p. 197), though he was an incomparably better historian. He began in this department with a life of his father-in-law, Julius Agricola, dwelling especially on his campaigns in Britain, still a source of perennial interest to archaeologists, and therefore describing the island in some detail and with not a few inaccuracies; it has been unkindly said that if it were not for Tacitus, Livy would be the worst geographer of all historians. Next, perhaps, came the famous *Germania*, the fullest account we have of that country in antiquity, and hence eagerly studied by Latinists and Germanists alike. After these preliminary essays, which already show his characteristic style, he embarked on his great work, a history of Rome beginning with the death of Augustus in A.D. 14 and continuing down to his own times. Of this we have two considerable portions, the *Histories* and the *Annals*, as they are commonly called. Both are imperfect. The former begins with the fall of Nero and ends abruptly, in the middle of a sentence, with the events of 70, thus covering only some two years in four books and part of a fifth. The latter begins, after a short introduction, with the death of Augustus, and by the end of Book iv has got down to 28; only a fragment of Book v is left to us, and Book vi begins at the end of 31; Books vii-x and the beginning of xi are lost, and then we have a continuous narrative (Books xi–xvi, the last being again imperfect) from 47 to 66, that is nearly to the beginning of the *Histories*. It is a period for the most part unhappy, containing the principates of Tiberius, Caligula, Claudius and Nero, and Tacitus does nothing to brighten it, but rather darkens the already sombre colours with transcendent art. He was, like very many of his high social standing, a Republican in principle, believing that the whole Imperial system was essentially bad, merely ameliorated by the coming of a good Emperor now and again. Therefore, although he is too honest to distort actual facts, he is always ready to impute the worst motives to their authors, finding for instance nothing better than dissimulation in Tiberius' more laudable, or at least tolerable actions, while now and then a sardonic comment on some indifferent event declares his attitude, for instance, among those of 32,

> At that time Lucius Piso the pontiff died a natural death, unusually for one so conspicuous. – *Ann.* vi, 10, 3.

And here it may be mentioned that Tacitus is very quotable, and sayings of his are to be found in the most unexpected places. For instance, in Somerset Maugham's novel *Cakes and Ale*, chap. i, comes the neat remark, 'Most of us, when we do a caddish thing, harbour resentment against the person we have done it to.' But the original, whether Maugham was conscious of imitating it or not, is briefer and neater still: *proprium humani ingenii est odisse quem laeseris*, 'hating the man you have wronged characterizes human nature' (*Agricola* 42). Everyone has said something is 'conspicuous by its absence', and everyone who does so is quoting *Annals* iii, 76, 5, and probably few who remark *omne ignotum pro magnifico* know that it is from *Agric.* 30.

The principates with which he dealt had much in them which not the most charitable historian could fairly praise, and Tacitus did not spare those concerned. To blacken the un-amiable character of Tiberius, emphasize Claudius' stupidity, and dwell upon the foolish and wicked conduct of Nero was clearly a congenial task, and one well fitted to his extraordinary ability for what ancient critics called *deinosis*, that is to say the presentation of events in their most horrible light. What he made of the criminal lunatic Caligula we cannot say, but certainly he would not flatter him. It is to be remembered that Tacitus had seen the early Empire at its worst, having lived through the reign of terror under Domitian, when no prominent man's life or reputation was safe from the swarming informers and even private conversations were spied upon. One would not expect a lenient handling of National Socialism in Germany from one who had spent the years between 1933 and the end of the late war in Berlin, and himself held liberal views. One result of Tacitus' terrible eloquence is that until recently there could hardly be found any historian who tried to take an unbiased view of any of the rulers of his time earlier than Nerva.

Perhaps that modern English writer who most resembles Tacitus in style, and incidentally in his sentimental regard for something called liberty, is a man of very different temperament, Macaulay. Both, especially when they have something impressive to describe, write in hammer-strokes, occasionally rather monotonous in their effect; the English writer said of the Latin that 'he stimulates till stimulants lose their power', and himself sometimes falls into the same defect.

Tacitus had a friend very unlike himself, the younger Pliny, nephew of the elder (p. 250) and his son by adoption, his natural father being Lucius Caecilius Cilo of Comum, hence his full name was Gaius Plinius Caecilius Secundus. He was of gentle and kindly disposition, brought up in more wholesome moral surroundings than those of Roman society, and consequently painting a much less dark picture of his times than either Tacitus or Juvenal (p. 261). Cicero was his obvious model, both in his literary style and, so far as was possible, in his public career. His dates are 61 or 62 to something short of

s

114; he held in turn all the usual magistracies, including that of *consul suffectus*[1] in 100. About 112 he was governor of Bithynia in Asia Minor, and there he came across a congregation of Christians, at that time a forbidden sect. He reported to Trajan that except for 'wrong-headed and unlimited superstition' there seemed to be nothing very harmful about them, and asked what further measures he should take. The Emperor, with his usual moderation, forbade him to seek the members of the suspected sect out or pay any attention to anonymous denunciations, but to let the law take its course if any were accused and convicted in regular form. This is the most noteworthy feature of his correspondence with the Emperor, which consists of 121 letters in all. Besides this, we have nine books of letters from Pliny to various correspondents, evidently revised for publication, for they contain details which would be known already to the recipient of the original letters, but might need explanation to a third person. They are, in effect, short essays, but even so they reflect their author's character, decent, amiable, kindly and charitable to those in need, but extremely vain and too ready to let his own good deeds be known. Pliny had a considerable reputation as an advocate, but the only oration we have of his is the published and no doubt elaborated version of his speech of thanks to Trajan on being appointed consul, his so-called *Panegyric*. It is correctly loyal in tone, its sentiments are admirable, it contains some pieces of useful information, and on the whole it is very dull. But there is no doubt that it was admired in its author's day and afterwards.

Pliny's friends included Gaius Suetonius Tranquillus, generally called Suetonius simply. His dates are about 69–140;

---

[1] There were always two consuls, hence if one died or resigned someone else must be appointed in his place. Such a substitute was known as *consul suffectus*, i.e. 'replacing consul'. Under the Empire, the regular consuls for the year commonly resigned after a short term of office, so that the title of ex-consul (*consularis*) could be held by a sufficiency of men to fill the posts open to those of that rank. Hence Seneca's joke (*Apocol.* 9, 2) about a *pomeridianus consul*, i.e. consul for one afternoon.

he was learned, and interested in biography, literary and other, though not in that alone. Being for a while secretary to Hadrian, he seems to have had access to documents belonging to the Imperial archives, and to have made use of them for his most famous work, the *Lives of the Caesars*, from Julius Caesar to Domitian inclusive. These biographies, written in an unpretentious but lively style, preserve a great deal of useful information, joined to a considerable amount of gossip and scandal; they were published about 121. In addition, he wrote lives of numerous scholars and literary men, whereof at least the substance of several has come down to us through various channels. His other works, dealing with a variety of topics, are lost save for some fragments. As a biographer he had imitators in late antiquity, and he, more than even Plutarch (p. 264), provided the form which the shorter compositions of this kind take in modern literature, for instance Johnson's *Lives of the Poets*.

Finally, Decimus Iunius Iuuenalis (Juvenal) was the last poet and the last satirist of importance in Latin literature. His life is imperfectly known,[1] partly because he came too late to be recorded by Suetonius and the biography of him which we have is a miserable affair. But this much is certain, that he was poor for most of his life, a native of Aquinum (near Monte Cassino), born perhaps about 60 and died after, but probably not long after, 127. He began to write, or at all events to publish, after the death of Domitian, whose cruelties had left an indelible impression upon him; how much he had personally suffered from them is uncertain, but Professor Highet is right (p. 9 of the work mentioned below, n. 1) when he detects a frightened tone in his writings. Poverty and the humiliating position of a hanger-on of wealthy houses (blisteringly described in his fifth satire) combined to sour a nature which perhaps was never sweet, and Juvenal vented his

[1] For established facts, eked out by intelligent and ingenious conjecture, see Gilbert Highet, *Juvenal the Satirist* (Oxford, 1954).

wrath on a society which he found corrupt to the core and at
the same time morbidly fascinating in its very corruption. His
satires number sixteen in all, and he published them in five
groups or books, whereof one consists of a single work, his
masterpiece, the long sixth, on women (particularly the
women of wealthy Roman society), while the rest vary from
three to five each. From Book 3 on (it begins with No. 7)
the tone becomes gradually less furious, which is not to say
that it is notably mild. Domitian's times were further away,
and someone, possibly Hadrian, seems to have relieved
Juvenal's wants to the extent of making him master of a little
estate on which he lived in modest comfort, as described by
him in the eleventh and twelfth satires.

If Juvenal can be said to follow any school of thought, it
was Stoicism. Certainly he resembles the Stoics in one paradoxical principle. They held that all vices were equally bad,
and Juvenal employs much the same tone of white-hot indignation when he describes the most hideous cruelties and
revolting sexual perversions and when he attacks a certain
Lateranus[1] for driving a carriage in public while he was consul.
But he has other resources, notably a terrible power of making
a rascal speak for himself and thereby reveal the depths of his
own villainy. He was a finished rhetorician, and when to
rhetoric is added no small skill in metre and real feeling combined with a good case, it can be devastating.

It is strange that so famous an author made no impression
on his contemporaries. None of them mentions him except
Martial, if the Iuuenalis of three of his poems is our Juvenal.
He is first named after his death by Lactantius, the 'Christian
Cicero', in 315, and after that, if not earlier, more or less
patent imitations of him, even a few quotations, occur in
various Christian and pagan writers. His poems were edited

[1] Apparently that Plautius Lateranus who was consul designate (i.e. elected
consul for the next year) in 65; but he never actually held that office, for he
came to his end in 65, being implicated in the same conspiracy which brought
about the deaths of Seneca and Lucan.

and commented upon (the details are obscure), only just in time, it would seem, for the sixteenth and last satire is incomplete, and the most likely explanation of this is that the editor or editors could find but one copy, which had lost its last page or two, if it was in shape like one of our books, or had its last few inches torn off, if it was a roll. But this neglect in antiquity has been abundantly made up for since the fourth century. The Middle Ages read him and copied him, not always well, for none of the surviving manuscripts is free from faults of various kinds. Moderns have generally shown a high regard for him, and besides actual imitations, such as Johnson's *London* and *The Vanity of Human Wishes* (respectively from the third and the tenth satire), echoes of him are to be heard almost everywhere when an author in a modern language has wished to express indignation or even, what Juvenal was not free from, spite.

About contemporary with Juvenal (again, we do not know his precise dates) was one of the most amiable and for a long while one of the most influential of Greek writers, Plutarch (Ploutarchos) of Chaironeia in Boiotia. A man of respectable though not particularly distinguished family, he had throughout his life three great interests, literature, philosophy and religion, if indeed the last two did not in his case reduce to one. He spent some time in Rome, where he went partly at least on public business, for deputations were constantly going there to get some privilege or exemption granted, take part in proceedings before the final courts of appeal, the Senate and the Emperor, or bring a formal message of congratulation on an appropriate occasion. There and elsewhere he gave lectures on philosophical or other topics, made a number of Roman friends, and learned a certain amount of rather inaccurate Latin, which proved useful to him, for becoming interested in Roman history and antiquities, especially sacral, he was able to make out something at least of Latin authors, including Cicero, Livy, perhaps Varro, certainly the Augustan antiquary

Verrius Flaccus. Besides a number of shorter writings which dealt with or touched upon Roman matters, he set about writing the most famous series of biographies in the world, the *Parallel Lives*, a full-length exposition of a topic such as he often expounded in his public lectures, namely that for every famous Roman there could be produced an equally famous Greek of like character and achievements. Hence the lives, of historical and occasionally mythical worthies, come in pairs, Romulus and Theseus, Cicero and Demosthenes, Mark Antony and Demetrios Poliorketes, and so forth, each pair having originally a short appendix in which a comparison was drawn between the Greek and the Roman, though several of these are now lost. In addition, since Plutarch obviously found biography an enthralling study, there are several lives (including those of Galba and Otho the short-lived Emperors) which do not form pairs, and we know of others again which are lost. The rest of his writings, with several pieces which have been falsely ascribed to him, are generally grouped together under the title *Moralia*, because most of them have an ethical interest, though by no means all. None of them shows much originality of thought, and that is almost a merit, since he had read widely in philosophical and other authors lost to us, and from him we know a great deal about their opinions and also the religious problems of the day and the many theories which were then current. For Plutarch was a deeply pious man, a priest of Apollo from 95 onwards, and fond of excogitating philosophical and especially ethical justifications for traditional religious practices, Greek and foreign. He regularly discovers some reason which satisfies his own moral sense, however grossly unhistorical it may be.

For a long while Plutarch formed part of the intellectual furniture of every educated European. Translated into French by Amyot (*Lives*, 1559; *Moralia*, 1572), he soon spread beyond France; in England, North Englished the *Lives* from Amyot's French and Philemon Holland translated the *Moralia* (respectively 1579 and 1603), and North was Shakespere's Plutarch. Since then he has been translated, edited and commented upon in sundry languages and by various hands; but during the last century or so his popularity has somewhat declined, partly because it has been realized that he was neither a first-rate original historian nor a profound philosopher. He never claimed to be either and, especially in the *Lives*, he gets his facts where he can, thus never being better than his source for the time being, and his chief interest is throughout in the moral and political lessons that can be drawn from the fortunes of his subjects and their good and bad qualities. Those who neglect him lose a charming companion and an admirable story-teller. For a modern reader, one of his merits perhaps is that he suffers little from being translated, if only it be done with tolerable accuracy, for he is not a first-rate stylist.

The age of the Good Emperors (Nerva to Marcus Aurelius) became unhappily an age of bad style and bad taste. Archaism came into fashion, and that superimposed on artificiality led to compositions in such Latin as never was spoken by anyone in ordinary life. The chief offender was M. Cornelius Fronto, a man of amiable character, known for his friendship with Marcus Aurelius, whose teacher he was, his polemic against the Christians, then a rapidly growing body who caused much anxiety to the State and led even the broad-minded Emperor to persecute them, and his fantastic style, in which new and old are blended in a manner rather irritating than effective. This he called the *eloquentia nouella*, approximately 'modern expression'. He was a native of Cirta in Numidia, thus being classifiable as one of the 'African' stylists. His exact dates are unknown, but he was born about 100 and died about 160. His private life was burdened with misfortunes which were not his fault, the deaths of his wife and their five daughters.

His archaism seems to have started with an interest in the work of the grammarian M. Valerius Probus. This man was a native of Beirut (Berytus in antiquity), and revived what

seems to have been almost dead, the study of the older Latin
authors. He wrote little for publication, was never a regular
teacher, although he would admit a few people to discuss
literary matters with him, and seems to have edited several of
the authors who lived before Cicero and some (Lucretius,
Vergil, Horace, perhaps Persius) who were contemporary
with or later than the orator. But his influence would seem to
have been considerable; Martial, for instance, who was about
contemporary with him, uses his name to signify 'implacable
critic' (Mart. iii, 2, 12). And this Probus (whose name is
usurped by more than one much later writer on philology)
was but one of a number of celebrated *grammatici* of whom we
know something from a little treatise on their lives and
activities written by Suetonius (p. 261). They are for the most
part of interest chiefly or wholly to specialists, but some of
their names are familiar in later times. For instance, the reason
why 'donet' in medieval English means a Latin grammar is
that in the fourth century A.D. there lived and wrote Aelius
Donatus, author of a grammar of his native tongue and of
commentaries on Terence and Vergil; while later still (he
flourished in the neighbourhood of 500) the famous Priscian
(Priscianus; we do not know the rest of his name) became
almost synonymous with grammar, so that to speak or write
incorrectly is 'to break Priscian's head'. Europe learned the
whole art of grammar from the ancients, and western Europe
specifically from the Latin writers, with the result that there is
still in common use a terminology and classification which
fit the ancient tongues well enough, but are merely misleading
if applied to some modern ones of totally different structure
and history, such as sundry Mongolian and African forms of
speech.

Here mention may be made of a few authors of Imperial
date whose subjects were not, or not wholly, literary or
historical. There was one writer on medicine long famous,
Aulus Cornelius Celsus, about contemporary with the

Emperor Tiberius, whose treatise on the subject formed part of a sort of encyclopaedia or compendium of sundry arts and sciences. The rest is lost, but the medical section is complete, written in a good plain style, and containing a great deal of information about the medical science of that day, for Celsus, whether he had any practical acquaintance with the subject or not, had read widely in the then approved authorities, with the result that he became an authority himself in later times, hence the boastful name of the famous Paracelsus, who thereby professed to have outdone the venerated ancient. He is, for us at least, the first of a long line of Latin writers on medicine, who on the whole become less and less scientific as time passes, till they degenerate into such mixtures of plagiarism, quackery and superstition as the notorious Marcellus of Bordeaux, sometimes called Marcellus the Empiric, who lived and wrote his compilation in the fourth and fifth centuries, and the earlier Quintus Serenus, of uncertain date and personality, who has left us 1,107 hexameters on medicine, including magical methods; e.g. he recommends as a cure for semi-tertian fever an amulet containing the famous word *abracadabra*, which he is the first surviving author to mention. There were also herbalists, one of whom has left a work falsely attributed to Apuleius (p. 269), for it is much later than his time. It was to have more than a few descendants in the Middle Ages.

Other technical writers included several whose subject was agriculture. Cato and Varro (pp. 167, 198) have already been mentioned; a good author was L. Iunius Moderatus Columella, a Spaniard of whose extensive writings we still have thirteen books, one, which deals with gardening, being in quite respectable verse, the rest in plain clear prose, the work of a practical man of good education who did not try to be fine in the wrong places. He lived under the early Empire; several writers on the same subject but of later dates have come down to us complete or in extracts. One of the latest,

Palladius Rutilius Taurus Aemilianus, has at least this claim to be remembered, that he mentions cats by their familiar modern name (*De agri cultura* iv, 9, 4, to keep down moles it is well to have *catti*, though many have tame weasels instead).

Roman architecture and engineering generally were of a high order, though their buildings never had the beauty of the best Greek work. Their most famous writer, a contemporary of Augustus, was Vitruvius Pollio, whose ten books *On Architecture* contain a vast deal of information, couched in an appallingly bad style.

Of miscellaneous writers two, of widely different date, deserve mention. The earlier is Aulus Gellius, born perhaps about 130 or a few years later, a man of undistinguished career and studious habits, who was caught in the archaizing current of his time and studied the older Latin authors diligently. He has left us one work nearly complete, the *Noctes Atticae*, that is 'Evenings in Athens', which was then practically a university town, living on the memories of its great past and on the students which it continued to attract. The title presumably suggested to 'Christopher North' his *Noctes Ambrosianae*, but there is not very much resemblance in contents between the older and newer work; certainly in Gellius there is nothing to correspond to the Gargantuan suppers which North and his cronies are represented as facing. The *Noctes Atticae* deal with chosen fragments of philological, historical and antiquarian information, including many extracts from books now lost, and anecdotes of scholars whom Gellius had met or read about.

The other compiler is much later, and his name was Ambrosius Theodosius Macrobius, generally known as Macrobius simply. He flourished about 400, and his sympathies were decidedly with those Roman aristocrats who were making a last stand in favour of the traditional religion of their country (or rather, of their conception of it, for they mingled much that was foreign and recent with their older practices) against the rapidly triumphing Christians. Like Athenaios

(p. 237), he imagines a number of friends, all of good social position and considerable learning, to meet at a dinner during the Saturnalia (December 17–23), which festival gives the work its title. In its seven books, which we have nearly complete, many topics are discussed, two outstanding ones being the solar religion of the time and Vergilian criticism, and in consequence we learn a great deal about works of scholarship known to Macrobius at first hand or otherwise, but not to us. He also wrote a very famous and long popular commentary on the Dream of Scipio with which Cicero concludes his *Republic* (see p. 190), and that has survived entire.

The artificial style which Fronto (p. 265) fostered was capable, in the hands of an artist, of producing interesting, even beautiful, results. An English reader may get some idea of them by sampling the strange but not ineffective English of some of William Morris' work, particularly perhaps *The Water of the Wondrous Isles*. The artist in question was Lucius Apuleius, or Appuleius, of Madaura (Mdaurusch) in what is now Algeria. He was born some time about 125, was elaborately educated, and read widely in both Greek and Latin, became a rhetorician and pleader, and increased his resources by marriage to a certain Pudentilla, a widow of fortune, older than himself, whose relatives accused him before the governor of his province of using magic to gain her affections. His defence, the *Apologia*, sometimes called the *De magia* (*Concerning Magic*), survives, and is a most interesting document both for its curious style and for the information it yields about contemporary beliefs, including his own, for he was a deeply religious man after his fashion and a mystic. Besides this and a selection of purple passages from his speeches, known as *Florida*, we have his masterpiece, the *Metamorphoses*, also called the *Golden Ass*. It is a picaresque romance for the most part, dealing with the adventures of one Lucius, who by using the wrong charm is turned into an ass, passes into the hands of a number of masters, generally of far from edifying life, and finally by the grace of Isis recovers his human shape and becomes her devotee. The hardest thing for a modern to realize is perhaps that it is a deeply religious work, culminating in Lucius' spiritual experiences; the easiest to appreciate is a long episode consisting of the only folktale which has come down from antiquity professedly as such, the immortal *Cupid and Psyche*, which begins in the true manner, 'In a certain city there lived a king and a queen'. The atmosphere of marvels and unrealities, culminating in divine epiphanies and weird experiences during initiation, suits well with the strange style. The reader who does not venture to attempt the original is well served, if not too curious about accuracy in detail, by the Elizabethan translation of William Adlington (1566), and for *Cupid and Psyche* he has the alternative of Walter Pater's version in *Marius the Epicurean*. There are also a few short treatises on philosophical subjects by Apuleius.

History was but ill-served in Latin after the death of Tacitus, save for one remarkable exception to be mentioned presently. Besides several compendia, of no importance as literature but here and there preserving some fact not elsewhere recorded, the late Empire produced a rubbishy imitation of Suetonius' *Caesars* (p. 261), the *Historia Augusta*, or history of the Emperors, consisting of biographies, all short, of every one from Hadrian down to Carinus, i.e. 117–285. These profess to be by six different authors, to draw on earlier writers and other documents, and to be of date not later than about 337. But it is practically certain that, although some of the authors cited may be real, the lives are actually all by one (unknown) scribbler, and the date not earlier than Julian the Apostate (360–3) and perhaps as late as Theodosius I (379–95). Of the documents allegedly reproduced, some at all events are manifest forgeries. However, for lack of anything better for much of that obscure period, this rubbish-heap has been patiently raked over by historians and the moderate amount of real information it contains extracted. For the non-specialist it hardly deserves mention, except that if he reads Gibbon he will often come across quotations from or references to it in his notes.

But in the deepening twilight of Latin literature and scholarship there arose one man who was really a historian, commendable for everything except his style. This was Ammianus Marcellinus, a Greek, born about 332, a soldier for a great part at least of his adult life, who set about continuing Tacitus down to his own times. We have rather more than half his work, Books xiv–xxxi, covering the years 353–78; evidently then he had attempted hardly more than a sketch of the earlier period, thirteen books for something consider-ably over 200 years, for he can hardly have begun later than the death of Hadrian, 138, and may well have started with his accession in 117, or even earlier. Ammianus was clearly a man of some reading and remarkable freedom from prejudice, witness his attitude towards Christianity (he was himself a pagan) and his criticism of Julian the Apostate, who is so to speak the hero of a great part of his narrative. When to this is joined practical experience, first-hand knowledge of many of the events he describes, and sober judgement, it is not surpris-ing that the result is good.

Oratory and poetry were much practised but produced little that was of worth, and still less that had any effect on later literature. Pliny's *Panegyric* (p. 260) has come down to us as one of a collection of such performances, all very ornate, very laudatory of the Emperors and other highly placed persons addressed, and all deadly dull. One of the last champions of paganism in Rome, Quintus Aurelius Symmachus, who was born about 340, had a high repute for eloquence, especially for the third of his *relationes*, that is to say official com-munications, which pleads for the restoration to the senate-house of the altar of Victory and also for the public maintenance of the Vestal Virgins. We also have his bulky correspondence, in which he shows a marvellous ability to say nothing in particular, clothing it in a multitude of words chosen from Latin of all periods. As to compositions in verse, they are numerous, in several metres and on a variety of stock subjects, pastoral, didactic and so forth, and with a very few exceptions such faint echoes of classical modes as not to be worth listing in a book of this kind. Here and there something better is to be found, notably the lovely *Vigil of Venus* (*Peruigilium Veneris*), of unknown authorship and date, but certainly not early. It is composed in trochaic tetrameters catalectic (the 'Locksley Hall' metre of English poets), supposedly on the eve of a spring festival of the goddess, and celebrating her power with a freshness totally unexpected in an age when the general tone of literature was one of stale weariness. It ends on a note of sadness; the poet asks when his spring is to come and laments that he has 'lost the Muse by keeping silent'. With this man, who was a poet, though but a minor one, we may contrast that extraordinary person Publilius Optatianus Porfyrius, who in the fourth century courted and won the lost favour of Constantine the Great (306–37) with a book of complimentary verses, in which he arranges the words so that they form squares (every line having the same number of letters, the poem the same number of lines as the letters in each one, and the perpendicular sides, also the diagonals, spelling words), or figures of one kind or another, or may be read backwards or forwards and still scan and construe. Another product of the degeneracy of literature was Decimus Magnus Ausonius, with whom in a sense French literature might be said to begin, for he was born in Burdigala (Bordeaux), early in the fourth century, rose to high office under successive Emperors, and continued throughout his life to pour forth copies of verse in various metres, mostly hexameters, on a number of subjects. His one product which is worth reading for its own sake is a pretty description of the Moselle. He was at least nominally a Christian; a far better poet was outspokenly pagan throughout what we know of his career (his first datable work is of the year 395, nothing is known of him after the death of his hero, Stilicho the great Vandal general, in 408, nor indeed for some little while before that). This was Claudian (in full, Claudius Claudianus), an Alexandrian Greek, to whom Latin was a foreign tongue. That he mastered it, at least for poetical purposes, is less re-remarkable than in the case of Terence (p. 158), for the Latin of poetry was by that time not much less a dead language than it is now, and there have been many writers since the Revival of Letters whose compositions in classical verse have been very respectable, e.g. Iohannes Baptista Mantuanus in Italy, George Buchanan in Scotland, Milton and several others in England. What is noteworthy is that at that late date Claudian handled his medium with the vigour of the early Silver Age, whether flattering the weakling Honorius, then nominal Emperor of the West, praising Stilicho, or abusing, with the utmost gusto, Rufinus and Eutropius, the powerful and un-worthy favourites of Arcadius, Honorius' brother and Emperor of the East. He also tried his hand at epic, and we have from him two incomplete poems, one on the battle of the gods and Giants, the other on the Rape of Persephone.

During all this period, i.e. from about the beginning of the third century A.D. till well into and beyond the fourth, the most meritorious Latin writers were almost without excep-tion Christians, for the new religion was daily attracting more of the best minds. It is unfortunately impossible to give any-thing like an adequate sketch of them in a book of this kind, partly because they are studied primarily by those interested in the history of Christianity, in Biblical scholarship, both textual and exegetical, and in the later developments of the non-Christian religions of antiquity, and partly because their direct literary influence, save perhaps on the style of the older theological works of modern times, is not very easy to trace. I therefore content myself with mentioning that, even purely as stylists, the most remarkable writers of that age, for both quantity and quality of output, included the great Africans Tertullian (Q. Septimius Florens Tertullianus) of Carthage, who flourished in the late second and early third centuries, Cyprian (Caecilius Cyprianus), doctor, bishop and martyr, beheaded in one of the numerous persecutions on September 14, 258, and, greatest of the three, Augustine (Aurelius Augustinus, bishop and doctor), 354–430. Africans again, certainly or probably, were Minucius Felix, about contemporary with Tertullian, and author of a really charming dialogue, *Octavius*, in which the Christian who gives the work its title defends his religion against slanders and converts an intelligent pagan, and Arnobius, who had the courage to turn Christian during the persecution of Diocletian (Emperor 284–305), and prove his sincerity by writing a hasty but interesting work 'against the Gentiles' (*aduersus nationes*), which we still have. Yet another probable native of the same province was Lactantius (Lucius Caecilius Firmianus Lactantius in full), already mentioned (p. 262), who was Arnobius' pupil in rhetoric and outdid his master in eloquence; his chief work was the *Divine Institutes*, reiterating the well-worn arguments against paganism and setting forth in excellent Latin the Christian doctrine as he conceived it. Italy had St Ambrose (Ambrosius, bishop of Milan, died April 4, 397), author of many surviving works, mostly but not exclusively theological. The little town of Stridon in Dalmatia was the birthplace of St Jerome (Eusebius Hieronymus, about 348–420), the greatest scholar of his Church and time, whose Latin version of the Bible, generally known as the Vulgate (i.e. *editio uolgata*, edition commonly circulated), still standard in the Church of Rome, was but part of his enormous activity, largely but not wholly in controversial divinity. Spain produced, by no means for the last time, a Christian poet, Aulus Prudentius Clemens, generally called by his second name only. It is every now and then the fashion to admire his verses, which are in a variety of metres and treat of pious subjects;

they include hymns, some fragments of which have found their way into collections used by modern congregations, passions of martyrs, allegories and polemic. The present writer finds most of his work dull and some of it disgusting, owing to his insistence on the gory details of the martyrs' deaths. Prudentius' quantities are sometimes false by classical rules, but excused by the pronunciation of his day; Commodian (Commodianus, perhaps of Arles and perhaps fifth century) was a worthy cleric who sought to set forth Christian doctrine and defend it against such paganism as was left in what he conceived to be hexameters. It is polite to call them accentual; in fact they illustrate the principle that to write verse it is well to have some knowledge of the prosody of the language one uses.

But during all this period Greek literature, pagan and Christian, went on vigorously, though the former never reached the old heights. The Latin doctors of the Church got most of their theology from Greek sources, especially from Alexandria, which does not mean that they were incapable of original thought. But the East was the lender, the West the borrower, for the most part. The Alexandrian Jews, and generally the broader-minded type of Jew, not hostile to Greek culture, had their share. Philon of Alexandria, often called Philo Iudaeus, who flourished about A.D. 30–45, was a Platonist, and discovered Platonism in the Torah, by the ingenious process of making everything in the Greek version, the so-called Septuagint, mean what it does not say. This started a whole school of allegorical interpretations of Scripture, a continuation, whether conscious or not, of the methods applied to Homer (p. 20) and sometimes to Vergil also. Josephus (his name regularly is Latinized, presumably to distinguish him from the Josephs of the Old and New Testaments), a Pharisee born in A.D. 37–8, fought against the Romans in 67, was captured and made his peace with Vespasian, becoming a Roman citizen, but retaining his Jewish patriotism in another

T

form. He set forth the history of his people in two works, the *Wars of the Jews*, i.e. the campaign resulting in the fall of Jerusalem to the Romans, with a long introduction giving the earlier history of wars from the days of the Maccabees, and the *Antiquities of the Jews*, i.e. Old Testament history in a style better suited to Greek readers than the often strange language of the Septuagint, continued down to A.D. 66. A shorter work, *Against Apion*, rebutted the slanders of an Alexandrian philologist of that name, whose account of the Exodus imposed on many Gentile readers, and an autobiography completes the list. Christian scholars and theologians produced much, notably the works of Clement of Alexandria (he was, however, of Athenian birth), about 150–216 at latest, whose chief theme was the superiority of Christian to pagan philosophy, and of others of the Alexandrian school, the greatest being Origen (Oreigenes Adeimantos, about 185–254), a profound Biblical scholar, a fantastically ingenious interpreter of its text, and a bold theologian, whose influence on later writers was enormous. Others, as St Gregory of Nazianzus (about 330–90) and the still more celebrated St John of Constantinople, surnamed Chrysostomos (Golden-Mouth), applied to the setting forth of their doctrines the methods of classical rhetoric and thus gave a new turn to the popular expositions of philosophical topics which had long been in vogue. They form part of what is now heavily at a discount, the tradition of pulpit eloquence. One interesting development of the reverence for antiquity which the Christians shared with the rest of the world was the study of chronology, for no purely scientific reason but to demonstrate that the new faith was really the oldest of all. Hence there were several Christian chronologers, such as Julius Africanus (third century), and the later Eusebios of Caesarea in Palestine (about 260–340), who used him, as he had used the Alexandrian chronologers, and then was Latinized by St Jerome, who supplemented him from Latin sources. Of all this, the last work has come down complete, much of the earlier ones can therefore be restored, and the net result has been a useful foundation for modern researchers. These few examples may perhaps indicate what a wide field there is for study in those writers who are collectively known as the Fathers of the Church.

Pagan Greeks were active throughout this epoch. Apart from controversies with the Christians (Celsus, a Platonist of the second century, Porphyry the neo-Platonist in the third, Julian the Apostate in the fourth, all brought out elaborate treatises against them, replied to in the first and last cases by Origen (p. 276) and St Cyril of Alexandria respectively), they produced a good deal of philosophy, though, save for the great neo-Platonist Plotinus, Porphyry's master, nothing really original. There were lecturers, such as Dion of Prusa, or Dion Chrysostom, who in the late first and early second centuries delivered a number of discourses, literary or mildly Stoic, to a variety of audiences over a great part of the then known world, or Maximus of Tyre, who put forth similar though rather inferior lectures of a Platonic tinge in the latter half of the second century. Plutarch (p. 264) might be reckoned among these; but better, or at least more earnestly sincere philosophers, were a slave and an Emperor, Epiktetos and Marcus Aurelius Antoninus. The former wrote nothing, at least for publication, but his hearer Arrian (p. 278) did posterity a service by setting forth his teachings, we cannot say how nearly in his very words, in two works, the longer *Diatribes* (meaning simply popular lectures or talks) and the shorter *Manual* (*Encheiridion*), a synopsis of his views. They are enough to show that Epiktetos was not simply a moralist who accepted Stoicism, but a saint of the cheerful and unpretentious type. Epiktetos' dates are about 55–135, and his master, himself a freedman, in turn set him free, after which he began to teach, first in Rome and later, when Domitian banished philosophers, at Nikopolis in Epeiros. The Emperor's dates and the main events of his life naturally were and are generally known; he was on the throne in the troubled years 161–80, and perhaps the most eloquent voice of those which have justly sounded his praises is that of Gibbon:

> His meditations, composed in the tumult of a camp, are still extant. . . . But his life was the noblest commentary on the precepts of Zeno. He was severe to himself, indulgent to the imperfections of others, and beneficent to all mankind. – *Decline and Fall*, chap. 3.

The 'meditations' bear the simple title *To Himself*, and are a sort of combination of autobiography and commonplace-book, published we do not know when or by whom. He and Epiktetos alike have been read and loved ever since by people of all beliefs and none, and in all manner of languages.

In history, the Greeks produced no one of anything like the first rank after Polybios (p. 147), but some few who were and are worth reading. Diodorus Siculus, as he is usually called, i.e. Diodoros of Agyrion in Sicily, wrote a compendium of universal history, of which several books survive, with large fragments of others. He was a mere compiler, unintelligent and uncritical, and of value only for the information, good or bad, which he preserves from the authors he excerpted.

A much better historian was Arrian (Flavius Arrianus), who lived and wrote in the second century A.D. and has already been mentioned (p. 277) in connexion with Epiktetos. A native of Nikomedeia, he was nevertheless a Roman citizen, who had an honourable career in the service of the State (*consul suffectus* some time in the twenties of the century, governor of Kappadokia 131–7) and afterwards retired to Athens, where he could indulge his amiable hobby of being as much like Xenophon as possible. Among other works in imitation of his model, he composed an *Anabasis* (cf. p. 121), but not having taken part in any comparable expedition himself, he took as his subject the campaigns of Alexander the

Great, compiling his book from the best authorities available to him and producing the most trustworthy account which has come down to us, in very readable style and not bad imitation-Attic, for he was an Atticist. About contemporary with him, perhaps about twenty years younger, was Appian (Appianus; we do not know the rest of his name), an Alexandrian by birth, whose subject was the history of Rome. Of the twenty-four books which he composed we have about half, dealing with the various sections of the Empire for the most part and explaining how and when they came into relations with Rome; five books treat of the civil wars which ended the Republic. He is simply a tolerable compiler, having access to some material lost to us.

Again of the second century A.D. was the famous Pausanias, to whom we owe an invaluable *Periegesis*, in other words a guide-book, of Greece. His style is bad, his matter of great interest, for he was far-travelled, inquisitive and widely read, consequently he gives us not only welcome information as to the whereabouts of ancient monuments of all kinds, but also concerning local legends, cults, traditions and so forth, mostly of course in Greece itself, but incidentally in other parts of the world, including his native Asia Minor.

The Greek novel has already been mentioned (p. 235); it flourished under the later Empire, producing such works as the *Chaireas and Kallirhoe* of a certain Chariton, otherwise unknown, who lived perhaps in the second century, the *Ephesian Adventures* (*Ephesiaka*) of Xenophon of Ephesos, who cannot be earlier than Trajan (97–117) and may be considerably later, and the *Ethiopian Romance* (*Aithiopika*) of Heliodoros, a man of quite uncertain date and personality, for it is alleged, according to Sokrates the ecclesiastical historian (*Hist. eccles.* v, 22, 51), that he was a Christian bishop, but the pagan tone of the story (its chief characters include a virtuous Egyptian priest skilled in magic) makes this very unlikely. The third century A.D. is a not improbable date; i.e. it may be contemporary with Longus (p. 236). Other romances are known to have existed and we have outlines of the plots of some two or three; but perhaps the most important is preserved only in a late Latin version. It is the famous tale of Apollonius of Tyre, the story which underlies the doubtfully Shakesperian *Pericles*.

To conclude this brief account of the later Greek writers, mention must be made of that one who has exercised the greatest influence, who indeed may be said to have given some of our own authors and those of other European nations lessons in the writing of humorously satirical works in prose. This is Lucian (Lucianus; again, we do not know the rest of his name) of Samosata in Syria, the best of all the Atticists for style and by far the cleverest for matter. His mother tongue was presumably not Greek at all, but perhaps Syriac, and he therefore composed in a foreign idiom; but he had learned the fashionable form more thoroughly than most native speakers of Greek, and he makes few mistakes. Besides some rhetorical exercises, clever but unimportant, we have from him several works on literary subjects, the most important of which is the ancestor of *Gulliver's Travels* and of the similar writings of other authors than Swift, for instance the adventurous voyage of Gargantua in Rabelais and the sundry explorations by heroes of European fiction in several languages of the moon and other unlikely regions. This is the *True History*, which justifies its title by announcing at the beginning that everything else in it is false. It is at least in part a parody on two kinds of writing which were then in vogue, one the philosophical romance, which laid its scene in places conveniently inaccessible, the other the hardly more truthful geographical treatises and books of travel of certain unscrupulous persons. Lucian makes his heroes start on a voyage of discovery across the Atlantic, during which they are caught up to the moon, visit the Islands of the Blessed, are swallowed by a sea-monster and so forth. It need hardly be said that this really comical story is full of incidental parodies and other jests at the expense of all manner of respectables, literary and other. Lucian had a keen mind, quick to perceive absurdities and inconsistencies, and was the sworn enemy of all kinds of superstition and fraud; but he was not a deep thinker, and although he treats of numerous philosophical doctrines, his understanding of them is superficial. This does not make his semi-philosophical works any less amusing, as when he supposes the most celebrated philosophers offered for sale on the slave-market and makes each of them put forth the most paradoxical of his doctrines to the amazement of prospective buyers (*Sale of Lives*). Among his most celebrated short pieces are the various *Dialogues* (*of the Dead*, *of Sea-People*, *of Courtesans*, *of the Gods*), full of burlesqued mythology and other such topics. When he sketches contemporary life, he can be as bitter as Juvenal, witness his treatise *On hired companions*, describing the miseries of those professed philosophers who attached themselves for meagre pay to great households, in a position not altogether unlike that of an eighteenth-century domestic chaplain or of such a dependant as Swift was in Temple's establishment. His attitude towards all religions was rather shallowly sceptical; his mentions of Christianity show little knowledge of it, and his attacks on religious innovators of the time (*Peregrinus* and *Alexandros*, *or the False Prophet*) represent them, whether fairly or not, as shams pure and simple. If he admired anyone, it was such a Cynic philosopher as the otherwise unknown Demonax, of whom he wrote a biography. Needless to say, the contemporary superstitions, magic, necromancy and the rest, got no mercy from him, as can be seen for instance from his *Philopseudes* ('Lover of Lies'), a collection of incredible tales supposed to have been told in the hearing of one Tychiades, who clearly is the mouthpiece of Lucian's own views.

One or two of his imitators have already been mentioned; it is worth noting that Ben Jonson had read his *Lexiphanes*, an attack on one who used obsolete words in forced meanings, and took hints from it for *The Poetaster*, Act v, Scene 1. His influence on Walter Savage Landor in his Dialogues is present, but not strongly marked; Landor had too independent a mind to imitate very closely, though in some ways he resembled Lucian in character.

Lucian's dates are from about 117 or earlier to about 180 or perhaps later. There is a curious group of four writers, all called Philostratos and all connected with each other by blood or marriage, whose combined lives extend well into the third century. They were sophists, that is to say rhetoricians, and apparently as credulous as Lucian was sceptical, for one of them, Philostratos III, wrote a life of Apollonios of Tyana, a wandering philosopher and alleged worker of miracles whose long career embraced most of the first century A.D. It is crammed with marvels, wholly unreliable, and doubtless was acceptable to Julia Domna, the pious wife of Septimius Severus (Emperor 193–211), who was his patroness. He also wrote a curious treatise, the *Heroicus*, in which the ghosts of sundry notable heroes converse amicably with a worthy old countryman. There exists a collection of letters attributed to one of the Philostratoi, which is worth mentioning because its No. 23 furnished Herrick with hints for the poem *To Anthea* ('Bid me to live . . .'); I have already mentioned it as the source of Ben Jonson's *Drink to me only*.[1]

Greek literature has never ceased, and that of Latin has given place to its descendants in the Romance languages, but these concern rather historians of medieval and modern times; our brief survey may end here.

[1] P. 236, n. 1.

Bibliography

I. CLASSICAL LITERATURE

H. J. ROSE, *A Handbook of Greek Literature*, London, Methuen, fourth edition, 1950.

H. J. ROSE, *A Handbook of Latin Literature*, Methuen, third edition, 1954.

For accounts of particular authors, see especially *Oxford Classical Dictionary*, 1949, under the relevant names.

No attempt has been made to include handbooks of English literature, which are very numerous and many of them very good.

II. MYTHOLOGY

H. J. ROSE, *Handbook of Greek Mythology*, London, Methuen, sixth edition, 1958. German translation, *Griechische Mythologie, ein Handbuch*, Munich, Beck, 1955.

H. J. ROSE, *Gods and Heroes of the Greeks*, London, Methuen, 1957.

The former of these works contains extensive notes; the latter is a short popular account without notes. Both have bibliographies.

H. HUNGER, *Lexikon der griechischen und römischen Mythologie*, Vienna, Hollinek, fourth edition, 1955. Gives brief but good accounts of the use made in post-classical times of each mythological character by artists and writers in various languages.

Index

As indicated in the Preface, Greek names are generally spelled Greek fashion. Exceptions are (a) a few whose Latinized form is so naturalized among us as to have become practically English, as Thucydides, (b) those who are cited from Latin authors only and therefore in Latinized forms, as Clinia (Kleinias). A Greek name is regularly followed by its Latinized form in brackets; in the case of a deity, that Latin one who was generally identified with the Greek is named. Principal references are in bold-faced type.

U